M000035656

NEIL RIDLEY is one of the UK's new breed of passionate young wine & spirits writers. He writes regularly for drinks and lifestyle publications and he is contributing editor to Whisky Magazine. He is also chairman of the World Whiskies Awards and in 2015 he was nominated as the IWSC Communicator of the Year. In the last 18 months he has hosted over 200 different spirits-based tastings from as far afield as Japan to Lithuania

GAVIN D. SMITH is a professional freelance journalist and author who specializes in the subjects of whisky and beer. Gavin now acts as contributing editor for www.whisky-pages.com, as well as contributing to other leading drinks magazines. He also regularly undertakes commissions for leading drinks companies and hosts whisky events. He lives in the Scottish Borders.

Let me tell you about WHISKY

Let me tell you about WHISKY

Neil Ridley
& Gavin D. Smith

PAVILION

Foreword by Rupert Wheeler of Whisky Magazine   *6*
Introduction   *8*

PART 1: WHAT IS WHISKY?

The history of whisky   12
The most common myths about whisky   17
Legal definitions   18
Whisky-making today   20
Single malt whisky   26
Grain whisky   28
American whiskey   30

PART 2: THE FLAVOURS OF WHISKY

Casks   34
Maturation   37
Terroir in whisky?   39
Old versus young whisky   40
Aroma and flavour   42
The flavour map   44
Consistency of flavours   45

PART 3: ENJOYING WHISKY

How to taste whisky   48
Buying whisky   51
Serving whisky   54
Three classics with a twist   57
Whisky and food   58
Whisky flavours and food   60
Whisky and cigars   64

Collecting and investing 66

Counterfeit whisky 72

PART 4: THE WORLD OF WHISKY

Scotland 76

Highlands 77

Speyside 86

Lowlands 94

Islay 100

Campbeltown 108

Islands 112

Blending 120

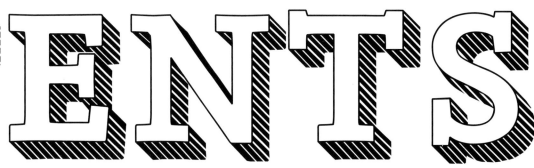

Ireland 126

Japan 134

US: Kentucky and Tennessee 148

Main US craft distilleries 162

Canada's main distilleries 172

Main distilleries in Europe 180

Asia 194

South Africa 198

Australia 200

Whisky vocabulary 204

Whisky bars 211

Specialist retailers 214

Whisky sources 216

Index 218

Acknowledgments 223

FOREWORD

Rupert Wheeler, Managing Editor of *Whisky Magazine*

The popularity of whisky and bourbon shows no sign of slowing down as shown by press coverage of the shortage of barrels in the United States and Bourbon and whisky producers declaring that they are unable to keep up with demand. The major problem for all distilleries is that because of the incredibly long lead times, whisky being bottled today was probably being produced on average about six to seven years ago. Estimating how much whisky to produce for six years hence can only be done on a guestimate and due to the current increasing demand this obviously means that the sums don't always add up. Recently a distillery announced that they were going to 'water' down a particular whisky because of a shortage due to its popularity in the States. This would in effect reduce its 90 proof to 84 proof. This caused outrage and the distillery had to back track.

In the beginning there was Scotch and from there whisky is now produced all over the world with more and more countries now distilling, in many instances, very fine whiskies. In 2015 at the World Whiskies Awards, presented by *Whisky Magazine*, the best single malt went to Kavalan (Taiwan) and the previous year was awarded to Sullivan's Cove (Tasmania). So you can see that the Scotch whisky industry has some serious competition.

Definitions in the whisky industry are very important. To be a single malt means that the whisky has to have come one distillery, and must have matured in Scotland for at least three years and one day in an oak cask. It must also be made from malted barley, yeast and water. Another important definition is Bourbon which must be produced in US (not necessarily in Kentucky), be made from a mash of not less than 51 per cent corn grain and matured in new, white oak barrels that have previously been charred or thermally degraded. No minimum maturation (length of time it spends in barrel) period is specified but Bourbon has to be aged for at least two years before it can be labeled 'straight Bourbon.'

The purpose of this book is to try and introduce you not only to the production of whisky but more importantly to many – the tasting. Whether you are a beginner or wanting to learn more, the authors (Neil and Gavin) guide you through the various processes and their knowledge has been acquired by visiting and tasting whiskies all round the world.

There is a certain amount of snobbery involved in the tasting of whisky. For me its not about whether you are having it with or without water; or whether it's a single malt or a blend. It's more the experience of the taste and taste can only come with experience. So go out and taste as many different whiskies as possible. Find out if you prefer a peaty whisky such as those that come from

Islay off the west coast of Scotland or whether you are more interested in the whiskies of Speyside in the Scottish Highlands or even further afield such as Japan or Australia? I suggest that you always have a tasting notebook near to hand so that you can write your thoughts down during your tasting which you can then refer back to. There is nothing more frustrating than tasting a really good whisky and then months later not being able to remember which one it was. With the huge variety on offer tasting notes are essential. I also highly recommend that you visit at least one distillery so you can better understand the production process. Many distilleries now have excellent visitor centre experiences which include a tasting. A good place to obtain good whiskies is when travelling abroad. The increase in the global travel retail market is colossal. Many distillery companies are now producing special releases that are only available in airport shops. Buy that special whisky when you are flying out on holiday – you won't notice the cost so much but you will certainly enjoy the dram.

Investing in whisky is now also very popular but you have to know what you are doing and if buying online I urge you to go to a reputable site. Many a reader of the magazine has written in complaining bitterly about being ripped off.

In the end drinking whisky is supposed to be an enjoyable experience. and one that I find even more enjoyable when in the company of other imbibers. Whisky clubs, shows and specialist shops are all places were you can enjoy your whisky and learn more about it in the company of like minded folk. You will inevitably end up with having a favourite whisky – I have.

LEFT: Whisky tasting at the Scotch Whisky Experience on the Royal Mile in Edinburgh, Scotland.

INTRODUCTION

NEIL RIDLEY

If you are reading this book you almost certainly have an interest in whisky, but where does that interest stem from? Many fellow imbibers were introduced to whisky under circumstances not conducive to obtaining anything meaningful from the spirit – I write from experience! An over-indulgent introduction to whisky via the family drinks cabinet often leaves you with a distinctly bad taste in the mouth – as well as a hangover from hell the morning after ...

But times and palates change. When shown a little respect, whisky is one of the most eloquent and rewarding of all spirits. For centuries, it has settled scores; influenced the creation of some of the greatest music, art and film; reinforced friendships; instilled us with courage; and given pleasure to countless generations of drinkers.

Today, the perceived barriers to the spirit of old no longer exist and the memories of that first fateful encounter fade quickly when you consider how the world has embraced whisky in the 21st century. From flavoursome and refreshing whisky-based cocktails at sundown to luxurious and warming single malts by the fireside, whisky has a time and a place in any social situation.

What was once seen as exclusively Scottish – and perhaps as traditional as the humble haggis and dear old 'Nessie' herself – is now successfully produced in over 27 countries: from newer producers such as New Zealand and Taiwan, to long-established regions such as Scotland, Ireland and Kentucky.

So wherever your initial encounter with this intriguingly complex yet so often misunderstood spirit first led you, it is now time to re-ignite the senses, tune up the taste buds and become acquainted with one of the most exciting and enduring of drinks.

Whisky, wherever you are from, we salute you!

Editorial Note:
Throughout this book the authors have used the spelling 'whisky', except when they are referring to an Irish or American liquor, when they have used 'whiskey'.

At its most prosaic, whisky is simply distilled grain, but given a dram or two of the stuff itself, the brain is apt to be less literal. Then whisky becomes the greeter of guests, the cementer of friendships, the centrepiece of convivial gatherings, the accompaniment to contemplation.

Formerly seen as the domain of aging, middle- and upper-class males, whisky is now enjoying greater popularity among younger consumers, and is becoming increasingly favoured by women. Just as their parents 'rebelled' against whisky as the drink of their fathers, so the latest generation of drinkers have rediscovered whisky.

There are also far fewer social constraints today on the way in which whisky is drunk. As whisky gains new aficionados around the world, so the manner of consumption sometimes changes; for example, many Chinese imbibers favour mixing their whisky with green tea.

Distillers all over the world are innovating in terms of production and maturation practices, and there is a greater choice of styles and brands across a wider range of 'price points' than ever before. Scotch whisky alone now sells in more than 200 countries, with emerging markets in Asia offering glittering prizes for distillers.

One significant phenomenon of the last couple of decades has been the extraordinary growth of interest in, and

GAVIN D SMITH

availability of, single malt Scotch whisky, while aged Scotch whisky blends of real quality and provenance are being seen as the equal of good single malts in many countries.

Meanwhile, in the USA the Bourbon industry has responded to the expansion of single malt Scotch with 'small-batch' and limited-edition bottlings, while Ireland is seeing a recent renaissance in pot-still Irish whiskey.

Whether you spell it the Scottish way, without an 'e,' or the Irish and US style, with an 'e', whisky is the most diverse and rewarding spirit in the world, with an extraordinarily rich heritage and narrative to explore.

PART 1: WHAT IS WHISKY?

As with any subject, the more you know about whisky, the more you can appreciate and enjoy it. In *Let me tell you about whisky* we aim to equip you with enough knowledge to be able to find your way around the whisky section of a specialist drinks retailer and to help you feel confident choosing a whisky in a bar or restaurant. At the same time, we don't intend to blind you with too much science or bog you down in irrelevant facts. We aim to demystify whisky, without taking away the magic.

In this first section, 'What is whisky?', we cover a little bit of the story of whisky, where it began and how and we demystify a few common myths about whisky and what it really is from a legal point of view. Then we then move on to whisky-making today, and through simple illustrations explain how the three main types of whisky – single malt, grain whisky and American whiskey – are made.

THE HISTORY OF WHISKY

UISGE BEATHA

Whisky moderately taken,

Sloweth age

Strengtheneth youth

Helpeth digestion

Cutteth the phlegm

It cureth the dropsy

It poundeth the stone and repelleth gravel

It preserveth the head from whirling

The tounge from lisping

The teeth from chattering

The throat from rattling

The heart from swelling

The guts from rumbling

The hands from shivering

The sinews from sinking

The veins from crumbling

The bones from aching

And is truly a sovereign liquor if it be orderly taken.

An early reference to whisky, by Raphael Holinshed in his **Holinshed's Chronicles of England, Scotland and Ireland** *1577*

Like most things that have resolutely stood the test of time, the history of whisky is shrouded in mystery, intrigue, mythology, legends galore and, undoubtedly, a barrel-load of old wives' tales! It has traversed continents, inspired songs and been the source of many heated debates about the exact origins of the spirit.

It isn't possible to pin down precisely when whisky was first produced, but here, we look back on a few key moments which have had a profound influence on the development of whisky. The art of distillation has been practised for over two millennia by alchemists, men of science and those in search of refined medical elixirs. The ancient Greeks are said to have pioneered the use of an alembic still (which has a 'swan neck' style of head and which is still used in most of today's modern pot stills) as far back as the 3rd century AD, but the techniques and reasons for the distillation have not been documented.

Before the Greeks, the Egyptians and Chinese were known to use distillation for extracting essential oils from organic material, but it is unlikely that the art of distilling alcohol for consumption was derived directly from this process. Instead, many historians have looked to the West, almost 800 years later, where strong opinion suggests that it was the Celts who first distilled a drinkable alcohol at a number of European monasteries, using techniques learned from the Moors. Old Celtic ruins near Cashel, in Tipperary, Ireland, include what might well be the remnants of bronze distillation equipment, and around the end of the 12th century, when the English army invaded Ireland, it is claimed that they discovered the inhabitants drinking *uisge beatha* – the 'water of life.'

At this time the origins of whisky as we know it begin to take shape. Over time, *uisge beatha* became corrupted to a more anglicised 'whiskybae', eventually being shortened to '*uishigi*' or 'whiski'. It is likely (although somewhat contentious, especially for the Scots) that whisky production took place in monasteries on the north coast of Ireland, from whence the process travelled across the sea to the Hebridean islands off the west coast of Scotland. The first recorded documentation of Scotch whisky dates back to 1494, and in particular the Rolls of the Exchequer, which document an order for 'eight bolls of malt to Friar John Cor wherewith to make aquavitae', also meaning the 'water of life'. This elixir was noted for its apparent medicinal effects and used to treat many complaints at the time, including smallpox, but later its heady, intoxicating properties became popular in a much wider social capacity.

Whisky distillation grew at a huge pace, with arguably one of the first licensed distilleries being located in County Antrim, on the north coast of Ireland, in 1608, now home to the old Bushmills distillery. In Scotland, farmers, whose crops of barley were used predominantly to make bread, were also distilling, making beer first, which would then be distilled once, giving the resulting spirit a harsh character with a lower alcohol strength. The spirit was drunk without any maturation time and with little thought to the processes or consistency involved. But as the quality and volume of spirit developed, several laws were passed to enable the collection

of tax on whisky, much to the irritation of the farmers and budding distillers. In 1660, the Scottish Parliament began to employ gaugers or excisemen to monitor how much whisky was being produced, pushing the world of whisky-making underground into the nooks, caves and hidden hollows across the Scottish Highlands. Notably, Scotland's favourite son, the poet Robert Burns, was an exciseman during the latter years of his life, which often influenced his writing.

During the mid-18th century there were tougher constraints on the production of whisky, but also a greater understanding of the production of a higher-quality spirit, matured in a variety of wood types to give it complexity and balance. Pioneers sought out new territories in which to make whisky, and Welsh distiller Evan Williams emigrated to Kentucky alongside other founding fathers of American whiskey, such as Elijah Craig; these innovators were making whiskey from non-barley grains such as corn and rye. In the 19th century, enduring Scotch distillery names such

ABOVE: Part of an engraving from a supplement to the *New and Universal Dictionary of Arts and Sciences* by J Barrow, published in London in 1754, showing the processes of distilling malt.

FACING PAGE: Chromolithograph showing the distillery buildings of William Jameson & Co in Marrowbone Lane, Dublin, in 1845. These fine Georgian buildings are now home to the Jameson Experience, and Jameson is Ireland's best-selling whiskey.

LEFT: Crowds loot a whiskey store of confiscated liquor in New York. Prohibition came into force across the US in 1920 and consequences for both the American whiskey and wine industries were disastrous. Front page of French newspaper *Le Petit Journal Illustré*, 1922.

The Glenlivet, Glenfiddich, Laphroaig and Talisker were established alongside highly successful blended whiskies and their blenders including Johnnie Walker, Dewar's and Chivas Brothers.

Boom-and-bust periods have changed the equilibrium of the whisky industry, especially during the latter part of the 20th century, when the number of Scottish distilleries was dramatically scaled down, some being mothballed, deactivated or, sadly, demolished. A few distilleries such as Port Ellen and Rosebank have left behind liquid legacies which have matured exceptionally over the past few decades.

Outside of Scotland, the Japanese established their first distillery in 1923 and quickly began to perfect the art of whisky production. Since the late 20th century whisky distilleries have cropped up all over the world, with varying

RIGHT: Advertisement for Johnnie Walker whisky from the 1920s. Johnnie Walker is the world's best-selling blended whisky and the marketing has always made much of its 'striding man' image.

BELOW: The modern face of whisky production today. Diageo's Roseisle distillery, opened in 2010, was the first malt distillery of scale to open in Scotland in over 30 years. The distillery pioneered the use of new computer-controlled systems.

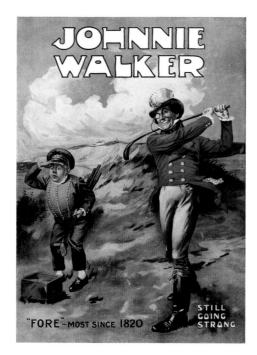

American whiskey to younger drinkers are developing at a swift pace, and whiskies infused with new flavourings, particularly, honey and cherry, are becoming hugely popular stateside.

Global whisky sales are today at an all-time high, with new markets such as China, Brazil, Russia and Taiwan beginning to enjoy whisky in many forms. Such is the predicted growth of the spirit that today, huge sums are being invested in Scotch, Irish, Japanese and American distilleries. High-tech distillery operations are opening up all over the world, taking an age-old production technique and bringing it firmly into the 21st century.

Since the development of whisky gathered pace in the 18th century, producers have often suffered from periods of high taxation and economic downturns. Today, however, producers are working in an international market – and it is an exciting one, too.

degrees of acclaim. In the US, despite an extensive period of Prohibition through the 1920s which threatened to obliterate the country's spirits and wine markets, many brand names have stood the test of time. New ways to present

THE MOST COMMON MYTHS ABOUT WHISKY

'Whisky! You stand before us today, charged with some of the most heinous crimes in the drinks world. How do you plead?'

Rather unfairly, the phrase 'innocent before proven guilty' has bypassed a few people concerning their first impressions about whisky, mostly based on old wives' tales, urban myths and previous bad experiences. So rather than see whisky condemned to a grizzly end at the hands of a biased jury, here are a few of the most common myths about whisky.

1 The Scots make the best whisky

Not necessarily. Despite perhaps learning the craft of whisky distillation from the Irish (a hotly debated subject in its own right), there's no doubt that Scotland has done wonders to promote whisky as a quintessentially Scottish drink. But times have changed over the last few decades. Now a thriving whisky scene exists across the globe, with arguably some of the world's greatest whiskies being produced in Japan, India and Europe, as well as the USA!

2 Whisky is definitely a man's drink

Not necessarily. Until the 1970s whisky was the fiery, powerful preserve of the alpha male. You only need to trawl through the outdated and embarrassingly sexist whisky advertisements depicting masculine pursuits and scantily clad women to realize just how far the spirit has come since then. Today, gender is no longer a boundary to discovering whisky, especially in emerging markets such as China and Russia, where whisky is becoming hugely popular with female drinkers.

3 Blended whisky is always an 'inferior quality' spirit

Nonsense. Blended whiskies are one of the most important and artisanal elements of the entire whisky business. No doubt there are cheaper, lower-budget blends, but the large majority of reputable blended whiskies are based on recipes dating back to the early 19th century and draw upon a palate of different- aged single malt and grain whiskies. As a result, the whisky blender's role is one of the most respected jobs in the entire industry.

4 Whisky should always be drunk neat

Nonsense. The golden rule is that there are no rules – it is a hugely versatile and refreshing drink, to be enjoyed on its own or mixed in a variety of ways.

5 Older and more expensive is most definitely better

One part of this myth is correct: older usually means more expensive. But when it comes to age as an indicator of quality, you're on a different playing field altogether. In recent years, some dazzlingly good (and youthful) whiskies have set the market on fire, but there are some pretty substandard old ones, too.

LEGAL DEFINITIONS

Essentially, making whisky is the same the world over, with distillers all using the 'holy trinity' of grain, water and yeast. But there are significant variations concerning grain varieties, methods of distillation and minimum legal maturation periods. Here are essential definitions of some of the main types of whisky being made today.

Scotland

There are five legally defined categories of Scotch whisky. To bear the name all Scotch whisky must be matured in Scotland in oak casks for a minimum period of three years.

Single malt is a Scotch whisky distilled at a single distillery from water and malted barley without the addition of any other cereals, and by batch distillation in pot stills. Single malt Scotch whisky must be bottled in Scotland. Contrary to opinion, there is no such thing as a 'double malt', but there are single malts that have been matured in two types of cask.

Single grain is a Scotch whisky distilled at a single distillery from water and malted barley, with or without whole grains of other malted or unmalted cereals, so it therefore does not comply with the definition of single malt Scotch whisky.

Blended Scotch whisky is a blend of one or more single malt Scotch whiskies with one or more single grain Scotch whiskies. Most blends are age-old recipes, expertly balanced by a master blender to keep the perfect consistency. **Blended malt Scotch whisky** is a blend of single malt Scotch whiskies that have been distilled at more than one distillery.

Blended grain Scotch whisky is a blend of single grain Scotch whiskies that have been distilled at more than one distillery.

Ireland

The legal definition of **Irish whiskey** states that the spirit must be distilled in Ireland from a 'mash of cereals', and then matured for a minimum of three years in Ireland. Although triple distillation is often regarded as one of the traditional characteristics of the style, there is no legal requirement to say that Irish whiskey must be triple distilled. Most Irish whiskey is a blend of patent still and pot still spirit, made using a mix of malted and unmalted barley. 'Pot still' Irish whiskey is triple-distilled in pot stills from a mash of malted and unmalted barley, and Irish distillers now use the term 'single pot still' for a range of such whiskeys. Just to confuse matters even more, single malt Irish whiskey is also produced by Cooley Distillery, using the Scotch whisky method of a pair of stills and malted barley.

LEFT: Between 1866 and 1868, New York City newspapers were full of reports of seized distilleries due to the necessary duties not having been paid. The illustration depicts a conflict in 1869, when General Pleasanton led a force of 1500 infantry and marines to destroy illicit stills and barrels of illegal whiskey.

The US and Canada

Bourbon whiskey production must take place within the US, but Bourbon can be made in any state, not just Kentucky, as is sometimes mistakenly thought. By law it must be made from a mash of not less than 51% corn grain and matured in new, white oak barrels that have previously been charred, or thermally degraded. No minimum maturation period is specified, but Bourbon has to be aged for more than two years before it can be labelled as 'straight Bourbon'.

Rye whiskey is produced in the US and Canada. In the US, rye whiskey by definition has to be produced from a grain mash of not less than 51% rye grain. In Canada, there is no such stipulation. The Canadian regulations merely state that Canadian whisky (Canadian rye whisky or rye whisky) should be distilled in Canada, and should possess the aroma, taste and character generally attributed to Canadian whisky.

Corn whiskey is a generic term for a rural, unsophisticated form of US whiskey, which has strong associations with 'moonshine' and is considered to improve very little with any aging. Legally, it must contain a minimum of 80% corn grain.

Tennessee whiskey is a Bourbon-style whiskey only produced within the state of Tennessee and subjected to a process of charcoal filtration – commonly known as 'the Lincoln County Process'.

Rest of the world

The rules governing whisky production around the world are not as strict as those of Scotland, Ireland and the US, and allow different grains, cask sizes and wood types to be used to great effect from as far afield as Austria to South Africa.

WHISKY- MAKING TODAY

ABOVE: This is Edradour, one of the smallest distilleries in Scotland and one of the prettiest to visit.

A look around any modern whisky distillery today will tell you two key things. First, very little has changed in the way of the actual production methods and the tools required to make whisky, from the mash tuns to the gleaming copper stills. Take a snapshot from 1900 and chances are the picture will look reasonably similar to any photo taken today. But if you take a closer look, you'll see a number of more recent changes – signs that production in the 21st century has embraced the digital age.

Except for the smallest artisanal operations, practically every distillery now uses some element of computer control. Stillmen sit at a computer console, monitoring temperatures and timings of spirit cut points and looking for any potential faults or changes to the production process. Use of the computer in the distillery has destroyed any romantic notion that whisky is still a totally handcrafted spirit, but it has led to a greater consistency with every production run. Gone, too, are the coal fires that once heated nearly every copper pot still, replaced by a more regulated steam coil or pan heating system, which makes it easier to maintain the correct temperature of a still – and is also less of a drain on natural resources.

In some of the largest distilleries, for example Diageo's impressive new Roseisle operation in Speyside, distillery operatives use wireless tablets, which means that any problems in production can be sourced quickly and repaired on the spot, rather than the operator having to leave the distillery floor to return to his office computer. The world's most high-tech distilleries are certainly a far cry from their 19th-century counterparts, but one thing will never change: yes, microchips can regulate production, but the human element will always remain the most important factor in determining a whisky's quality. As Dennis Malcolm, Master Distiller at the Glen Grant Distillery, observes, 'I can always tell if something is wrong just by using my nose. When I walk into the still room, if something smells different, I immediately know that all is not well!'

So it seems that the human nose always knows!

LEFT: A few Scottish distilleries still use operational floor maltings.

Inside the distillery

George Grant, owner of Glenfarclas Distillery in Speyside, recently noted, 'When I was a child I used to play hide and seek around the distillery and learned so much about the place just by doing that. The distillery was my playground.'

As playgrounds go, the modern distillery can conjure up all manner of delights – especially for the grown-ups. Visiting a distillery will not only give you a first-hand insight into how whisky is made, but it will also highlight that each one has its own slightly different take on making whisky, which then imparts a distinct set of flavours and aromas into the spirit when it is ready to be bottled.

Basically, whisky production in its (very) rawest state is a little like making a strong beer: boiling up the liquid a couple of times, collecting and condensing the vapours back into a liquid, then transferring it into wooden casks to age. But if it were that simple, everyone would be doing it! The production of whisky is a highly skilled process that requires not only an understanding of the chemical processes involved, but also a keen eye for detail and a well-developed nose and palate. You could say that the secret to making a great whisky is getting the right balance between science and art – and without either, the magic just wouldn't happen.

Today's distilleries, no matter where they are located in the world, usually comprise four key production areas, which we will look at in greater detail in the diagrams in the following pages: malting, mashing, fermentation and distillation.

Although a broad church with many international variants, whisky can be broken down into the following simple component parts, sometimes described as a 'holy trinity':

* Water
* Malted grain (of which there are many types)
* Yeast

ABOVE: Japanese whisky distillers have long appreciated the importance of the purity of the water used in the whisky-making process.

The water of life

Without a pure water source, no distillery could ever operate efficiently, so most have historically been built next to or near a plentiful supply – a river, borehole or loch. Scottish water tends to be softer in character, with a lower calcium and mineral content, which is believed to be the ideal type for producing whisky. Water from the islands on the west coast of Scotland tends to have a high peat content because the rivers and streams running through peat bogs give the water a brown tinge. Whether or not this has any direct effect on the overall flavour of the whisky is debatable, but there's no doubt that every distillery treats its water with the highest-possible regard. In Japan, for instance, the link between the purity of water and

the ancient Japanese tea ceremony had a profound influence over the location of the country's very first whisky distillery, Yamazaki (see page 145).

So when it's pouring with rain, raise a dram to the greying skies and think to yourself that today's rain is really tomorrow's whisky!

Grain: the real brains behind the spirit

For thousands of years, grain has been the building block of some of our most basic foodstuffs, and when fermented and turned into rich, malty ale it has also been responsible for much merriment.

Malt whisky production across most of Europe and Asia relies on barley as its base grain, and this little gem of flavour comes in a variety of strains. The most common varieties used by the whisky industry are Oxbridge, Optic and Chariot, and other more rare strains are used, too. The distiller is looking for the maximum yield of alcohol from the grain used and barley is therefore an ideal choice, given that it is particularly high in starch. This starch is turned into fermentable sugars by the process of malting – the first step in creating a wonderful malt whisky. Across North America and in Europe craft distillers are also experimenting with a number of more unusual grains, including varieties of corn, spelt and buckwheat.

Step 1 Marvellous malting A large proportion of the barley used in the production of whisky, from Scotland

to Japan, is grown on Scottish soil. Many distilleries now purchase their barley ready-malted. To malt the barley the grains are soaked in water. This encourages the first stages of germination in the grain, where the starchy insides are slowly converted into a type of sugar, known as maltose, to feed the germination process.

This process, whereby little shoots begin to emerge from the grain, takes up to six days. The maltster knows when to start the drying process (using peat smoke or hot air), which then stops any further growth and stops the grain from becoming rotten. Historically, most distilleries contained malting floors and a handful, such as Highland Park, Kilchoman and Balvenie, still malt a small proportion of their barley in this traditional fashion. Turning the slowly germinating barley by hand is a very laborious process, and in the past distillery workers often succumbed to a painful condition known as 'Monkey Shoulder' – a moniker adopted today by a popular blended malt whisky!

Step 2 The monster mash Once the perfectly malted barley is dried, it is ground into a mixture of coarse flour and grist (the husks of the grain). This mixture is then steeped in gallons of hot water in a huge vessel called a mash tun. Mashing separates the solids from the sweet sugars and the process is repeated twice more. The end liquid is sweet and hot and is called the wort. The wort is now ready for the third and hugely important stage of fermentation, where the third ingredient, yeast, comes into play.

Yeast

In order to create alcohol, yeast is combined with the wort in large fermentation vessels, called either fermenters or washbacks. Most distilleries in Scotland still have wooden washbacks, while newer ones and older expanding ones prefer to use stainless steel, which is much easier to keep clean. However, some distillers insist that the very fact that wooden vessels are less sterile, contributes to the character of the spirit that is ultimately produced.

The wort is pumped into the vessels and yeast is added to start the fermentation process. Most distilleries now use dried rather than creamed yeast. The yeast multiplies at a rapid rate, and in doing so uses up oxygen and creates carbon dioxide. It then begins to consume the sugar in the wort, producing alcohol as a result.

Over time, yeast varieties have been developed especially for use in distillation, and they tend to be higher-yielding and more stable and predictable than the brewer's yeast often used in the early years. Even so, the fermenters or washbacks are still usually fitted with revolving blades, or switchers, which cut down the foaming head of the fermenting wort as the yeast works its magic.

The crucial stages of fermentation take place in the first 48 hours, by which time all the sugar has been used up. Many

ABOVE TOP: Malted barley is used in the production of single malt Scotch whisky. Other types of grains are used globally to make whisky, helping to define a unique flavour in the process.

ABOVE: The whisky-making process is monitored continuously to ensure the very highest quality.

ABOVE: Copper pot
stills are a wonderful
sight to behold. This
is the still house at
Roseisle Distillery
in Speyside, where
the 14 copper stills,
called plain stills, are a
squarer-sided varation
on the lantern shape.
traditional plain shape
with squarer sides.

distilleries allow the process to continue for much longer – up to 70 hours – as different chemical reactions occur in the liquid, which is now called wash rather than wort, and which is essentially a kind of beer. Longer fermentation times tend to lead to fruitier notes in the spirit created at the next stage, when the wash undergoes distillation.

The copper

Distillation occurs in the still house, and one of the most memorable parts of any distillery visit comes when you enter the building and get your first impression of the pot stills: gleaming, curvaceous copper, hissing, hot to the touch and almost alive. This is the true heart of the whisky-making process.

But why are pot stills always made of copper? Why not stainless steel or any other heatproof, non-porous material? For a start, copper is relatively easy to work, mould and shape into the sort of designs you see in the still house, and it is also a good conductor of heat. Better still, contact between the liquid in the stills and the copper they're made from dramatically reduces undesirable sulphur compounds in the spirit ultimately produced. Whenever people have tried making pot still whisky without the use of expensive copper, the results have never been good!

Pot still whisky-making involves two consecutive distillations, the first of which takes place in what is known as the wash still, while the second happens in the spirit still. Essentially, each still is a copper kettle, nowadays usually heated by an internal steam coil. Because alcohol boils at a lower temperature than water, the alcohol vapours rise from the still before the water vapours. The alcohol vapours are then condensed into liquid when they pass through coiled copper pipes or 'worms', immersed in vast, water-cooled wooden vats or, more usually now, modern 'shell and tube' condensers, which function in much the same way.

After initial distillation in the wash still, alcohol with a strength of around 28% alcohol by volume (abv) is re-distilled in the spirit still in order to raise its strength. Throughout the distillation process the stillman uses the spirit safe to obtain the most pure 'cut' of spirit that will mature into whisky. The product of the spirit still is usually in the region of 70% abv.

In Ireland, and traditionally in the Scottish Lowlands, triple distillation is practised using three stills rather than two, and the result is a spirit that is lighter and more subtle in character.

Pot stills vary greatly in size, shape and technical design, and this diversity is one of the variables that contribute to the style of spirit made. As a general rule, small, squat stills will produce a bigger, more robust style of spirit, while tall, elegant stills will deliver a lighter, finer spirit.

The product of the spirit stills is referred to as 'new make' or 'clearic', a clear liquid that is reduced with water from its natural strength to around 63%

COPPER POT STILLS

There are three main types of pot stills:
* The **onion still** gets its name from its onion shape and is the most common.
* The **boil ball still** has a bulb fitted between the pot and the neck
* The **lantern still** has a narrow waist between the pot and the neck.
Visit the following distilleries to see some impressive pot stills:
* **Glenmorangie** In 2008 two pairs of stills were added which were exact replicas of those installed in 1843.
* **Glenkinchie**. Due to its closeness to Edinburgh, it has over 40,000 visitors a year.
* **Bruichladdich** on Islay has a strange-looking still called 'Ugly Betty'.
* **Penderyn** has a unique pot still.
* **Adnams** has a new 'Copper House'.

or 64% abv, as this is usually considered the optimum maturation strength. The next stage is maturation, which takes place in wooden casks (see page 35).

The illustrations on the following pages show the whisky-making process-es in a simplified form.

ABOVE: Onion-shaped copper stills at the Isle of Arran distillery.

SINGLE MALT WHISKY

1. Malting and drying Malt whisky is made using barley, steeped in water to make it germinate. The malted barley is then dried, either using hot air, or in the case of peated whisky, the smoke from a peat-fired kiln, giving the malt a smoky flavour and aroma.

2. Milling and mashing The malted barley is ground down into a mixture of coarse flour and grist (the husks of the grain). It is then transferred to a mash tun, where it is combined with hot water. This process creates a hot, sweet liquid called wort.

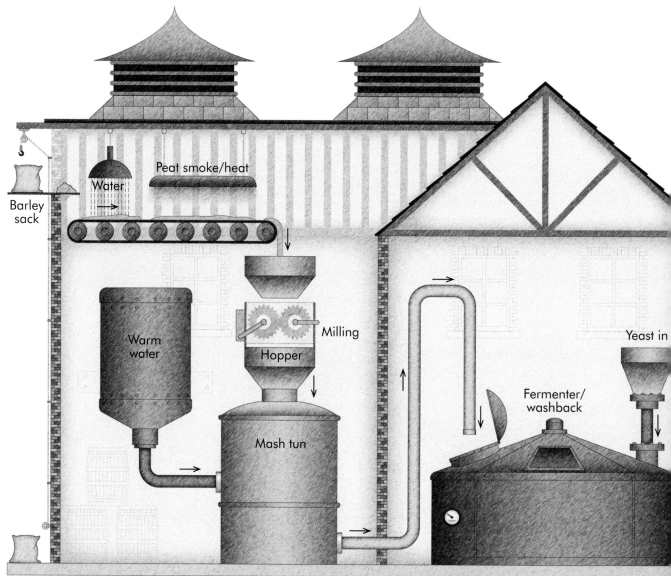

Peat smoke/heat

Water

Barley sack

Warm water

Milling

Hopper

Mash tun

Yeast in

Fermenter/ washback

3. Fermentation The wort is cooled and piped into huge fermenters or washbacks. Yeast is then added. The mixture starts the fermentation cycle (where the sugars in the wort are consumed by the yeast and turned into alcohol). The resulting liquid is called wash (or beer), with an alcohol strength of around 7–8% by volume.

4. Distillation The wash makes its way into the first of a two-stage distillation process, using a pair of copper pot stills (wash and spirit stills). When heated, the wash evaporates and the alcohol vapour rises and condenses back into a liquid. The process is repeated in the second still, the spirit increasing to around 70% abv, where it is collected, then slightly diluted, ready for filling into casks.

5. Maturation The new-make spirit is filled into used oak casks, which are most likely to have previously held American Bourbon or Spanish Sherry. The spirit matures slowly, developing a range of flavours and aromas from the wood. The spirit must be matured for a minimum of three years before it can legally be called Scotch malt whisky.

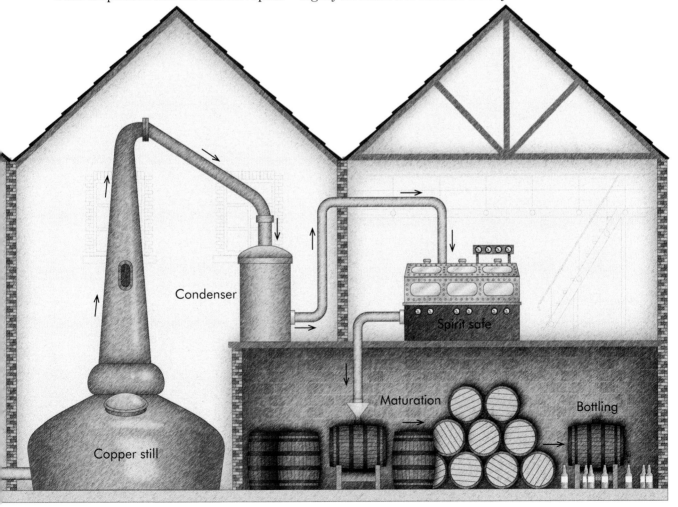

Condenser

Spirit safe

Maturation

Bottling

Copper still

GRAIN WHISKY

The mash bill for grain whisky usually comprises a high percentage of unmalted cereal, commonly wheat, along with an amount of 'green' malted barley (barley that has started to germinate and has not yet been dried), which is included to promote fermentation. Maize (corn) is sometimes used as an alternative to wheat, but its high cost compared to wheat has led most distillers to switch to wheat in recent years.

1. Milling and mashing The wheat or maize is milled and then cooked in large pressure cookers in order to soften the husks and release starch. The liquid is mixed with malted barley in a mash tun, where the barley converts the starch into fermentable sugars.

2. Fermentation The liquid, now called wort, is pumped into fermenting vessels, where yeast is added. The resulting wash has an abv of 6–7%.

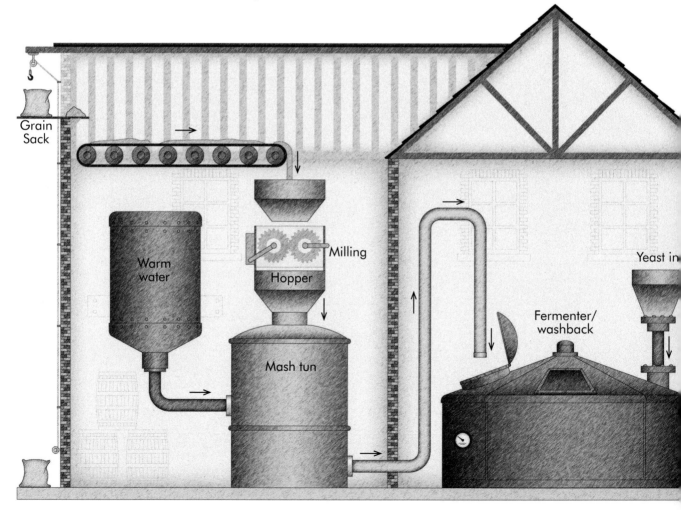

Grain
Sack

Warm
water

Milling

Hopper

Mash tun

Fermenter/
washback

Yeast in

3. Distillation The column still consists of two interconnected stainless steel columns called the analyser and the rectifier. Steam is fed in at the base of the analysing column, while hot wash enters at the top. When the wash boils, the alcohol vapour and uncondensed steam rise to the head of the column. The alcohol vapour is pumped into the base of the rectifying column. This second distillation stage strengthens the spirit, which subsequently passes through the water-cooled condenser to the spirit safe.

4. The strength of the spirit collected in the spirit safe is significantly higher than that produced in pot stills – usually between 90% and 94.8% abv, with the latter being the highest strength allowed by law in Scotland and Ireland.

5. Maturation Maturation almost always takes place in ex-Bourbon casks, usually of the first-fill variety. By law in Scotland and Ireland, the spirit must be matured for at least three years.

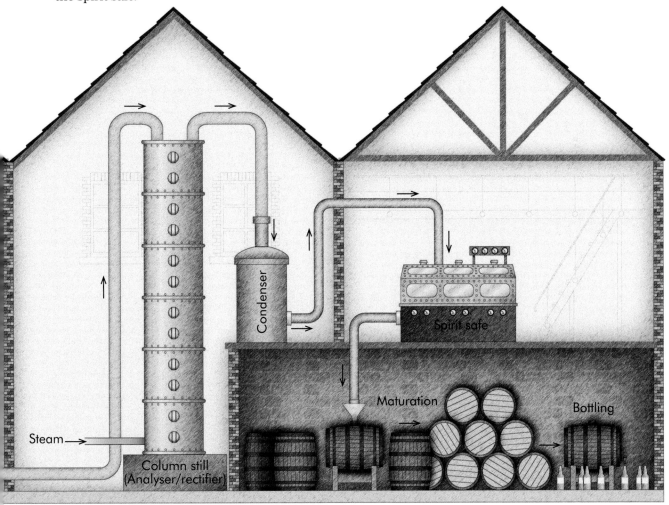

Condenser

Spirit safe

Maturation

Bottling

Steam ⟶

Column still
(Analyser/rectifier)

AMERICAN WHISKEY

There are four main types: Bourbon, rye, corn and Tennessee (*see* page 19 for a fuller explanation). Each distillery designs its own unique mash bill recipe. Bourbon is predominantly made up of three grains: corn (maize), with a minimum of 51% required by law, rye and malted barley. Each grain brings a different level of flavour to the finished product. Sometimes wheat is also used to give more flavour.

1. Milling Corn is a difficult grain to ferment and distil so it is often milled and cooked separately.

2. Mashing The three grains are steeped in water, with an additional sour mash (the leftover residue from a previous mash), which brings an acidic note and helps fermentation.

3. Fermentation Yeast is added. As well as generic dried or creamed yeast, Bourbon distilleries have numerous

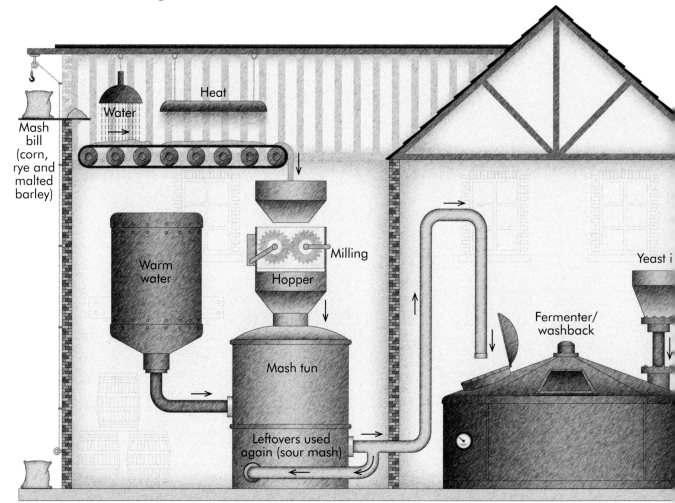

Mash bill (corn, rye and malted barley)

Water

Heat

Warm water

Milling

Hopper

Mash tun

Leftovers used again (sour mash)

Fermenter/ washback

Yeast i

local strains of yeast (some even preserved from the distillery's past) to give a wider range of flavour to the mash. Fermentation usually lasts for around three days.

4. Distillation The column or continuous still is the most popular method used, with the wash or beer being pumped into the top of the first, analysing column. The alcohol vapour is condensed into a liquid for the second distillation in the rectifying column. This process intensifies the abv of the spirit. In the production of Bourbon, the distillate collected from the still must not exceed 80% abv. Tennessee whiskey uses the Lincoln County process whereby, the new-make spirit is slowly dripped through layers of maple charcoal to purify or filter it.

5. Maturation The spirit (reduced to around 60%) is filled into brand new, charred white American oak casks. Bourbon must be matured for a minimum of two years and the casks cannot be re-used for Bourbon – many are shipped overseas for use by the whisky industry worldwide.

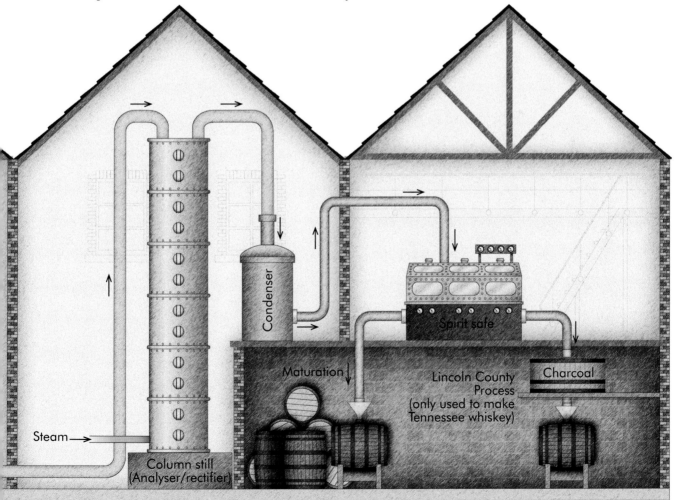

Steam →

Condenser

Column still (Analyser/rectifier)

Maturation

Spirit safe

Lincoln County Process (only used to make Tennessee whiskey)

Charcoal

PART 2: THE FLAVOURS OF WHISKY

In this section we cover the aromas and flavours found in whisky. It is reckoned that about 70% of these aromas and flavours come from the maturation process in oak casks. We also discuss whether environment and factors such as climate, the grain and where it is grown, the water used in the production process and the age of whisky play a part in its final flavours.

There is much more to describing a particular whisky than simply labelling it as good or bad, but there is no such thing as a secret code of vocabulary used by experts to describe its many aromas and flavours. We all have our own set of words we use and build on every time we taste a whisky. Most of us use memories and associations to expand our own personal database.

CASKS

Once the new-make spirit is ready to leave the spirit stills (see page 25), the next stage is to fill it into casks. The cask – or 'wood' as it is often known in distilling circles – is particularly important because it serves two purposes: it is both a storage vessel, and it is where the vital process of maturation takes place. New-make spirit develops its colour and the large majority of its aroma and flavour from the inside of the cask. The three mostly commonly used casks are the Bourbon barrel (200 litres/44 gallons), the hogshead (250 litres/55 gallons) and the butt (450–550 litres/100–120 gallons).

Oak is the best wood for whisky casks because it is hard, yet relatively easy to work, and has just the right degree of porosity, allowing the spirit to 'breathe' within the cask without it leaking out. By law, most of the principal recognized styles of whisky, wherever produced, must be matured in oak casks. The two main types of oak are American white oak (*Quercus alba*) and European or 'Spanish' oak (*Quercus robur*). American white oak grows faster, is tighter-grained and has fewer knots. It is not better but simply different in the way it interacts with the spirit in it and the character it gives that spirit, though it tends to be easier for coopers to work with.

Aging of Scotch whisky was traditionally carried out in Spanish oak casks, as there was a ready and inexpensive supply because of the popularity of imported Spanish Sherry in Britain during the 18th and 19th centuries. The use of cheaper American oak casks in Scotch whisky was a 20th-century innovation, largely brought about by the US legal requirement for all Bourbon whiskey to be matured in newly charred casks that could only be used once. It followed, therefore, that there were plenty of ex-Bourbon casks looking for new homes once their Bourbon-aging days were over. The Scotch whisky industry eagerly snapped up this new source of casks, which coincided with a dramatic decline in the British love affair with Sherry.

The result is that today only around 5% of the 18 million casks of whisky quietly maturing in Scottish warehouses are ex-Sherry casks. These casks are also around ten times more expensive than ex-Bourbon ones.

FACING PAGE: In Scotch whisky production the traditional art of coopering is as important today as it was a century ago. The role of the cooper is to rejuvenate and reassemble old casks ready for the maturation process.

BELOW: By law Bourbon whiskey is matured in new oak casks that can only be used once.

RIGHT: The insides of a cask are charred to precise degrees to help release the natural sugars and flavour compounds within the oak in order to enhance the flavour profile of the whisky.

Today some Scottish distilleries use only American oak casks, while many use a mixture of American and European oak casks. The whiskies from these different casks are then blended together in varying proportions. For example, the proportions may be altered for bottlings of different ages. A few traditionalists, such as The Macallan, Glenfarclas, GlenDronach and The Dalmore, concentrate on the use of ex-Sherry casks, and their single malts have a dedicated band of consumers around the world.

Old casks are reconditioned by coopers before filling with the new spirit. The coopers spend a lengthy apprenticeship learning how to assemble, re-assemble and repair the casks to make them watertight again. No nails, glue or other 'trickery' are used. The art of coopering involves very precise jointing and fitting and, while labour-saving devices have taken much of the back-breaking toil out of the business, nothing can replace the pure craftsmanship of the cooper when the (wood) chips are down!

MATURATION

We don't know when someone discovered that if you left fiery, raw, new spirit in wooden casks for a period of time the quality improved, but we can speculate that it probably happened by accident. Imagine a distiller coming upon a mislaid cask of his whisky after months or years, maybe expecting it to be ruined, only to be pleasantly surprised by its mellowness and rounded character.

While science can explain almost every part of whisky production, there remain aspects of maturation that elude even the most determined chemists, and for most of us this element of mystique makes the spirit taste even sweeter.

Broadly speaking, maturation takes place as part of a three-way 'conversation' between the spirit, the cask and the external atmosphere. In a small cask the spirit has much greater contact with the wood than in a large one, and so the smaller the cask, the faster maturation will occur. This is a generalization, since a cask that has previously held Bourbon or Sherry and is being used for whisky

BELOW: The empty old casks at Glenfiddich's distillery at Dufftown, Speyside, Scotland, are seasoned outside for a few months before being filled with whisky.

ABOVE LEFT: The 'angels' share' seen above refers to the small amount of evaporating spirit, which escapes naturally from the casks over time.

ABOVE RIGHT: Traditional malt whisky distilleries in Scotland often used low-lying stone buildings, called dunnage warehouses. The walls are thick and the floors are often packed earth to encourage humidity during the maturation process

maturation for the first time – known as a first-fill cask – has a greater influence than a cask being used for the second, third or even fourth time.

Different types of spirit mature at varying rates, with some lighter styles reaching an acceptable rate of maturation after half a dozen years, while others may need twice that span or even more to realize their true potential.

In addition, the type of cask plays a major part in determining the character of the mature whisky. Ex-Sherry casks tend to generate raisin and prune flavours in the whisky and give it a more viscous character, while the use of ex-Bourbon casks leads to vanilla, banana and spicy oak notes.

During maturation, changes in volume and strength occur, with casks losing between 1–2% in volume per year, usually referred to as the 'angels' share'. Both alcohol and water evaporate during maturation, and if the humidity is relatively high, as in Scotland and

Ireland, there is less evaporation of water, leading to a lowering of strength.

By comparison, in the southern US whiskey-making heartlands of Kentucky and Tennessee, temperatures tend to be higher and humidity lower, so water losses are more substantial, resulting in an alcoholic strength that may actually increase during maturation. In India and Taiwan, two of the world's newest whisky-producing nations, the high temperatures and humid climates mean that spirit evaporation with a cask happens at a much faster rate than in Scotland. As a result whiskies are bottled there at a much younger age, usually at between two and six years.

It is estimated that up to 70% of the character of the whisky we drink develops during maturation, so it's far more than just the colour of the whisky that is transformed from clear to varying shades of gold and brown during all those years slumbering in warehouses.

TERROIR IN WHISKY?

Wine writers will tell you that the 'terroir' of a certain vineyard has a profound effect on the overall style of a quality wine. First developed in France, the notion of terroir, put simply, is the relationship between climate, soil and exposure to the sun of a particular vineyard and how it affects the wine from the grapes grown there. Does the same apply to whisky? After all, wine and whisky are unquestionably elemental drinks.

Would even the most discerning of palates be able to detect any differences between whisky made using barley grown in Mr McTavish's bottom field and the one, over yonder hill, behind the tree and the babbling burn?

Whisky's raw materials

If we consider the raw materials of whisky – malted barley, water and yeast – and how they are processed, the real differences in character of the newly made spirit become more apparent.

The strain of barley – for example, the highly efficient Oxbridge, Optic or Chariot varieties – can give a greater crop harvest per acre, and a higher yield of fermentable sugars for the distiller to convert into alcohol. But they won't necessarily add a noticeable difference to the spirit's flavour. More important is a distillery's individual approach to malting, milling and mashing the barley, which will create the embryonic character of a whisky's flavour.

Although an abundant supply of clean water is integral to every distillery, the type of water (hard, soft, high in certain minerals and so on) has only a minor effect on the flavour of a whisky at the final stage, when the alcohol strength of the whisky is diluted in the bottling hall.

Peat is also a crucial element in the terroir of a whisky. Peated Scotch whisky has become synonymous with the islands of Islay, Skye and Orkney and the peated malts from here do have distinctive flavour differences. Whiskies produced on Islay could be described as having a distinct style – smoky – but this description is not unique to the island.

The type of vegetation from which the peat forms differs from island to island (for example, Orkney has very few trees and is covered in floral heather), and some people argue that these differences do have an effect on the end flavours. But as a generalization, the whiskies produced on these islands have historically developed smoky styles out of necessity. For centuries peat provided an abundant source of fuel and has directly influenced the production and style of the whiskies in the region.

Another factor is the storage conditions of the whisky casks. The cool, damp conditions may vary from warehouse to warehouse – so much so that certain warehouses are said to have 'sweet spots'.

ABOVE: Peat cutting is a hugely important job on the islands of Islay, Skye and Orkney. Peat is still cut for domestic fuel, although not nearly as much as in the past, as well as for use in whisky production. It is traditionally cut by hand into bricks, then left to dry naturally in the open air. For use in whisky production it is burnt in kilns to give a distinctive smoky characteristic to the barley, which in turn imparts that character to the actual spirit.

OLD VERSUS YOUNG WHISKY

If there's one thing that sparks many a bar-room debate (and possibly the occasional tipsy argument) between whisky-lovers, it is a discussion about the nature of what makes whisky such an exciting and topical spirit: its age.

Although there's no denying that filling some newly made spirit into a quality oak cask will have a profound effect on the resulting whisky, there is the recurring question of when does 'it's ready' actually mean it's ready. Since 1915, the UK Immature Spirit Act has required all whisky to be matured for a minimum maturation period of no less than 'three years and one day'. More recently, under the guidance of the Scotch Whisky Association, the law now requires that the only age statement that can appear on the label of a whisky bottle is the age of the youngest whisky contained inside.

A straightforward or down-right complicated issue?

What this essentially means is that if a batch of, for example, 12-year-old single malt whisky has been produced and bottled by a distillery, the whisky within the bottle must be no younger than 12 years old. What this doesn't account for is that there might well be some older whiskies in there, too, helping to give the overall whisky a greater complexity and texture. It is not uncommon for distilleries to undertake this practice because of the need consistently and accurately to re-create a recipe across multiple batches of a brand of whisky.

Is older actually better?

The longer a whisky matures in a cask, the more likely it is to develop a complexity of flavour, as well as to lose some of the perceived 'harsh', spirity characteristics associated with very young whisky. A cask of maturing whisky loses around 1.5% of its volume year on year, as well as developing a lower abv, as the water evaporates. Rather like a well-reduced sauce, the longer a whisky rests, the more concentrated the flavours become and the more the whisky will begin to take on characteristics of the type of cask in which it is housed. But sometimes whisky can begin to take on the undesirable characteristics of maturing in wood: slightly bitter, woody notes, thin, dry flavours and in the worst of cases, being completely overwhelmed by the oak, losing all its character and therefore its quality. There is a very fine balancing act between knowing when a cask is just right and whether it's about to fall off the cliff into an oaky abyss.

As the demand for whisky around the world increases year on year, there is a greater pressure on distilleries to make their stocks go further, and whiskies that have been maturing for less time can effectively be bottled and enjoyed by drinkers more quickly! To highlight this, the growth of Scotch whiskies released with no age statement at all means that so long as it's older than three years and a day, whisky can be bottled, with the likelihood that the overall balance of flavour and aroma will be rounded off with some older, more mature whisky to help give a greater complexity.

Although young whiskies have had less time to develop a character of their own, this doesn't mean that they are without merit. Some of the most exciting and surprising whiskies are aged for less than five to six years. More often than not, younger whiskies exude less complexity but more than make up for it by offering a fresh, spritely and direct personality, and it is this style that is becoming popular around the world.

The moral is not to mistake age for beauty or to choose wisdom in preference to youth. Sometimes all is not what it seems, and every whisky tells its own unique story.

YOUNG WHISKIES TO TRY

KAVALAN CLASSIC — MATURED FOR 2 YEARS

AROMAS OF WOODY SPICE, TROPICAL FRUIT, VANILLA AND SWEET SPONGE CAKE. VERY EASY-DRINKING, WITH FURTHER NOTES OF VANILLA AND OAK ON THE PALATE.

THE BELGIAN OWL — 3-YEAR-OLD

LIGHT CITRUS NOTE MIXED WITH VANILLA AND SWEET MALTED CEREAL ON THE NOSE, WITH SOME DELICATE VANILLA, FRESH ORCHARD FRUIT AND A TOUCH OF FRESH MINT ON THE PALATE.

KILCHOMAN MACHIR BAY
— A VATTING OF 3-, 4- AND 5-YEAR-OLD WHISKY

A NOSE OF SWEET PEAT AND VANILLA, UNDERCUT BY BRINE, KELP AND BLACK PEPPER. FILLED ASHTRAYS IN TIME. LOTS OF NICELY BALANCED CITRUS FRUIT, PEAT SMOKE AND GERMOLENE ON THE PALATE. THE FINISH IS RELATIVELY LONG AND SWEET, WITH BUILDING SPICE.

AROMA AND FLAVOUR

ABOVE: Nosing a whisky in the warehouse in which it has been maturing is always an exhilarating experience.

On the facing page we have outlined four simple aroma and flavour groups that seem to work for our noses and palates. The divisions are not hard and fast but we hope they will help to link together certain aromas and flavours you may find within your whisky, and also offer some useful descriptive words so that you can recall it in the future. The more whiskies you try, the more your own whisky vocabulary will develop. This is particularly helpful when tasting one of the growing number of new international whiskies that are now available, as these may bring unusual notes you may not be able to identify immediately.

Some people find it useful to identify aromas and flavours by certain colours or, in some cases, by seasons. For example, the lighter, softer and more floral and fresh notes found in a whisky can be associated with lighter, more vibrant colours and are subsequently more often suited to being drunk in spring and summer. Darker, heavier notes, such as dried fruits, peat smoke and woody spices, tend to be associated with darker colours and are perhaps better suited to being drunk in autumn and winter.

But again, there are no firm rules. If you happen to enjoy a lightweight soft, floral, fruity whisky in the middle of winter, then so be it: simply fill your glass and enjoy!

How do you start learning about the fundamental aromas and flavours of a particular whisky and what makes it smell and taste the way it does? One of the best ways is to separate whiskies into simple categories.

Fresh, floral and fruity

Cut grass, hay, jasmine tea, rose petals, citrus fruit, red berries, orchard fruit, perfume, freshly cut pine, nail polish remover, mint, menthol, fresh herbs, white wine.

Buttery, smooth and sweet

Vanilla, candyfloss, malty cereal, ice cream, golden syrup, dairy fudge, milk and white chocolate, icing sugar, cream, sponge cake, candle wax, wet cardboard.

Rich and spicy

Polished furniture, oak, honey, toffee, dried fruits, cinnamon, woody spice, red wine, Sherry, Christmas cake, black pepper, cedar, coffee, rubber, dark chocolate, nuts.

Smoky and peaty

Burnt bonfire, soot, cigar smoke, salty sea spray, bandages, medicine, disinfectant, seared meat and barbecue, tar, engine oil, soil, wet leaves, moss.

THE FLAVOUR MAP

SMOKY

LIGHT

RICH

DELICATE

Sainsbury Islay 10 Yr Old

Ardberg 10 Yr Old

Laphroaig 10 Yr Old

Laphroaig Quarter Cask

Ardberg Uigedail

Lagavulin 12 Yr Old Special Release

Lagavulin 16 Yr Old

Ledaig 10 Yr Old

Caol Ila Cask Strength

Caol Ila 12 Yr Old

Port Ellen 24 Yr Old

Lagavulin Distillers Edition

Caol Ila Distillers Edition

Talisker 10 Yr Old

Port Ellen 29 Yr Old

Talisker Distillers Edition

Caol Ila 18 Yr Old

Talisker 57 North

Bowmore 12 Yr Old

Laphroaig 25 Yr Old

Talisker 18 Yr Old

Talisker 25 Yr Old

F&M Islay Bowmore 9 Yr Old

Talisker 30 Yr Old

Longrow 10 Yr Old

Brora 30Yr Old

Highland Park 12 Yr Old

Highland Park 30 Yr Old

Springbank 10 Yr Old

Ardmore Traditional Cask

Glenfiddich 12 Yr Old Caoran Reserve

Bowmore Legend

Johnnie Walker Green Label 15 Yr Old

Highland Park 21 Yr Old

Highland Park 18 Yr Old

Jura Superstition

Brora 25 Yr Old

BenRiach 16 Yr Old

Highland Park Single Malt 16 Yr Old

Highland Park 40 Yr Old

Bells Special Reserve

Glen Ord 12 Yr Old

The Singleton of Glen Ord 18 Yr Old

Teaninich 10 Yr Old

The Singleton of Glen Ord

Glenlossie 10 Yr Old

Glenfarclas 25 Yr Old

Oban 14 Yr Old

Cragganmore 12 Yr Old

Oban Distillers Edition

Cragganmore Distillers Edition

Glendullan 12 Yr Old

Old Pulteney 21 Yr Old

Bruichladdich 15 Yr Old

Dalwhinnie Distillers Edition

Mortlach 16 Yr Old

Dalwhinnie 15 Yr Old

Mannochmore 12 Yr Old

Singleton of Glendullan 12 Yr Old

Blair Athol 12 Yr Old

Benrinnes 15 Yr Old

Dailuaine 16 Yr Old

Glenmorangie 25 Yr Old

Clynelish Distillers Edition

Singleton of Dufftown 12 Yr Old

Oban 18 Yr Old

Clynelish 14 Yr Old

Glenmorangie Signet

Glenmorangie 18 Yr Old

Macallan 18 Yr Old

Glenfarclas 21 Yr Old

Linkwood 12 Yr Old

F&M Speyside Braeval 9 Yr Old

Cardhu 12 Yr Old

Glenmorangie Nectar D'Or

Aberfeldy 21YO

Glenmorangie AStar

Balvenie 21 Yr Old

Macallan Select Oak

Macallan 10 Yr Old

AnCnoc 12 Yr Old

Glen Elgin 12 Yr Old

Glenmorangie Original

Glenlivet 25 Yr Old

Macallan Makers Edition

Dalmore 15 Yr Old

Royal Lochnagar 12 Yr Old

Aberfeldy 12 Yr Old

Dalmore 12 Yr Old

Scapa 16 Yr Old

Macallan 10 Yr Old

Glenfarclas 15 Yr Old

Glenfiddich 30 Yr Old

Bruichladdich 10 Yr Old

Arran 10 Yr Old

Longmorn 16 Yr Old

Glenrothes 1991

Glenmorangie La Santa

Glenfiddich 21 Yr Old

Glenkinchie 12 Yr Old

Glenmorangie Quinta Ruban

Glenrothes Special Reserve

Glenkinchie Distillers Edition

Balvenie 14 Yr Old Golden Cask

Balvenie Double Wood

Inchgower 14 Yr Old & F&M Highland Blair Athol 9 Yr Old

Smiths Glenlivet 15 Yr Old

Cardhu Special Cask Reserve

Glen Moray

Glenlivet Archive 21

Glenfiddich 18 Yr Old

Glenlivet 12 Yr Old

Aberlour 12 Yr Old

Glenlivet Nadurra 16 Yr Old

Balvenie Signature

Glenfiddich Solera

Aberlour 15 Yr Old

Tormore 12 Yr Old

Strathisla 12 Yr Old

Monkey Shoulder

Aberlour 16 Yr Old

Aberlour 10 Yr Old

Auchroisk 10 Yr Old

Glenfiddich 12 Yr Old

Bunnahabhain 12 Yr Old

Aberlour A'bunadh

Strathmill 12 Yr Old

Knockando 12 Yr Old

Sainsbury Speyside 12 Yr Old

Balvenie Founders Reserve

Jura 10 Yr Old

Glenlivet 18 Yr Old

Rosebank 12 Yr Old

Scapa 14 Yr Old

Bruichladdich 16 First Growth Haut Brion

Auchentoshan Classic & Sainsbury Highland 12 Yr Old

Auchentoshan 12 Yr Old

Auchentoshan 3 Wood

Glen Spey 12 Yr Old

Glenlivet 15 Yr Old

44   THE FLAVOURS OF WHISKY

CONSISTENCY OF FLAVOURS

Whisky-lovers rightly celebrate diversity and quirkiness, enjoying sampling anything new and slightly different. Limited editions of single malts made using unusual barley varieties or matured in out-of-the-ordinary casks, for example, tend to sell out very quickly. This is at odds with what most distillers want to achieve with the vast bulk of the whisky they make: consistency.

We should always remember that however exciting the world of single malts might be, more than 90% of all Scotch whisky produced is sold in the form of blends, and one of the primary objectives of whisky blenders is to ensure that every bottle of a specific brand you buy tastes identical to the last one you bought, and to the one you buy next time.

Accordingly, all large-scale whisky producers work very hard to ensure that one batch of malt whisky produced in an individual distillery is as close as possible to all other batches.

To achieve this, producers have increasingly turned to scientists who have analysed each stage of the whisky-making process from a chemical and biological point of view, determining just why things turn out the way they do. Understand why various practices and procedures produce particular results and you can be that much more confident of making a consistent spirit.

Scientific research has led to the development of new barley varieties that give higher spirit yields, and to new yeast varieties, which are more stable than in the past, when tun-room workers could often be seen beating down the froth of washbacks with heather switches!

The different stages of whisky production used to be affected by far more variables than is the case today. The malting of barley used to take place in individual distilleries, where it was a labour-intensive process, with peat being burnt in a kiln to dry the 'green malt', as it is known, and to halt germination and impart flavour. Now many of the distilleries buy their barley 'ready malted' for both consistency and cost reasons.

The ultimate consistency is produced when computer programmes are used in the distillery to control production processes. But most of us like to think that the whisky we drink is a handcrafted product, and the producers encourage such thoughts in their marketing.

FACING PAGE: Use this flavour map of 138 different Scotch malt whiskies to try some new whiskies. It has been prepared by the independent whisky expert, Dave Broom, together with Diageo and is widely used to help people understand the multitude of different flavours in whisky.

PART 3: ENJOYING WHISKY

Whether it's a refreshing blended whisky and soda over ice in the summer, or a generously proportioned warming dram of single malt in the winter, enjoying whisky is about making the most of your location and the company you happen to be with.

At its best, whisky is a wonderful conversation starter with friends and a terrific social lubricant. It is also one of the most rewarding spirits when approached in the right frame of mind – with enough time to get under its skin and have a good root around you can discover many unique flavours.

This section gives you easy tips on how to taste, buy and serve whisky with confidence and how to enjoy whisky either on its own or as part of a cocktail. When paired with food whisky needs careful consideration and we cover the do's and don'ts of whisky and food pairing. Whisky and cigars have long been a classic combination and we describe some great matches to enhance your smoking experience. Next, the subject of collecting and investing is explained – which distilleries are the most collectable, whether for your own small collection to enjoy at home or for collecting for profit – followed by the world of counterfeit whisky and its potential pitfalls.

HOW TO TASTE WHISKY

ABOVE: The usual number of whiskies sampled at a tasting would be five or six, starting with the lighter in character and moving to the heavier styles. Style is usually more significant than age of the whisky.

It's an exciting moment sitting there about to taste your first whisky rather than just treating it as any old drink.

First, look at your whisky

The colour of a whisky will invariably tell you very little about what to expect from the flavour and aroma, unless the label on the bottle explains that there is additional caramel colouring, or E150, to give it its official title. In small amounts, E150 is flavourless and odourless. It is more likely to be present in whisky bottled by large distilleries as they place more emphasis on a consistent appearance in the end product. Independent, small-batch companies place less emphasis on a consistent appearance. If you pour a whisky that

is cloudy, especially with the addition of water, this is most likely because it hasn't been through the process of 'chill filtration'. This process is essentially to ensure visual conformity in the whisky and that there is no cloudiness when water is added. It is reckoned that not chill-filtering gives a better texture and additional flavour elements to the whisky.

All in all, the most important thing to look for in a whisky's appearance is what are cheekily called the 'legs'. Swirl your glass round several times and a line of fine beads or globules will form around the rim. These then slowly ooze back down into the whisky, forming 'legs' as they do so. Thicker, slower-forming 'legs' often indicate a more viscous, mouth-filling whisky.

A nose knows

After you have taken a good look at the colour it's the turn of the nose – but before you take a deep breath, close your eyes and dive straight in, spare a thought for the senses you're about to call on. The truth is that rather than rely on any one sense, tasting whisky properly relies on all your senses ... well, perhaps not hearing, unless you happen to hear the drip, drip, drip from a cracked glass.

The link between your sense of smell and taste is perhaps not very well known but it is worth pointing out. Just behind the top of your nose lies a pretty incredible organ, the olfactory gland, which we still know little about, other than its importance in the process of detecting, deciphering and helping the brain assess aroma and taste. And one thing's for sure: you need to keep it healthy in order to taste anything properly.

Try pinching your nostrils together when you take your first swallow of whisky – you won't taste anything at all! This is precisely why we lose our sense of taste during a cold, as the pathways between the nose and the olfactory gland become blocked and are unable to allow the transfer of aroma into the olfactory receptors in the brain. Upwards of 70% of 'perceived flavour' is generated this way; our tongues and the minute papillae which cover them can only detect bitter, sweet, sour, salty and umami sensations.

As we have already mentioned, whisky is a feisty beast, so avoid diving straight in the glass with your nose! The strong alcohol content of whisky will invariably have a numbing effect on your senses. Find a comfortable distance between the glass and your nostrils and slowly inhale the aromas from deep inside the glass. Close your eyes, visualize what you can smell and note down your findings. Several long, slow sniffs will begin to reveal the depth of character within the whisky.

Allow the whisky some time in the glass to breathe, nose again and you'll begin to notice marked differences from the first time. The key to visualizing aroma is hidden within the

EASY STEPS TO A TASTING NOTE

Make a note of the **distillery/brand** and the **age/strength (abv) of the whisky.**

Then make notes on:
Nose Note down your first findings (initial aromas) e.g. spices, fruit, smoke. Then try to evaluate the aromas further: What kind of spice/smoke? Is it citrus or orchard fruit? Fresh or dried? Then you can add a little water to the glass and note the changes in aromas.

Palate Note down the flavours from your first sip – is there anything overpowering? Take a further sip and look for any changes in flavour.

Finish Note down what flavours are left on the palate. How long do they linger?

Overall Try to sum up your thoughts: whether you loved, liked or disliked it, so you can refer to the tasting note in years to come. A score out of ten is useful.

LEFT: So now you know what whisky 'legs' look like. These are the globules of whisky that ooze slowly back down the sides of the glass after you have given it a good swirl. The thicker the legs, the more mouth-filling the whisky.

its complexity – the richer and thicker the body of a whisky, the more natural oils and flavour emerge. If it is sipped at cask strength (around 54–60% abv), a few drops of water will certainly unlock more character and remove some of the slightly harsh, alcoholic overtones. Some people advocate holding the whisky in the mouth a second for every year of the whisky's age – try and get past 20 seconds before the burn begins to set in! Professional whisky tasters do spit, just as wine tasters do, as these tasting can include up to 50 or so different whiskies to try – but, of course, you don't have to when you're with friends.

The grand finale

As the initial taste gives way and dies down, the finish of the whisky will remain and leave a lasting impression, an echo or just a trace, sometimes imparting further qualities and character to the palate. The longer the finish to a whisky, the more well-balanced and enjoyable it becomes.

Writing tasting notes

Whether you get 'leather on willow' or the 'smell of Grandma's apple pie', every tasting note is personal to you. It takes time to develop a set of descriptive skills, so it's worth documenting your notes in a diary whenever you try a new whisky. That way, when you revisit it, you have a reference point ... has your description changed the second time around? Have fun and surprise yourself!

ABOVE: A whisky tasting may include up to five or six whiskies. A normal measure at a tasting is 25ml (1 fl oz) or lower.

BELOW: Use a whisky tasting diary for those all-important whisky-tasting notes.

mysterious olfactory gland. When you detect a familiar aroma, the olfactory gland triggers memories, or olfactory 'hallucinations' of where you were, how old you were and what you were doing when you first smelled the aroma! Throughout life, we collect thousands of aromas, all personal to each of us, and that is why no one person has a definitive set of notes on the aromas in a particular whisky.

A taste sensation

Take a small sip and allow the spirit to envelop the whole of the mouth and tongue. Try to hold the whisky in the mouth for a few seconds before swallowing. What are the first impressions? The mouthfeel of a whisky often gives an indication to

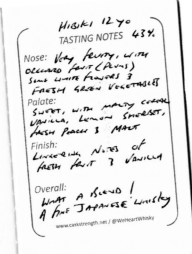

BUYING WHISKY

From the moment you walk through the door of a decent whisky shop, you're presented with the wonderful, if ever so slightly mesmerizing sight of shelf upon shelf of fabulous-looking bottles. For many of us, this is just as exciting a moment as your first visit to a sweet shop all those years ago (we still get hot under the collar just thinking about it). But for the novice it can be a pretty intimidating experience – especially if you don't know exactly what you're looking for.

Most whisky shops are staffed with knowledgeable assistants who share a common love for the spirit. Remember, too, that they were once beginners like you might be, so you're in good hands.

Make sure you explain to the assistant what style of whisky you have enjoyed previously – and, perhaps more importantly, any styles that you really didn't enjoy. The assistant can help you draw up a profile of the type of flavours you've experienced and point you in the right direction. Many shops arrange their whiskies by region and country: for example, Islay, Speyside, blended, American, Japanese and so on. A good shop will often have samples of numerous styles of whisky open. Be adventurous and allow your palate to be challenged. Ask as many questions as you can: what gives the whisky this flavour? What are the differences between these regions? Explain clearly if you are working to a budget, and don't be tempted to spend more than you want. There should be a number of options in every price bracket. Most decent shops have an extensive range of miniatures. These can provide you with a great way to try new and exciting whiskies for very little outlay, so it's worth asking the staff to suggest a broad selection of styles from a range of distilleries and countries.

Finally, spend time getting to know your local retailers. They will no doubt enjoy talking about their passion for whisky, so indulge them – they may end up learning something new about the spirit from you!

LEFT: A favourite shop of ours, Cadenhead in Edinburgh. The firm of William Cadenhead Ltd, Wine and Spirit Merchants, was founded in 1842 and is Scotland's oldest independent bottler. The company was in the ownership of the same family until taken over by J & A Mitchell & Co. Ltd in 1972, the proprietors of Springbank Distillery.

A Connoisseur's Whisky Menu

All whiskies are served in 25ml (1 fl oz) measures

Scotland: Islay

Caol Ila 1996, 40% ABV
A very good bottling of Caol Ila; for those who like their whiskies smoky, but not too intense. £3.75

Scotland: Islands

Highland Park 18 year old, 43% ABV
Toffee, honey and heather with a gentle lift of sweet peat on the finish. One of Scotland's great whiskies. £6.00

Scotland: Highland

Duncan Taylor, Glencraig 1974, 40.8% ABV
Rare single cask, cask strength bottling from the now defunct North Port Distillery in the eastern Highlands. £14.00

Scotland: Campbeltown

Springbank 15 year old, 46% ABV
Springbank distillery is one of the only three remaining distilleries in the whisky-producing region of Campbeltown and possesses a wonderfully unique flavour. £4.80

Ireland

Midleton Very Rare 40% ABV
Much-loved elegant and complex mature Irish blend. Delicate fruit intermingles with creamy malt. £14.00

Wales

Penderyn Single Malt, 46% ABV
Gentle and light single malt whisky that gains spicy complexity from a short stint in Madeira casks. £4.00

USA

Evan Williams Vintage Single Barrel Bourbon 43.3% ABV
A superb drinking Bourbon – the corn spirit lends a rich but not overpowering sweetness. Best enjoyed neat or with just a touch of water. £3.75

Japan

Suntory Yamazaki 12 year old, 43% ABV
Rich toffee- and caramel-laden malt from Suntory's Yamazaki distillery. £4.00

India

Amrut Indian Single Malt, 46% ABV
Bangalore's Amrut distillery is producing world-class whisky. With a gentle creamy sweetness, it could easily be mistaken for a top Speysider. £3.75

Blended Malt Whiskies

Compass Box—The Spice Tree 46% ABV
Coastal Highlander Clynelish provides the base to this superb whisky from the innovators at Compass Box — a cult. £5.50

Reproduced with permission from a more extensive whisky menu available from
The White Horse Hotel & Brasserie, Market Place, Romsey, Hampshire SO51 8ZJ

Understanding a whisky menu

While every visit to a pub or bar should be a fun experience, when it comes to ordering a whisky, some menus can be a little daunting. Many hotel and restaurant bars now have well-presented lists helping you to make an informed choice. The best menus should be simple and jargon-free, but if you have any doubts, ask to speak to the bartender who seriously knows his whisky – a good one should help you steer a clear course to the right one for your palate.

Before ordering, ask to see what type of glasses the bar uses for whisky. The right kind (see pages 54–55) will greatly enhance your drinking experience. Also, don't be afraid to ask for a side order of water to dilute the whisky slightly – this, too, can greatly help open up the whisky's flavour and aroma.

One important thing to remember is that if a bar stocks a wide range of whisky, it might not have a huge turnover of bottles. If you plan to try something which is expensive or rare, always ask how long the bottle has been open and check out how much is left. Although whisky doesn't 'go off', if there's only a small amount left, it could be slightly oxidized and won't give you the same experience as if it was poured from a full, freshly-opened bottle.

Jargon on the whisky menu

ABV On a good menu, whiskies should be listed clearly with their alcoholic strength (abv), which ranges from a standard 40% to cask-strength bottlings of around 58–60%.

Age The age of a whisky will undoubtedly determine its price, but not necessarily its quality – or whether you'll enjoy it. The majority of older whiskies offer a more diverse complexity of flavour, but again, a good bartender should be able to point you towards younger examples, which are not only cheaper, but still retain huge character.

Rare whiskies The flagship of any whisky bar tends to be releases that disappeared from production a long time ago, often from closed distilleries. These are often bottled by independent companies and tend to cost a great deal more, so ask the bartender for a detailed description before parting with any money.

Region Whisky menus sometimes group their bottles into production regions – in Scotland: Highlands, Islands, Lowlands, Speyside and Campbeltown – as well as by country (e.g. Japan, USA, India). Whiskies within each region can also vary, so ask the bartender for a description of what to expect.

Single casks Some limited edition whiskies are bottled as single casks, meaning they are limited in release, with the whisky drawn from one cask. They are usually bottled at a greater strength than regular whiskies. They can differ from the 'house style' of a distillery, so ask for a sample before ordering.

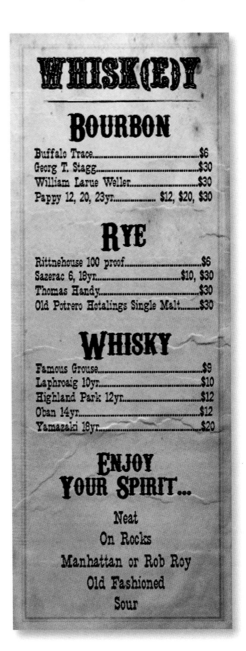

WHISK(E)Y

BOURBON

Buffalo Trace	$6
Georg T. Stagg	$30
William Larue Weller	$30
Pappy 12, 20, 23yr	$12, $20, $30

RYE

Rittnehouse 100 proof	$6
Sazerac 6, 18yr	$10, $30
Thomas Handy	$30
Old Potrero Hotalings Single Malt	$30

WHISKY

Famous Grouse	$9
Laphroaig 10yr	$10
Highland Park 12yr	$12
Oban 14yr	$12
Yamazaki 18yr	$20

ENJOY YOUR SPIRIT...

Neat
On Rocks
Manhattan or Rob Roy
Old Fashioned
Sour

SERVING WHISKY

Whisky is one of the most evocative spirits in the world. It is also perhaps one of the most misunderstood and, to some, challenging of drinks. Its high strength is sometimes enough to give imbibers cause for concern, so when learning to serve whisky properly, it is worth spending a little time getting to know exactly what's in your glass. Unlocking the inner secrets to your favourite dram is like having a conversation with it – there's no point diving in feet first and missing all the details!

As with many of life's great pleasures, taking time and learning the correct techniques to enjoy whisky are the fundamentals to successful and contented dramisfaction.

Glassware

Is the glass purely a vessel to contain your precious dram – or so much more? Well, quite a bit more as it turns out. The glass you decide to use for nosing and tasting whisky can have a huge impact on the flavour and aroma of a whisky, so much so that specific styles of glassware have been developed to heighten the experience.

1. Tulip-shaped glass This is based on the traditional *copita*-style glass, used to sample Sherry. It has evolved into several fairly unique designs, but this shape is ideal for nosing and tasting whisky because of the narrow dimensions at the rim of the glass and the wider, bowl-shaped base. The narrow rim means that the aromas of the whisky are much more concentrated, giving you a precise nose, bursting with complexity. The thinner stem on a tulip-shaped glass allows it to be cradled easily in the hand and allows the spirit to warm gently, which also helps to release more aroma in the whisky.

2. Glencairn This is a tulip-shaped glass, specifically designed for whisky. It has a narrow rim and a heavier bowl-shaped base, with a thicker stem.

3. Tumbler This the traditional style of whisky glass. It is perfect for filling with ice, soda and a generous measure of blended whisky. You can't knock the tumbler for simplicity and versatility, but as the rim is fairly broad, it is not ideal for specifically nosing whiskies. Also called a rocks glass.

4. Snifter This the classic brandy balloon-style glass, often associated with gentlemen's clubs, leather armchairs and cigars. Although some drinkers prefer them for the way they cup majestically in the hand, snifters are pretty rubbish for seriously nosing any spirit around 40–50% abv. Their broad, chubby base and extremely tight

rim concentrates the harsh alcohol whiffs above any subtle aromas you may hope to find. Please avoid.

It's getting hot in here...

The idea of putting a few blocks of ice in with your whisky is likely to spark a fierce debate in some quarters. One view is that it totally ruins the aroma and flavour of a single malt whisky. Our view is that no one has the definitive 'my way is better than yours' and whichever way you prefer to drink whisky – with or without ice – it is the right way! A chilled whisky gives off less of an aroma than one at room temperature, but in some cases chilling a whisky right down can be a new (and highly enjoyable) experience. Try sticking a bottle of decent blended whisky in the freezer for a few hours – pouring out chilled shots of the luxuriously viscous spirit takes whisky to another dimension indeed! Similarly, see how the Japanese have embraced the culture of using high-quality ice in their whisky on page 139.

Just a splash

All whisky is bottled at or above 40% abv, with many bottlings significantly higher in strength. Some cask-strength bottlings weigh in at a whopping 60% or more abv. The effect of a high-strength spirit hitting the tongue and palate is almost akin to being anaesthetized, so in many cases the addition of a little splash of water not only helps to bring the strength down to a more manageable level, but it also helps to open out and unlock the flavours you'll find in the whisky.

Try a small sip of the dram undiluted and decide for yourself if you think it needs the addition of water, but be careful not to drown it! It's interesting to note that when nosing and tasting whiskies in the blending lab, many master distillers and whisky blenders reduce their samples with a mixture of 50% whisky and 50% water in the glass.

Mixing it up a bit

There is an old story that some time ago a whisky producer offered a customer a dram of his most prized and expensive whisky. As he poured out the ancient liquid with a mixture of pride and excitement, his beaming smile turned to an expression of utter disbelief and horror as the customer proceeded to top the dram up with warm Irn-Bru. This is perhaps the most extreme example of 'whisky terrorism', and adding any sweetened fizzy mixer to a highly sought-after vintage whisky is probably a bit foolish. But the idea of drinking whisky with cola, ginger ale, tonic, lemonade or soda water really isn't a crime, and in the right environment, poured into a tall glass with ice and

The Biltmore

PAUL WHITEMAN *plays again! You may catch his smart rhythms drifting across the* **PALM COURT** *from Le Casino Bleu and into this famed room, as you enjoy the cocktails born at its magnificent bar. In this* **MADISON ROOM** *of gay continental mood, discriminating New Yorkers dine and wine, as of old. In the Palm Court they enjoy an apéritif. In* **LE CASINO BLEU** *they come for tea, dinner and supper dancing.*
BOWMAN-BILTMORE HOTELS CORPORATION • OPERATORS OF THE BILTMORE AND THE COMMODORE

ABOVE: Cocktail hour at the Biltmore Hotel, New York, in 1935. In recent times the hotel bar has epitomized the chic nature of classic whisky cocktails, such as the Manhattan and whisky sour.

a decent mixer, whisky can be a perfect way to cool down in style. In some bars in China it is now commonplace to drink blended whisky with sweetened green tea as an undoubtedly unique refreshment.

Suave times

Over the last few years the culture for enjoying whisky cocktails has grown enormously in popularity, thanks to a renaissance for all things vintage. Television programmes like *Mad Men* have once again put the spotlight on some terrific vintage drinks, such as the old-fashioned Manhattan and whisky sour. So what better way to explore the huge gamut of flavour in whisky from around the world than with a suave, elegant and perfectly balanced mixed drink?

CLASSIC BOURBON MINT JULEP

50ml/2 fl oz quality Bourbon
2 teaspoons water
2 teaspoons granulated sugar
    (or, if using a simple sugar
    syrup, omit the water)
4 fresh sprigs of mint.

Add the sugar, mint, water and some crushed ice into a Collins-style glass and muddle together. Then add the Bourbon, more crushed ice, stir and top with another fresh sprig of mint. Serve with a straw and imagine you're at a sundown cookout in Kentucky!

THREE CLASSICS WITH A TWIST

WHISKY SOUR

USING REDBREAST 15-YEAR-OLD IRISH POT
STILL WHISKEY

In a cocktail shaker, add 2 teaspoons of egg white and shake (without ice) vigorously, until fluffy. Then add 50ml/ 2 fl oz Redbreast 15-year-old Irish whiskey, 25ml/1 fl oz freshly squeezed lemon juice and 12.5ml/½ ounce sugar syrup (homemade, using a 2:1 sugar to water ratio)

Fill with ice and shake vigorously again, until frothy and creamy. Strain over ice into a tumbler and drip several dashes of Angostura bitters over the froth. Garnish with a pitted fresh cherry and a slice of lemon.

OLD-FASHIONED

USING KAVALAN SOLIST TAIWANESE WHISKY

This simple cocktail has a wonderful, yet complex balance of flavours. Using Kavalan Solist adds rich, spicy, sherried note – and a distinctly Asian feel!

Fill a tumbler with ice and add 25ml/2 fl oz of Kavalan Solist. Stir slowly, diluting the ice. Add more ice, a few dashes of Angostura bitters and 1 teaspoon of brown sugar syrup. Stir again, add a piece of orange zest and another 25ml/2 fl oz of Kavalan Solist. Keep stirring, adding more ice.

The result after all your hard work stirring is a wonderfully rich, spicy yet refreshing cocktail.

MANHATTAN

USING YAMAZAKI 18-YEAR-OLD
JAPANESE WHISKY

In a mixing glass pour 50ml/2 fl oz Yamazaki 18-year-old whisky, 25ml/ 1 fl oz quality sweet vermouth, such as Punt e Mes or Antica Formula Capano, and several dashes of aromatic bitters (for a richer note try The Bitter Truth Xocolatl Mole chocolate bitters!).

Add ice and stir gently. Strain into a chilled Martini glass and garnish with a cocktail cherry and a small piece of orange zest, or for a more Japanese feel a piece of Mikan Mandarin orange. The photograph below shows Manhattan cocktails.

WHISKY AND FOOD

Whisky is undoubtedly a drink for many occasions, whether gluggable when mixed with soda water or a refreshing mixer, or sipped and savoured as a nightcap. But paired with food it needs some careful consideration.

As a highly flavoured and powerfully complex spirit, you wouldn't ordinarily think that whisky pairs at all well with foods, especially given the potentially anaesthetizing effect a few whiskies can have on the tongue and palate. But let's break down the component parts of what makes for a good food and drink pairing: complementary flavours, texture and aroma, and, above all, balance and harmony across the palate.

Classic food and wine combinations are well known (from a top-quality red Bordeaux with a tender, perfectly cooked chateaubriand steak, to vintage Port and a generous slice of ripe Stilton cheese) but whisky and food combinations are less well known and talked about.

Looking closely at a single malt whisky in particular (its age, its abv and how it has been matured) will reveal a huge amount about the potential of finding a tasty dinner table treat to enjoy with it.

The strength within

The golden rule is that any spirit over 40% abv drunk neat will dominate the taste buds and demand your full attention. Any food wanting to get a look-in is going to need to have enough potency of its own, or at least work around the power of the whisky, with a combination of mouthfeel (texture), complementary flavour and development – how it changes and works with the whisky to produce gastronomic nirvana.

Casks and flavours

The type of cask that whisky matures in imparts about 70% of the overall flavour to the bottled whisky. The type of cask used will also give you an idea of what sort of flavours you should expect to find, helping you choose a food pairing that is both complementary and enjoyable.

As a rule of thumb, whisky matured in Sherry casks (especially dark, oloroso and Pedro Ximénez sherries) tends to take on a nutty, spicy, woody and dried-fruit character, so you can find foods that also mirror these flavours, or ones that will work sympathetically. Heavily sherried whiskies are often the perfect foil for rich fruit cake and desserts like crumble and tiramisu. Foods with more autumnal and winter flavours, including heavily spiced dishes, also go well with these whiskies.

Whiskies matured in Bourbon casks tend to develop buttery, sweet, vanilla, marzipan and coconut aromas and flavours, so pairings with lighter foods, including sweet shellfish, creamy desserts and summer fruits, work extremely well.

The smoky and peaty whiskies such as Lagavulin, Ardbeg, Caol Ila, Bruichladdich, Talisker and Laphroaig, as well as some heavily peated Japanese and Indian whiskies (for example, Amrut Peated and Hakushu Heavily Peated), are completely different. They can be difficult to pair with food because of their dominance on the palate. Even so, some of the best and most enduring food and whisky pairings come from mixing peated whisky and similarly dominant flavours: try these whiskies with smoked fish, briny shellfish, aromatic peppery meat and blue cheese.

Hammer and tongues

The bottom line is that one man's steak is another man's roadside burger. Any pairing suggestion might work superbly well – or miss the mark entirely. Taste, and the perception of what defines a 'complementary flavour', are incredibly subjective, so the best advice is to try your whiskies first, get to know their profiles on the nose and palate, and then think about what you're looking for from your menu.

Experiment and have fun: food and drink are surely some of the greatest pleasures in life!

BELOW: Fresh oysters go well with peated single malts.

WHISKY FLAVOURS AND FOOD

Smoky and peaty

Likes! Barbecue notes, spice, strong cheese, dark chocolate, shellfish, sea fish.

Dislikes! Salads, mild, delicate food, tropical flavours.

Suggestions

- **Talisker 10-year-old** Oak-smoked salmon, capers, cracked black pepper and oatcakes, with whisky drizzled liberally over the salmon
- **Yoichi 12-year-old** Barbecued mackerel fillets on toast
- **Bowmore Darkest** Cherry and dark chocolate mousse
- **Caol Ila 12-year-old** Butterscotch ice-cream sundae with toffee pieces
- **Lagavulin 16-year-old** Lancashire Blacksticks blue cheese and ginger chutney
- **Bruichladdich 10-year-old** Flash-fried scallops, black pudding and samphire
- **Ardbeg 10-year-old** Fresh oysters

Fresh, floral and fruity

Likes! Citrus zest, orchard fruit, white fish, green vegetables.

Dislikes! Heavily spiced meat, dried-fruit desserts, blue cheese.

Suggestions

- **Redbreast 12-year-old Irish whiskey** Fresh tropical fruit salad
- **Balblair 1997** Summer fruit panna cotta
- **Yamazaki 12-year-old** Served as a highball with soda and ice with stir-fried chicken and noodles and seared green beans
- **Glenkinchie 12-year-old** Greek salad with lemon zest shavings
- **Miyagikyo 10-year-old** Cornish crab cakes with sweet chilli dipping sauce
- **Strathisla 12-year-old** Lemon posset
- **Auchentoshan 12-year-old** Dover sole, new potatoes and hollandaise sauce
- **Cutty Sark blended Scotch whisky** Served on the rocks or with soda water with grilled asparagus and lemon butter
- **Glenmorangie Original** Cranachan, with fresh raspberries

Rich and spicy

Likes! Red meat, dried fruits, root vegetables, fresh herbs, chocolate.
Dislikes! Delicate fish, light summer berries.

Suggestions
- **Glenfiddich 18-year-old** Seared venison with redcurrant sauce
- **Springbank Vintage 10-year old** Slow-roasted lamb with red cabbage and roast potatoes
- **Woodford Reserve Bourbon** Sticky seared baby back ribs, barbecued beans and coleslaw
- **Hakushu 18-year-old** Ginger- and soy-marinated lamb chops with sesame-dusted bok choy
- **Glenfarclas 15-year-old** Christmas or plum pudding or rich fruit cake
- **Aberlour A'bunadh** Spicy Italian hunters chicken casserole with black olives
- **Benrinnes 15-year-old** Cottage pie, roasted squash and carrots
- **Oban 14-year-old** Mackerel pâté and toasted wholemeal bread
- **The Balvenie Doublewood** Crème brûlée and Balvenie Doublewood-soaked raisins

Buttery, smooth and sweet

Likes! Honey, apples, pastry, sweet meat.
Dislikes! Smoked food, hot spices.

Suggestions
- **Dalwhinnie 15-year-old** Apple and blackberry tarte Tatin with vanilla custard
- **Nikka All Malt** Chicken yakitori with sweet and sour sauce
- **Highland Park 12-year-old** Crispy bacon and avocado salad with honey and balsamic vinaigrette
- **Johnnie Walker Gold Label** Frozen and poured over real vanilla dairy ice cream
- **Clynelish 14-year-old** – Smooth duck liver pâté and wholemeal toast
- **Glenlivet Nadurra** Baked apple with cinnamon butter and muscovado sauce
- **Isle of Arran 14-year-old** Pears poached in white wine and vanilla
- **Macallan Fine Oak** Chicken and apple casserole, with buttery mash

Some more 'world' whiskies

Four Roses Single Barrel Bourbon
Served on the rocks with a medium-rare
cooked burger, with Monterey
Jack cheese and barbecue relish

- **Amrut Cask Strength Indian whisky** Dry spiced chicken tandoori
- **Hakushu 12-year-old** Tempura-battered vegetables
- **Kavalan Solist Taiwanese whisky** Stewed prunes with clotted cream
- **Penderyn Sherry Cask Welsh whisky** Pan-fried black pudding, seared scallops and rocket
- **Sazerac Rye American whiskey** Cold cuts: chorizo, pastrami, rye bread, olives and sundried tomatoes
- **Three Ships 10-year-old South African whisky** Smoked eel and spiced apple chutney
- **Yamazaki 18-year-old** Home-made brown-sugar rice pudding, with cinnamon and raisins (for more on Japanese whisky and food, *see* pages 138–9).

Still hungry?

Try these mouthwatering recipes,
which benefit from a generous
measure of whisky:

- Scottish Tablet with a dash of whisky – this traditional hard, sugary fudge comes alive with the addition of something buttery and waxy, like **Clynelish 14-year-old**, or sweet and peaty such as **Bruichladdich 10-year-old**.
- Barbecue and whisky marinade – either use a smoky but fruity whisky, such as **Ardbet Uigeadail**, or American Bourbon, such as **Maker's Mark**, for some additional sweetness.
- Whisky and cinnamon ice cream – time to dust off that ice-cream maker. Add a sprinkling of powered cinnamon and a few teaspoons of a sweet but spicy whisky, such as **The Singleton of Dufftown 12-year-old** or **Amrut Fusion** Indian whisky to the ice-cream maker.
- Very adult gingerbread men – add some additional spice to your gingerbread mix with a splash of **Compass Box Spice Tree** blended whisky.

HAGGIS AND WHISKY: SURELY A PAIRING MADE IN HEAVEN?

On Burns Night, 25 January, the traditional celebration is to enjoy a dram alongside your haggis, while toasting Scotland's most famous son. The ritual of addressing the haggis, by reading lines from Robert Burns' famous poem, 'Address to a Haggis', has become a very theatrical affair for some hosts, who violently (but skilfully!) plunge a knife straight into the middle of the haggis to release its 'reeking' aroma for the assembled audience. Burns would no doubt be proud that the dish still invokes such passionate performances over 200 years after his poem was written.

However, not everyone agrees with pairing whisky and haggis. Macsween, which is undeniably the most popular and well-known producer of the spicy beasties, recommends enjoying a whisky before commencing your Burns Night feast, or to savour afterwards, but not with it: 'I've personally always found that whisky can overpower the haggis,' explains Director Jo Macsween, 'so I've favoured pairing it with beer – they were meant to be together!'

If you are still thinking about pairing a whisky with your haggis, we recommend the peppery, robust flavours found in Talisker 10-year-old as the perfect complement. You could even try a big, sherried Yamazaki 18-year-old from Japan … but don't tell Jo!!

WHISKY AND CIGARS

ABOVE: The Soho Whisky Club in London is a comfortable and elegant club where members can try over 300 malts, as well as other spirits and wines. There is also a smoking terrace where you can enjoy a selection of the finest cigars. Members can enjoy a series of tutored tasting events throughout the year.

Cigar-smoking still conjures up an image of mature gentlemen sitting by the fireside in a dark-panelled and exclusive club library or 'smoking room', perhaps reading *The Times* and complaining about how the youth of today have no sense of discipline. Often the drink of choice with their cigar would have been a glass of Cognac.

But times change, and more and more younger people are enjoying the occasional luxury of a fine cigar, and – whisper it quietly – some of the ladies have joined in, too. Make no mistake: a hand-rolled cigar from Cuba, the Dominican Republic or Honduras is an expensive treat. Because of the various indoor smoking bans, it's become increasingly difficult to find anywhere to light up a 'stick' in comfort. However,

despite the challenges, cigar-smoking is thriving, and some whisky distillers have taken the opportunity of encouraging smokers to pair fine malts with their cigars, instead of the traditional Cognac.

There are a number of parallels between great cigars and great whiskies. Both are handmade products in which the integrity of ingredients and processes are crucial. Some whiskies suit certain moods, times of day or occasions, and the same is true of cigars. So which whiskies work particularly well with cigars, enhancing the smoking experience, and which cigars are best suited to a glass of good whisky?

The Dalmore distillery has gone so far as to produce a bespoke whisky by the name of The Dalmore Cigar Malt Reserve (see facing page), featuring the use during maturation of a relatively high percentage of oloroso Sherry casks. Master Blender Richard Paterson, who developed The Dalmore Cigar Malt, is also an avid cigar-smoker himself, so here's the word straight from the blender's mouth.

Paterson's pairings

'When I choose a whisky to accompany a cigar, I'm looking for some of the characteristics of the whisky to be reflected in the cigar itself. With the first puff of the cigar you know whether it's going to be light, medium or heavy in style and, as with the aftertaste of a whisky, you're looking for a similar connection that will be reflected on the palate.

'For example, if you had a Speyside malt you'd perhaps go for a lighter tobacco, such as a Dominican Republic cigar or a floral Havana, like some of the Cohiba range from Cuba. Heavy Islay malts go with heavyweights such as the Punches and the Bolivars. There's a degree of sweetness in all malt whiskies, so the cigar must be well-rolled and blended to avoid bitterness.

'Personally, I'm looking for something with medium flavour in terms of both the whisky and the cigar. Neither must be too light. Choose an Upmann, a Hoyo de Monterrey, a Romeo y Julieta, a Montecristo or a Partagas. They are all medium in character, but with a bit of body and weight without being too overpowering.

'Most cigars have some subtle sweetness: oranges, vanilla, caramel and even bananas, along with spicy, peppery notes towards the end. Because bitterness sometimes comes through in a cigar, the sweetness of a more sherried malt helps to balance the smoking/drinking experience. You've got to have weight in the whisky, and 'silkiness' is very important, too.

'If I had to choose another whisky to go with a cigar, besides The Dalmore Cigar Malt Reserve, I'd opt for a 21-year-old Glenfarclas or an old Glenrothes. I'd go for an 18-year-old Glenfiddich or a Balvenie Double Wood with a lighter cigar, and, perhaps surprisingly, an aged Old Pulteney goes perfectly with a Bolivar. The smokiness of Talisker also lends itself well to a cigar, but it needs to be well-aged to get that real sweetness coming through. The age is crucial.'

More suggestions

- Romeo y Julietta Churchill (Cuban) and Highland Park 25-year-old
- Santa Damaniana (Dominican Republic) and Glengoyne 17-year-old
- El Rey del Mundo (Cuban) and Auchentoshan Three Wood

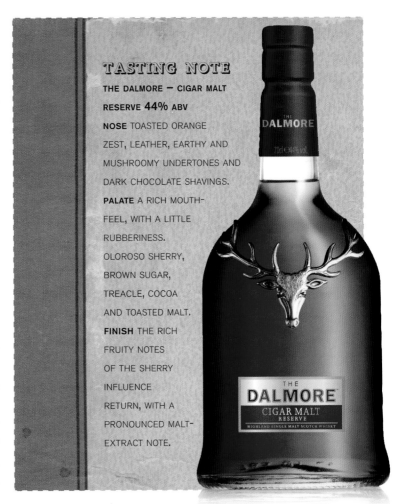

TASTING NOTE

THE DALMORE — CIGAR MALT RESERVE 44% ABV

NOSE TOASTED ORANGE ZEST, LEATHER, EARTHY AND MUSHROOMY UNDERTONES AND DARK CHOCOLATE SHAVINGS. PALATE A RICH MOUTH-FEEL, WITH A LITTLE RUBBERINESS. OLOROSO SHERRY, BROWN SUGAR, TREACLE, COCOA AND TOASTED MALT. FINISH THE RICH FRUITY NOTES OF THE SHERRY INFLUENCE RETURN, WITH A PRONOUNCED MALT-EXTRACT NOTE.

COLLECTING AND INVESTING

ABOVE: The Macallan single malt Cire Perdue sold at Sotheby's in New York in 2010 for $462,992 (£289,600). It is now in the *Guinness Book of World Records* as the most expensive whisky in the world.

First, let us explain that there is a difference between 'collecting' whisky and 'investing' in it. Collectors usually specialize in a particular distillery or region, while investors are purely purchasing with future profit in mind.

Collectors may slavishly buy every new expression of a particular whisky – for example, Bruichladdich – that appears on the market. Investors, meanwhile, will always have an eye on the long-term main chance, usually purchasing very limited editions of whisky from desirable distilleries. They may buy a few releases from a certain distillery, but they will be ultra-selective, and certainly won't buy them all.

So just which distilleries are most desirable, whether you wish to collect for pleasure or potential profit?

As things stand at present, Scotch whiskies are unquestionably the most popular with collectors and investors. Top auction houses specializing in whisky sales include Christie's (which held its first specialist whisky sale in New York in 2007) and Bonhams also auctions whisky in New York and even in Hong Kong, too. McTear's in Glasgow has seen such an increase in demand for fine and rare whiskies that it has recently doubled its auctions to ten a year.

The international growth of interest means that collectors are also now starting to buy old and rare Bourbons, Irish malts and even Japanese whiskies, particularly those from now-lost Japanese distilleries with high reputations such as Karuizawa. The market for collectible 'vintage' bottles of Bourbon is growing. As a result, a few interesting old bottlings do turn up at auction, and many cocktail bars are snapping them up, offering their guests the opportunity to try 'vintage' classic cocktails, made from whiskey, vermouth and cocktail bitters bottled decades ago.

Silent stills

Rarity is usually guaranteed to add value to any commodity, so distilleries that are now permanently closed or even demolished may be a good place to start, whether in Scotland or other parts of the world.

Whiskies from some 'lost' distilleries are more bankable than others, so if your budget stretches to it, consider the likes of Port Ellen, Brora and Rosebank – habitually the most coveted Scotch whiskies no longer being made. Other lesser known malts that fall into the 'lost' category and may be worth collecting include Banff, Lochside and St Magdalene. But bear in mind that although these malts come from distilleries that are no longer in production, there are still sizeable stocks of them in warehouses up and down Scotland, so don't expect your £35 Gordon & MacPhail-bottling of a 1994 Caperdonich to double in value any time soon.

One of the pleasures of collecting whiskies from defunct distilleries is that you may learn more about the heritage of the whiskies in question and even try to visit some of the places where they were made. Sadly, this is not always possible, since many have been knocked down and their sites are now occupied by retail parks, car parks, supermarkets or housing developments.

Record-breakers

Two working Scottish distilleries stand out as being eminently collectable; namely The Dalmore and The Macallan. Both regularly release limited editions of old and rare whiskies which have then gone on to break many price records. For example, in 2011 the last of just 12 bottles of 62-year-old Dalmore fetched an eye-watering £125,000 (US$197,500) when sold in Singapore. less than a year after a

TOP TEN BOTTLES UNDER THE HAMMER

1 The Macallan
64-year-old Cire Perdue
£289,600 ($462,992)
Sotheby's, New York, 2010

2 Glenfiddich
Janet Sheed Roberts
Reserve 1955
£46,850 ($74,900)
Bonhams, Edinburgh, 2011

3 The Macallan
Vintage 1926
£33,750 ($54,000)
Christies, New York, 2007

4 The Dalmore
Oculus
£27,600 ($44,000)
Bonhams, Edinburgh, 2009

5 Glenfiddich
64-year-old 1937
£25,200 ($40,000)
Bonhams, Edinburgh, 2010

6 Bowmore
Mutter
£25,000 ($40,000)
Mctear's, Glasgow, 2007

7 The Dalmore
62-year-old Kilderorie
£22,000 ($35,200)
McTear's, Glasgow, 2002

8 Springbank
1938
£20,000 ($32,000)
McTear's, Glasgow, 2010

9 The Macallan
60-year-old 1926
£18,000 ($28,800)
McTear's, Glasgow, 2002

10 The Macallan
60-year-old 1926
£15,000 ($24,000)
McTear's, Glasgow, 2001

Headlines from whisky auctions around the world give added publicity to the ever-increasing popularity of buying whisky at auction. Detailed above are the top ten bottles, along with the prices they achieved at auction. *Source:* Whisky Magazine *2012*

FAULT FINDING

Happily for consumers, there's very little badly made whisky nowadays. Any faults you may find in a new bottle tend to be the result of the effects of a rogue cask or batch of casks. These are very rare, and are more likely to be found in whisky released in small quantities by an independent bottler than in the large-scale offerings from major producers.

If a newly opened bottle of whisky has a musty note on the nose, and an aroma or taste of something close to vinegar, the cask or casks in questions will have been contaminated by stale rainwater while being stored empty.

If you detect notes of sulphur in your whisky, this could be because it has spent some time in ex-Sherry or ex-wine casks that have been sterilized with sulphur candles. The smoke from these candles settles on the inner surfaces of the cask staves and easily taints a subsequent filling of whisky. Although to most of us sulphur is an 'off note', there are whisky-lovers who enjoy that particular characteristic!

RIGHT: The Dalmore Trinitas is one of the world's most expensive whiskies, with only three bottles being offered for sale, each with a price tag of £100,000 ($160,000).

64-year-old bottle of Macallan, complete with rare Lalique crystal decanter, sold at a charity auction in New York for US$462,992 (£289,600). Macallan went on to set a new world record for the most expensive whisky sold at auction when an M Imperiale 6-litre Lalique decanter sold for US$628,000 (£397,000) in Hong Kong in 2014.

First division

It is also possible to buy other, less expensive but still collectible bottlings from both The Dalmore and The Macallan. Other, more affordable options may include whiskies from the group of distilleries that can be seen as the Scottish 'first division'. There is no definitive list of these distilleries, but shrewd judges tend to cite the following

(listed here in alphabetical order): Ardbeg, The Balvenie, Bowmore, The Dalmore, Glenfiddich, Glenmorangie, Highland Park, The Macallan, Rosebank and Springbank. Another option is to buy older bottlings of 'standard' single malts aged 8, 10 or 12 years, and perhaps dating from the 1960s and 1970s, as these are still relatively cheap and easy to find. They may be relatively affordable and should always hold their purchase prices, provided the bottles – and ideally the cartons, too – are in good condition, without damaged labels and too much loss of contents through evaporation.

It is also worth bearing in mind that blended Scotch whiskies do not have the same cachet as single malts, so it's possible to put together an array of brands like Haig, Dewar's, Teacher's and White Horse from the 1960s and '70s for less than £50 ($80) per bottle. Ideally, buy two bottles – keep one as a collectible item and open the other. Indeed, you could also compare and contrast

'then' with 'now'. Take a 1972 bottling of Teacher's Highland Cream and taste it alongside a 2012 bottling of the same brand and you will be amazed at the differences. The same also applies to older bottlings of single malts. Doing your own comparison goes some way to pacifying the anti-collecting and anti-investment lobby, which insists that whisky is made to be drunk, rather than kept in a cupboard or display cabinet, and that not to drink it is an insult to all the craftsmen who lovingly created and nurtured it over the years.

Seller beware

A word of warning if you are thinking of putting together a portfolio of whiskies in the hope that they may keep you in your old age. Although it is possible to sell your bottles through a website such as eBay, the main channels for exchange are auction houses, which will charge you a significant seller's fee. Even if the bottle has increased in value during its time in your keeping, you could still end up out of pocket. There are no guarantees when buying and selling whisky, but at least if the bottom ever falls out of the whisky market, you will have some rare and interesting drams with which to drown your sorrows!

Storing

Whether it's a £15 blend or a £15,000 rare malt, there are a few basics to bear in mind when it comes to looking after your whisky. Whisky bottles should be stored upright, rather than on their side,

like wine bottles sealed with corks. It may seem obvious, but store your whisky bottles away from bright sunlight and extremes of temperature and humidity.

There's some debate about whether whisky improves or changes at all in a sealed bottle if kept for a lengthy period. The common view is that no changes occur, but a growing number of people now believe the character of the whisky may change as air can get past even the most apparently secure corks or screwcap closures, leading to an oxidized flavour sometimes described as 'rancio'.

Whether the whisky is better as a result of this, or simply different, is a moot point, but the important thing is that it isn't 'bad'. Old bottles of whisky with all their seals intact often show an element of what is known as 'neck creep', where the level of liquid has fallen because of evaporation.

Once a bottle of whisky has been opened, it is advisable to drink it over a period of weeks or months, rather than

ABOVE: An auction house employee holds one of the world's rarest whisky miniatures, which sold for £1500 ($2400) at McTear's, Glasgow in 2009. The miniature of Springbank, which was distilled in 1919 and comes with a letter of authenticity, attracted international attention. If opened, each measure would work out at £750 ($1200)!

USEFUL WEBSITES

Major auction houses with specialist whisky sales include:

* Scotch Whisky Auctions wwwscotchwhiskyauctions.com

* Bonhams wwwbonhams.com

* Christies www.christies.com

• McTear's www.mctears.com

Whisky Highland is a specialist whisky investment consultancy www.whiskyhighland.co.uk

Whisky Magazine provides an index of auction best-sellers, updated each issue, along with an 'auction watch', previewing forthcoming specialist sales. www.whiskymag.com

RIGHT: This 57-year-old bottle of The Macallan is another example of the distillery's work with highly regarded crystal glass designer Lalique and will set you back a cool £15,000 ($24,000) from specialist retailers.

years, but you don't need to worry that it will develop off notes after a day or two in the same way that wine does.

The effects of increasing 'headspace' above the liquid – as more is drunk from the bottle – results in evaporation of the most volatile top notes as the alcohol escapes, and eventually the aroma becomes 'flattened', with a loss of vibrancy and some elements of the original 'nose'. It tends to depend on the original character of the whisky in question, too. If the whisky has intense peatiness, you won't notice the effects of oxidization for a long time. You will notice it sooner in a lighter-bodied whisky.

We don't advocate the old Scottish custom of throwing away the cork when you open your whisky, but if you do open a really expensive bottle, it is best not to keep it for 10 years – as if you would!

THE JEWEL OF ORKNEY

Highland Park Distillery, situated on the Orkney Islands, worked very closely with the multi-award-winning jewellery designer Maeve Gillies on the packaging for the oldest release in its portfolio: Highland Park 50-year-old. Having visited Orkney on many occasions since she was a child, Maeve was able to use the island as her inspiration for the design of the packaging. The concept behind the design is a marine theme to make the carton look as if it has been washed up on the beach after 50 years. The outer casing 'designed to resemble a net', is handcrafted from solid sterling silver, and the particularly tactile carved wooden box gives the overall package a distinctly timeless appeal. A stone mason who works at Orkney's 12th-century St Magnus Cathedral showed Maeve a stretch of beach where you can find worn pieces of the sandstone, and so she designed the centrepiece on the front of the bottle to be made from Orcadian sandstone sourced from the very same quarry used to build the cathedral.

The whole project took about two years to complete, with only 275 bottles being produced. For those lucky enough to afford one (it costs around £10,000/$16,000) there is a further treat to enjoy, should they decide to open the bottle and drink the contents. Inside the bottle, on the back of the sandstone centrepiece, there is a sterling-silver replica of the cathedral's rose window, which you can only really see when the whisky has been drunk.

The whisky is a vatting of five casks distilled in 1960. Like all Highland Park whiskies, the 50-year-old has been cask-harmonized – that is to say, refilled into casks upon reaching maturity in order to ensure perfect balance and consistency in the end product.

TASTING NOTES

HIGHLAND PARK – 50-YEAR-OLD – BOTTLED 2010 – 275 BOTTLES – 44.8% ABV

NOSE INITIALLY SOME SWEETENED, SPICY JAVA COFFEE, DAMSON JAM, MADEIRA WINE AND A WISP OF DELICATE SMOKE, FOLLOWED BY LEATHER, MINT/MENTHOL LOZENGES, FRUIT COMPOTE AND SOMETHING SLIGHTLY FISHY/SEAWEED, ALL WRAPPED UP WITH PLUM JAM RICHNESS.

PALATE FIRST A WOODY DRYNESS, FOLLOWED BY HAZELNUTS, LIGHT PEAT, LIQUORICE, HINTS OF MUSTY CASKS, POLISHED MAHOGANY AND SOME SALT. VERY, VERY RICH IN TEXTURE.

FINISH LINGERING HEATHER NOTES, DRY SHERRY, SEA SALT AND A LITTLE COASTAL SPRAY.

COUNTERFEIT WHISKY

DETECTION

A new method to tackle the counterfeiting of Scotch Whisky using laser technology has been developed by St Andrews University. Researchers have claimed that they can work out a whisky's brand, age and cask by using a ray of light the size of a human hair.

The technique involves researchers placing a tiny amount of whisky on a transparent plastic chip no bigger than a credit card.

Using optical fibres, the whisky sample is illuminated by light using one fibre, and collected by another. By analysing the collection of light scattered from the whisky, the researchers say they are able to diagnose the sample.

The key lies in the ability of the laser to detect the amount of alcohol contained in the sample – genuine whisky must contain at least 40% abv. For those geeks out there, the method exploits both the fluorescence of whisky and the scattering of light and shift in energy when it interacts with molecules, known as its Raman signature.

The world is full of fake designer goods, with replica Rolex watches and Gucci handbags widely available for a fraction of the cost of the real thing. It should therefore come as no surprise to find that fake whisky, and in particular fake Scotch whisky, is also on the market. Apart from the obvious point that consumers are often being conned into parting with their money for inferior goods, which damages the reputation of genuine brands, there is the additional problem with whisky, and all other types of alcohol, that the substitute product could damage your health and even kill you. So it is in everyone's interests to make sure that no matter where in the world you buy a bottle of 'Scotch whisky', that is indeed what you are getting.

Scotch Whisky Association

The Scotch Whisky Association [SWA] is charged with policing the integrity and image of the product itself, and has a legal affairs department which takes action against any number of distillers and bottlers in a wide range of countries. Its three main tasks are:

- To act as the guardian of the regulatory framework
- To stop infringements of the laws relating to Scotch Whisky
- To provide advice to members and non-members on compliance with the law

The SWA's Legal Affairs Department (LAD) does not carry out brand protection; that is the responsibility of the brand owners. LAD's responsibility is to stop any misrepresentation that states or suggests a whisky is Scotch whisky, or comes from Scotland, when that isn't the case. It also protects the industry from general forms of unfair competition to help ensure there is a level playing field among all brands sold as whisky, whatever the origin. The situation has been helped by the recognition of 'Geographical Indication' status for Scotch by many countries, including China, the EU, India, Malaysia, Panama, Thailand, Turkey and Vietnam, which theoretically safeguards Scotch, but having legislation in place is a very different thing from being able to enforce it worldwide.

Scotch around the world

The international reputation of Scotch whisky is so good that it often commands high import taxes and therefore high retail prices when imported, particularly when compared with domestically produced spirits. So there's an obvious incentive for counterfeiters to produce look-alike – if not taste-alike – 'Scotch' and for unscrupulous barmen to refill empty genuine Scotch whisky bottles with something inferior.

There's a story that one major Scotch whisky distiller actually pays bar staff in certain countries to smash empty bottles of its brands once they have been drained of their original contents!

Many bottles destined for export sales are fitted with supposedly tamper-proof capsules designed to ensure that spirit can only be poured out and not back in, but people can become ingenious when a quick and unlawful buck is there to be made.

Sometimes 'faking' takes the form of using Scottish names and images on bottles, without actually claiming the contents is Scotch. It's all about the power of suggestion. Copying packaging without forging actual brand names is also popular, as in the case of a batch of bottles of look-alike Grant's Family Reserve blend, which was discovered in China and carried the name 'Great's' – which it probably wasn't.

Beware of scams at home

We tend to think that passing off poor-quality whisky as Scotch as something that only happens overseas, but British bar owners are occasionally not above diluting their drams or re-filling an expensive bottle of premium blend or single malt with something they bought cheaply at the cash & carry. However, scientists have developed various ways of testing the authenticity of specific brands, one of which is to use lasers to analyse a sample the size of a teardrop, telling you the brand, age, strength and even details about the casks in which maturation took place (see box).

Counterfeiting can be an even more expensive problem for individuals in the world of rare and collectible whiskies, which can be worth several thousand pounds each. Forgeries may be very cleverly produced, with great attention to detail, fooling even real experts. A few years ago the producers of one of Scotland's most highly regarded and collectable single malt brands were caught out, discovering that the 'antique 'bottles of whisky for which they had paid large sums had actually been knocked out by Italian forgers!

PART 4:
THE WORLD
OF WHISKY

Travel to practically anywhere in the world and the chances are you will find a well-known Scotch whisky brand behind the local bar. This may seem nothing out of the ordinary today, but it's worth pausing to think about how far the spirit has travelled from its relatively humble origins. Today the Scotch whisky business is worth a staggering £4.2 billion ($6.7 billion) and exports to new and emerging markets are increasing yearly.

But such is the current popularity of whisky that it has led to a global explosion of local distilleries – each with its own unique take on what was once quintessentially a Scottish or Irish spirit. So whether it's a new and emerging Tasmanian micro-distillery, a highly esteemed Japanese single malt or a well-known English brewery trying its hand at distilling whisky, the options for your tasting glass are now truly international.

This section is not an exhaustive library of whisky distilleries from around the world, but we have highlighted some of the essential must-try whiskies as well as some of the most entertaining, educational or just plain picturesque to visit.

SCOTLAND

For many people all over the world, Scotch whisky is synonymous with whisky itself. No matter that whisky is now produced in some 25 countries, for countless aficionados only Scotch is the real deal. And certainly Scotland boasts far more distilleries than any other country, producing a stylistically varying range of single malts that increasingly stand alone, but also allow for the creation of an extraordinary number of blends. The country is home to some of the most iconic names in the history of whisky, and you will find bottles of Johnnie Walker and Glenfiddich in bars from Nova Scotia to Rio de Janeiro and Lagos to Nagasaki. So let's explore the diversity that is Scotch whisky in all its many forms. The Scotch Whisky Association groups distilleries into five producing regions: Highlands, Speyside, Lowlands, Islay and Campbeltown.

HIGHLANDS

From a geographical point of view, the Highlands is the largest of Scotland's five regions of malt whisky production. The Highlands region includes all the mainland north of the theoretical 'Highland Line', which runs from the Firth of Clyde in the west to the Firth of Tay in the east, with the exception of the Speyside region, and the Islands. However, in this book we have given the Islands their own section and map.

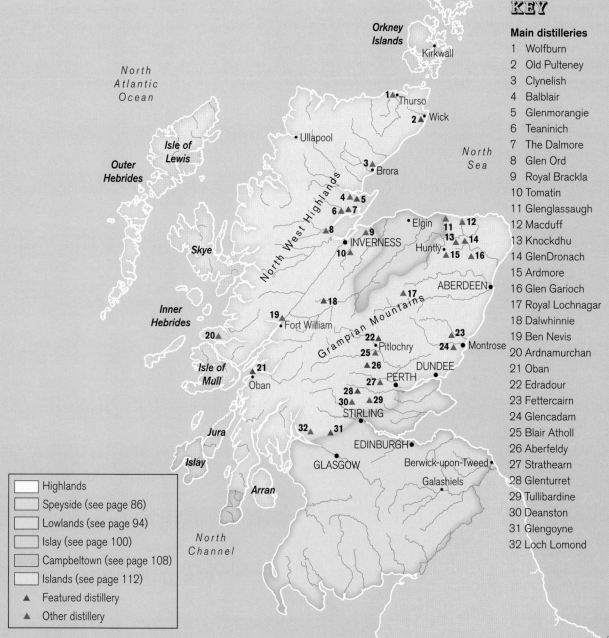

North Atlantic Ocean

Orkney Islands

Kirkwall

North Sea

1 • Thurso
2 ▲ Wick

• Ullapool

Isle of Lewis

Outer Hebrides

3 • Brora

4 ▲▲5
6 ▲ ▲7

8 ▲ 9 ▲
▲ INVERNESS
10 ▲

• Elgin 11 ▲ ▲12
13 ▲ ▲14
Huntly 15 ▲ ▲16

ABERDEEN

17 ▲

North West Highlands

Skye

Inner Hebrides

18 ▲

19 ▲• Fort William

20 ▲

Grampian Mountains

22 ▲ 23 ▲
▲• Pitlochry
25 ▲ 24 ▲• Montrose

26 ▲ DUNDEE
27 ▲ PERTH

28 ▲ 29 ▲
30 ▲ STIRLING

32 ▲ 31 ▲

Isle of Mull

21 ▲
• Oban

Jura

Islay

Arran

EDINBURGH •

GLASGOW

Berwick-upon-Tweed •

Galashiels

North Channel

KEY

Main distilleries
1 Wolfburn
2 Old Pulteney
3 Clynelish
4 Balblair
5 Glenmorangie
6 Teaninich
7 The Dalmore
8 Glen Ord
9 Royal Brackla
10 Tomatin
11 Glenglassaugh
12 Macduff
13 Knockdhu
14 GlenDronach
15 Ardmore
16 Glen Garioch
17 Royal Lochnagar
18 Dalwhinnie
19 Ben Nevis
20 Ardnamurchan
21 Oban
22 Edradour
23 Fettercairn
24 Glencadam
25 Blair Atholl
26 Aberfeldy
27 Strathearn
28 Glenturret
29 Tullibardine
30 Deanston
31 Glengoyne
32 Loch Lomond

Highlands
Speyside (see page 86)
Lowlands (see page 94)
Islay (see page 100)
Campbeltown (see page 108)
Islands (see page 112)
▲ Featured distillery
▲ Other distillery

THE DALMORE

Website www.thedalmore.com
Founded **1839**
Location **Alness, Ross-shire**

This once low-profile single malt from north of Inverness has been attracting plenty of headlines in recent years for the record-breaking prices achieved for some of its oldest and rarest whiskies. The distillery has taken the view that, although very few people would be willing to pay £100,000 ($160,000) for one of only three bottles of The Dalmore Trinitas produced, they would be attracted by the prestige of the brand and buy into it at a much more modest level.

The Dalmore has been able to position its top whiskies as some of the most expensive on the market because the character of The Dalmore spirit itself is rich and full, and lends itself well to extended aging. It also loves Sherry wood. So, fill new-make Dalmore into high-quality ex-Sherry butts, put them in the warehouse, and wait for several decades. In fact, you don't need to wait quite that long as The Dalmore is a full-bodied, rich, sherried whisky after only a dozen years, and a number of different bottlings, all costing considerably less than the Trinitas are always available.

However, if collectable single malts are your thing, 2012 saw a remarkable new line-up from The Dalmore under the Constellation label, comprising no fewer than 21 single-cask bottlings, ranging in distillation dates from 1964 to 1992. Prices vary from £20,000 ($32,000) for a bottle of the Vintage 1964 to £2,000 ($3200) for a bottle of Vintage 1992, with the entire collection costing a cool £158,000 ($254,500).

Whether or not you plan to invest in Constellation rather than buy that new Ferrari you always promised yourself, The Dalmore distillery itself is well worth a visit if you are in the northern Highlands. It boasts a fantastic setting beside the Cromarty Firth – look out for the bizarre sight of oil rigs resting in the Firth between jobs – and one of the quirkiest still houses in the business. Around £1 million ($1,611,000) was spent upgrading the visitor experience during 2011 and it's now one of the classiest around.

TASTING NOTES

The Dalmore – 12-year-old – 40% abv

Nose Aromatic spices and orange marmalade.
Palate Rich and elegant, with citrus fruits, sherry and vanilla.
Finish Long and warming, with oranges, ginger and a hint of smoke.

DALWHINNIE

Website **www.discovering-distilleries.com**
Founded **1897**
Location **Dalwhinnie, Inverness-shire**

Dalwhinnie is a picture-postcard distillery, located beside the main A9 Perth-to-Inverness road in wild and romantic mountain-and-loch scenery (see image page 76). Painted white, the building boasts a pair of copper-topped kiln 'pagodas' – what could be more archetypal?

The distillery dates from the end of the 19th century and, though its location must have seemed remote then, when the road was filled with horses and carts rather than today's caravans and tour buses, the site was selected partly because the Perth-to-Inverness railway line runs right past the still house.

The distillery is owned by Diageo, the biggest Scotch whisky distiller in the business, which has no fewer than 28 malt distilleries in its portfolio. Dalwhinnie is one of its flagship operations, and a founder member of the Classic Malts collection in 1987. Dalwhinnie is also one of a dozen Diageo distilleries that are open to visitors. Some of the first of several unusual features you see during your tour are two vast wooden 'worm tubs' in which the spirit from Dalwhinnie's pair of stills is condensed.

Most distilleries today use what are known as 'shell and tube'

condensers, but a few, including Dalwhinnie, stick to the old-fashioned method of a long, coiling copper pipe, or 'worm', immersed in a wooden vessel containing cold water. This helps to give the Dalwhinnie spirit a more robust character, which Diageo likes for blending purposes.

The water in those Dalwhinnie worm tubs tends to be pretty cold as, at 327m (1073ft), Dalwhinnie is the second-highest working distillery in Scotland, after Braeval on Speyside.

TASTING NOTES
Dalwhinnie – 15-year-old – 43% abv

Nose This nose really jumps out of the glass at you. Spices galore: cumin, cinnamon, black pepper. But also a hint of summer fruit, fresh butter and sweet dessert wine.

Palate A big hit of white pepper and liquorice on the sides of the tongue, followed by fresh blackberries, butter and cream.

Finish Lovely and warming, with lengthy baked apple notes.

GLENGOYNE

Website **www.glengoyne.com**
Founded **1833**
Location **Dumgoyne, Stirlingshire**

Unlike many of Scotland's famous distilleries hidden away at the end of a single-track road in a remote part of the country, Glengoyne is easily accessible: just 15 miles north of Glasgow, straddling the busy A81 road heading into Loch Lomond and the Trossachs National Park.

When we say 'straddle' the busy road we really mean straddle, as the spirit is made on one side of the road, which geographically is within the 'Highland' region of malt whisky production, and the filled casks are transported across the road to the warehouses, which are actually in the Lowlands. Indeed, until the 1970s Glengoyne was categorized as a Lowland rather than a Highland distillery.

Glengoyne stands in an area that once boasted 18 illicit stills; the whisky was smuggled into Glasgow to be sold. Glengoyne is also at the heart of 'Rob Roy country': Highland outlaw Rob Roy MacGregor once hid from the English army in the dense woodland that is still a feature of the area.

Glengoyne is owned by the independent company Ian Macleod Distillers Ltd, which boasts that the malt used is totally unpeated, allowing the natural character of the spirit to shine through. Glengoyne is also distilled more slowly than most of its competitors, creating a more subtle, complex whisky in which all the delicate flavours are freely allowed to express themselves.

Today Glengoyne is a very popular visitor destination, with a great variety of tour options ranging from the standard and excellent Glengoyne Tour to the Glengoyne Masterclass, which claims to offer the most in-depth and comprehensive distillery tour in Scotland. The well-equipped distillery shop, based in one of the original warehouses, offers the full range of Glengoyne variants, from 10 to 21 years of age, along with an ultra-rare 40-year-old and single-cask releases. You can also buy something unique: the 'Teapot Dram.' Back in the old days before 'Health & Safety' legislation and drink-driving laws, distillery workers were 'drammed' several times a day, often with new and un-matured spirit at a very high strength. At Glengoyne, dramming took place in the staff canteen, with the distillery brewer dispensing drams from a copper teapot – hence the name of this distillery-exclusive bottling.

TASTING NOTES

Glengoyne – 10-year-old – 40% abv
Nose Sweet and a little nutty, with toffee, popcorn and green-apple notes.
Palate Grassy, with more apples, barley and a touch of liquorice.
Finish Long, sweet and malty.

GLENMORANGIE

Website **www.glenmorangie.com**

Founded **1843**

Location **Tain, Ross-shire**

Glenmorangie is one the best-known single malts in the UK, and second only in terms of sales to Glenfiddich. The distillery enjoys a beautiful location close to the Dornoch Firth, some 30 miles north of Inverness.

Owned since the early 20th century by the family company of Macdonald & Muir Ltd, Glenmorangie and its 'sister' distilleries of Glen Moray and Ardbeg were acquired in 2004 by French luxury goods group LVMH, which already boasted such classic brands as Moët & Chandon Champagne and Hennessy Cognac before venturing into the field of Scotch whisky.

Glenmorangie Distillery, like a number of others, started life as a brewery, and when it was converted into a distillery during the 1840s it was kitted out with ex-gin stills from London, rather than the more usual smaller, squatter pot stills common to Scotch whisky production.

That tall, slender style of still has been retained here, and a visit to the Glenmorangie still house is definitely worth the trip. At 5.14m (16ft 10¼in) the Glenmorangie stills are the tallest in Scotland, and as the distiller proudly points, out they are the same height as a fully grown adult giraffe! In practical terms this means that only the very lightest and purest vapours make it to the top of the

long copper necks, leading to a smoother, purer and more elegant whisky.

In 2008 and 2009, a major expansion programme took place, increasing the number of stills from six to ten. True to tradition, the stills were 'sweetened' by one of the stillmen prior to their first run, using a secret blend of herbs, juniper and heather, intended to take the sharp edge off the copper and guarantee the unique taste of the whisky being produced.

Glenmorangie pioneered the art of 'finishing' whiskies in casks that had previously held another alcoholic drink other than Bourbon or Sherry. This provides a number of variations on the 'house' style. Current offerings include Quinta Ruban (Port), Nectar d'Or (Sauternes) and Lasanta (Sherry).

TASTING NOTES

Glenmorangie Original – 10-year-old – 40% abv

Nose A big hit of vanilla and freshly cut oak, a hint of green grass and some mint tea. Fresh, without being too zesty.

Palate The vanilla notes from the nose are enhanced on the palate, and the freshly cut oak develops into fresh pine. Slight hints of coffee and ginger. Easy-drinking.

Finish The woody notes linger. The ginger becoming more pronounced, and smooth vanilla returns for a clean, refreshing finish.

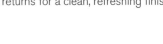

OBAN

Website www. discovering-distilleries.com
Founded 1794
Location Oban, Argyllshire

Oban is one of the oldest distilleries in Scotland, and the modern west-coast port and tourist centre of Oban really grew up around it from a tiny fishing village. Today, ferries from Oban serve many Hebridean islands, and the busy town has been a magnet for visitors since the latter decades of the 19th century, when steamers began to call with their cargoes of holidaymakers and the railway network finally reached the town. The fact that Oban expanded and developed around the existing distillery explains why the operation is on a cramped site beneath a steep cliff on the bustling harbour front, rather than enjoying the luxury of a rural setting like so many other distilleries.

But we all know that good things come in small packages, and compared to many other distilleries owned by Diageo, Oban is small indeed. It boasts just a single pair of stills and its annual capacity is one of the most modest of all Diageo's 28 malt distilleries. Only Royal Lochnagar on Deeside is capable of making less whisky.

Oban has been welcoming members of the public since the visitor centre opened in 1989 and, like its fellow Highland distillery of Dalwhinnie, Oban was one of the original 'Classic Malts.' Along with Ben Nevis in Fort William, Oban is the only full-scale distillery in the western Highlands, and while many single malts have only become commercially available in relatively

recent times, Oban single malt was selling as long ago as the 1880s.

During the distillery tour visitors may nose the new-make spirit and sample whisky straight from the cask. They are also invited to try the Oban 14-year-old along with a piece of crystallized ginger: a true taste sensation! While the 14-year-old is Oban's best-selling whisky, lovers of cask finishes may also like to try the Oban Distillers Edition bottling. This has spent a period of time undergoing secondary aging in ex-Montilla fino Sherry casks, and the dry, slightly briny, light character of the Montilla fino ideally complements the essential Oban single-malt style.

TASTING NOTES

Oban – 14-year-old – 43% abv

Nose Citrus fruits blend with a coastal saltiness and a whiff of peat.

Palate Smooth and delicious; ripe oranges and honey, with smoke and a tang of seaweed.

Finish Silky, medium to long, with dried fruits and a touch of oak.

OLD PULTENEY

Website **www.oldpulteney.com**
Founded **1826**
Location **Wick, Caithness**

Most distilleries are named after their location, or some local geographical feature, so Pulteney is unusual in taking its name from an individual. Sir William Pulteney was governor of the British Fisheries Society and responsible for developing Pulteney into a thriving fishing harbour and community adjoining the town of Wick in the early 19th century.

Despite having a local distillery, one of Wick's claims to fame is that prohibition was in force there from 1922 until 1947, and Wick was a 'dry' town. Prohibition didn't just happen in Chicago and New York. This came about in part because of the notorious reputation earned by Wick for drunkenness among the fishermen and associated folk who descended on the port during the herring-fishing season. Indeed, it is claimed that at one point in the 19th century as many as 500 gallons of whisky were being drunk each day in Wick – though as this figure was supplied by the Church of Scotland, which at that time supported temperance, there is always the possibility that it was exaggerated for dramatic effect!

Pulteney is the most northerly distillery in mainland Scotland, and, like Oban, it has an urban setting, although it is almost within sight of the sea. The single malt is always referred to as Old Pulteney, and in the ownership of Inver House Distillers Ltd it has gained a much higher profile during the last few years, being energetically marketed as 'The Genuine Maritime Malt'.

Pulteney's stills are a sight not to be missed. The single pair is shoe-horned into a very confined space, and the spirit still has no real head and neck, unlike most other stills. It is sometimes claimed that, long ago, when a new still was delivered to Pulteney, it was too tall to fit into the still house, and so the top had to be cut off in order to accommodate it!

Not only can visitors see the stills and purchase a range of whiskies, they also have the opportunity to fill, label and purchase bottles of whisky from one of several individual casks lined up at the back of the visitor centre.

TASTING NOTES

Old Pulteney – 12-year-old – 40% abv
Nose Malt, vanilla, walnuts and spice, with just the faintest tang of sea salt.
Palate Smooth and sweet, with caramel, while a little Sherry develops and the salt persists.
Finish Slightly oily, citrus fruits, becoming drier.

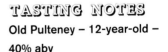

OTHERS TO TRY

ABERFELDY

Website www.dewarswow.com

Founded 1896

Location Aberfeldy, Perthshire

Traditional Victorian distillery with an excellent interactive visitor centre in the shape of 'Dewar's World of Whisky'. The malt at the heart of Dewar's blended Scotch whisky.

Tipple to try Aberfeldy – 12-year-old

EDRADOUR

Website www.edradour.com

Founded 1825

Location Balnauld, Pitlochry, Perthshire

One of the smallest and prettiest distilleries in Scotland, Edradour makes as much whisky in a year as some distilleries do in a week. Noted for its use of ex-Sherry casks.

Tipple to try Edradour Caledonia – 12-year-old

GLENTURRET

Website www.thefamousgrouse.com

Founded 1775

Location The Hosh, Crieff, Perthshire

A contender for Scotland's oldest surviving distillery, Glenturret is home to 'The Famous Grouse Experience', which vies with 'Dewar's World of Whisky' at Aberfeldy for its originality and visitor-friendly features.

Tipple to try Glenturret – 10-year-old

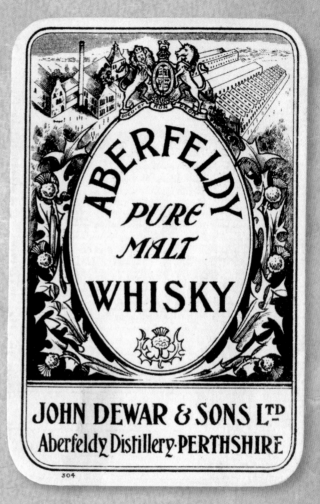

RIGHT: Moving casks of Glengoyne single malt in the early 1930s, when horses still played a part in the rural economy of Britain, though fast being replaced by motorized transport.

SPEYSIDE

The Speyside region of single malt production is located in the north-east of Scotland and contains around half of all the country's malt distilleries, including many of those producing the most famous brands in the world.

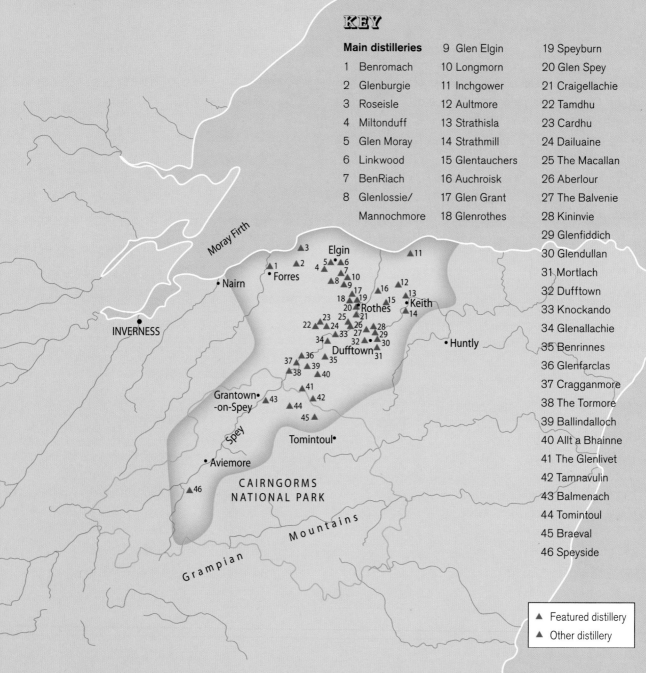

KEY

Main distilleries

1	Benromach	9	Glen Elgin	19	Speyburn
2	Glenburgie	10	Longmorn	20	Glen Spey
3	Roseisle	11	Inchgower	21	Craigellachie
4	Miltonduff	12	Aultmore	22	Tamdhu
5	Glen Moray	13	Strathisla	23	Cardhu
6	Linkwood	14	Strathmill	24	Dailuaine
7	BenRiach	15	Glentauchers	25	The Macallan
8	Glenlossie/	16	Auchroisk	26	Aberlour
	Mannochmore	17	Glen Grant	27	The Balvenie
		18	Glenrothes	28	Kininvie
				29	Glenfiddich
				30	Glendullan
				31	Mortlach
				32	Dufftown
				33	Knockando
				34	Glenallachie
				35	Benrinnes
				36	Glenfarclas
				37	Cragganmore
				38	The Tormore
				39	Ballindalloch
				40	Allt a Bhainne
				41	The Glenlivet
				42	Tamnavulin
				43	Balmenach
				44	Tomintoul
				45	Braeval
				46	Speyside

▲ Featured distillery
▲ Other distillery

CARDHU

Website **www.discovering-distilleries.com**

Founded **1824**

Location **Knockando, Moray**

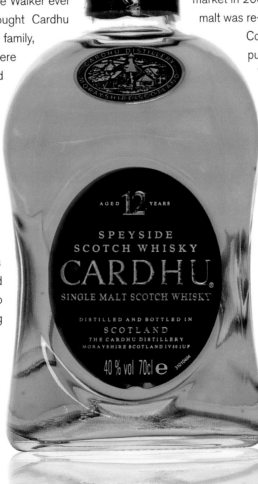

Cardhu is the best-selling single malt in the Diageo portfolio, and a founder member of the 'Classic Malts' range. It's also one of the principal malts included in the make-up of the Johnnie Walker collection of blended Scotches that lead the world in terms of whisky sales. There has been a strong connection between the distillery and Johnnie Walker ever since John Walker & Sons bought Cardhu from its founders, the Cumming family, in 1893. The original distillers were husband and wife John and Elizabeth Cumming, who distilled without the bother of taking out a licence for some 20 years before going 'legit' in 1824.

Unlike some malts, where the range of different expressions on offer can be quite baffling, it's all very straightforward with Cardhu. There's a 12-year-old, and that's it. Today, international demand for it is so strong that it is hard to find in the UK, with Spain having long been its main market.

Cardhu was at the centre of controversy a few years ago, when Diageo announced that, due to exceptional overseas demand, Cardhu would no longer be bottled as a single malt but as a 'Pure Malt' using whisky from the Cardhu Distillery along with other, unspecified Speyside malts, and the distillery reverted to its original name of Cardow. Vociferous opposition to the changes led to the withdrawal of Cardow Pure Malt from the market in 2004, and Cardhu 12-year-old single malt was re-launched the following year.

Considering that it's part of the well-publicized official Speyside 'Malt Whisky Trail,' and nicely located, it's surprising that Cardhu only attracts around 5000 visitors a year. But if you're on Speyside, do make sure you pop in for a dram and a look around.

TASTING NOTES

Cardhu – 12-year-old – 40% abv

Nose Approachable and sweet, quite light, with milk chocolate and honey, apples, pears and brittle toffee.

Palate Malty and sweet in the mouth. Easy-drinking, without being simplistic or bland.

Finish A wisp of smoke, a hint of peat, medium in length.

GLENFARCLAS

Website **www.glenfarclas.com**
Founded **1836**
Location **Ballindalloch, Banffshire**

By any standards Glenfarclas is one of the great Speyside single malts. Uncompromisingly matured in ex-Sherry casks, despite the expense, Glenfarclas vies with The Macallan as a traditional, regional classic.

The distillery is one of very few to remain in private ownership – in this case the Grant family, though a branch with no obvious connections with the Grants of Glenfiddich. Or the Grants of Glen Grant. Quite a popular surname in those parts!

The advantage of not having to keep legions of shareholders happy is that the owners can do pretty much as they like, and what they like to do is to offer a wide range of aged expressions of their single malt – from 10 to 40 years old – with minimum packaging and at sensible prices. The aim is to get consumers drinking the whisky, even the really old bottlings, and then come back for more. Essentially, this is a whisky for drinkers, not collectors.

The Glenfarclas Family Casks range was launched in 2007, and comprises a single-cask bottling at cask strength from every year between 1952 and 1994. That's the sort of thing an independent family company can choose to do.

Glenfarclas is part of the Speyside 'Malt Whisky Trail', and in 1973 it was one of the first distilleries to create a visitor centre. The Ship's Room is complete with oak panelling from the ship RMS *Empress of Australia*, 1913–1952.

Glenfarclas is very rare among Scottish distilleries in that it continues to use a direct flame, powered by gas, to fire its stills, with almost every other distillery in Scotland having switched to internal steam heating by way of coils or 'pans.' The Glenfarclas team once tried using a steam coil by way of experimentation, in order to see whether the spirit produced would actually vary at all. It turned out to be a totally different beast altogether, lacking the usual characteristics of Glenfarclas, so a rapid return was made to the naked flame, which remains in place to this day!

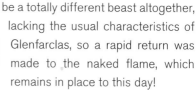

TASTING NOTES
Glenfarclas – 10-year-old – 40% abv

Nose Sherry, malt, delicate smoke and spice. Pleads to be tasted.
Palate Sherry, malt and smoke carry over from the nose, and are joined by dried fruits, cloves and cinnamon.
Finish Smooth and profound. Old for its years. A very polished 'entry level' Glenfarclas.

GLENFIDDICH

Website www.glenfiddich.com
Founded 1886
Location Dufftown, Banffshire

Even if you know nothing about Scotch whisky you've probably heard of Glenfiddich. You may not know it's a single malt but you're certainly familiar with the name. Glenfiddich is on sale everywhere, from your local mini-mart to the cocktail bars of the world's most prestigious hotels.

It's the world's best-selling single malt and its global success dates back to the early 1960s, when owners William Grant & Sons Ltd took the bold step of putting a great deal of resources into marketing their malt, at a time when Scotch blends were almost totally unchallenged by their 'pedigree' cousins. They also adopted the distinctive triangular green bottle that is still such a part of the brand, complete with its distinctive stag emblem.

Because it's so widely available, there is inevitably a degree of snobbery about Glenfiddich. If so many people drink it, the stuff can't be that special, the argument runs. The fact remains, however, that in blind samplings, many people pick it as one of their favourites, and older expressions in particular have won a great number of awards.

Glenfiddich comes in many forms today, from the standard 12-year-old right up to a 50-year-old, along with any number of highly regarded special editions and an eagerly awaited annual Vintage Reserve. While most best-selling brands are now owned by global conglomerates, it's good to see that Glenfiddich remains firmly in the hands of the Grant family, who created it on a shoestring budget in the late 19th century.

Glenfiddich was the first distillery in Scotland to create a dedicated visitor centre, which opened in 1969. This is one of Scotland's largest distilleries, but despite it's size it's still attractive to visit – on your tour around the site you will see no fewer than 24 washbacks and 28 stills. And best of all, those nice members of the Grant family who still own and run the distillery won't even charge you for the privilege!

TASTING NOTES

Glenfiddich – 12-year-old – 40% abv
Nose Very approachable, fresh and fruity, with green apples, pears, honey and almond.
Palate Smooth, soft and very drinkable. More almonds and soft fruit, butterscotch and a note of oak.
Finish Medium in length, nicely mellow.

GLEN GRANT

Website **www.glengrant.com**
Founded **1840**
Location **Rothes, Banffshire**

Glenfiddich may be the world's best-selling single malt, but nobody's told the Italians. They have an enduring love for Glen Grant, distilled in the village of Rothes, which is actually home to four distilleries. In fact, they love it so much that in 2006 the Italian Campari company bought the distillery.

The Italians like their Glen Grant young and pale, and beyond the age of five they seem to find it overly mature! However, it's actually a whisky that ages really well and can cope with decades in ex-Sherry casks when required, coming out as a lovely, rich, full-bodied dram.

Glen Grant distillery is named after its 19th-century founders, brothers John and James Grant, and was significantly extended by James's son, also called James and universally known as 'The Major'. He lived the life of a typical Victorian stalking, shooting and fishing Highland laird, but was also fond of big game hunting.

On one trip to Matabeleland in Africa he rescued an abandoned local boy, Biawa Makalanga, and took him home to Rothes in 1898. Biawa worked as the Grants' butler until the Major's death in 1931, developing a broad Rothes accent, which must have been at odds with what would be seen at the time as his somewhat exotic appearance. Biawa lived on in Glen Grant House until his death in 1972, and he is buried in Rothes cemetery, which lies alongside Glenrothes Distillery.

Glen Grant is one of the few distilleries where a visit to the garden is recommended almost as much as the distillery. Major James Grant laid out the spectacular grounds and even installed a 'dram safe' in the banks of a burn flowing through the site, so that he could amaze visitors by retrieving a bottle of Glen Grant from it to accompany the cold burn water.

Not that you should ignore the distillery itself, of course. Glen Grant has four pairs of very unusually shaped tall stills, fitted with purifiers which contribute to the crisp, light character of the whisky produced.

TASTING NOTES

Glen Grant – 10-year-old – 40% abv
Nose Quite delicate, with toffee apples and the merest wisp of smoke.
Palate Easy-drinking, but far from bland. Sweet, fruity and malty, with vanilla notes and a touch of peat.
Finish The finish is medium in length, with a little liquorice. Good, honest malt whisky.

THE GLENLIVET

Website **www.theglenlivet.com**

Founded **1824**

Location **Ballindalloch, Banffshire**

Along with Glenfiddich, The Glenlivet is one of the most immediately recognizable names in single malt Scotch whisky. It's currently the global number two behind its biggest rival, but owner Pernod Ricard has ambitions to change all that and claim the number one spot for itself.

This explains why, in 2009, a major new production area was developed at the remote distillery, adding six new stills to the existing eight and increasing capacity to 10.5 million litres (12.5 million gallons) per year, making it one of the largest distilleries in Scotland.

It's also one of the country's most historic distilleries, being famous as the first to be granted a licence after the passing of the 1823 Excise Act, which made legal distilling more commercially attractive and paved the way for the modern Scotch whisky industry. However, the distillery was only moved to its current site in 1858–59.

The Glenlivet's founder was George Smith, who had previously distilled illegally, without a licence, and Smith defended himself and his distillery against angry illicit distillers who felt he had sold out – using a pair of hair-trigger pistols presented to him by a local landowner, the Laird of Aberlour.

The Glenlivet area enjoyed a high reputation for the whisky distilled there, much of it illegal, and by the second half of the 19th century so many other distilleries were using the Glenlivet name that owner John Gordon Smith took legal action – the result of which was a ruling that only Smith could call his whisky The Glenlivet.

Today, The Glenlivet comes in a wide variety of expressions, ranging from a 12- to 25-year-old in the principal line-up. There are also a number of versions exclusive to travel retail outlets, which are worth keeping an eye open for when passing through airports. Notable among these is a 16-year-old by the name of Nadurra – the Gaelic word for 'natural.' The jewel in The Glenlivet crown is its Cellar Collection, which is made up of very small bottling runs of whisky bearing vintage dates, with the oldest so far released dating back to 1959.

TASTING NOTES

The Glenlivet – 12-year-old – 40% abv

Nose Wafts of spiced cooking apple, ripe bananas, toasted pine nuts and clear apple juice.

Palate Fresh vanilla pods, underripe bananas, honey and white pears.

Finish Medium, with a hint of spice. A true 'session' whisky.

THE MACALLAN

Website www.themacallan.com
Founded 1824
Location Craigellachie, Morayashire

For lovers of Sherry-influenced single malts, The Macallan is the Rolls-Royce of whiskies. Not only is it widely admired as the long-standing leader of this style, but it's also the most collectable whisky in the world. Just look at some of the records achieved at auction and you'll see how desirable this dram can be. In November 2010 a unique Lalique decanter of its 64-year-old became the most expensive whisky in the world when it sold at a charity auction for US$462,992 (£289,600)!

Coming back to earth to more affordable levels, The Macallan has established itself as the third best-selling single malt internationally, behind fellow Speysiders Glenfiddich and The Glenlivet. In order to keep up with anticipated future demand, the distillery has re-commissioned a major production area mothballed in the 1980s.

One key feature of The Macallan is the large number of small stills on the premises – no fewer than 21 to be exact. Another notable aspect of the operation is the immense trouble the distillery goes to to secure first-class ex-Sherry casks for maturation, although they can each cost up to ten times that of an ex-Bourbon cask.

Although best-known for its use of Sherry wood, since 2004 the Sherry Oak expressions of The Macallan have been accompanied by a Fine Oak range, matured in a mixture of ex-Sherry and ex-Bourbon casks, and intended to appeal to less traditional whisky-drinkers.

The Macallan is well-known for its collaborations with companies and individuals outside the Scotch whisky industry. It has enjoyed a particularly fruitful association with French glassmaker Lalique, but the brand has also ventured into the world of photography, working with Scottish-born Rankin, Albert Watson and Annie Leibovitz.

In the case of Rankin, each of the limited edition 1000 bottles of 30-year-old Fine Oak came with a unique and original Polaroid image of an aspect of the distillery or its surroundings, most of which featured Rankin's muse and now wife, Tuuli, but at £900 ($1450) each, there were clearly cheaper ways of buying artistic soft porn – though like most limited edition Macallans, the bottles in question almost instantly became collectors' items.

TASTING NOTES

The Macallan – 10-year-old – 40% abv
Nose Enticing, Christmas-like aromas – Sherry, dried fruits and toffee.
Palate Smooth and well-rounded; deep, rich and sensuous. Sherry, ripe oranges, spice, more dried fruits and wood smoke.
Finish Long and silky. A great introduction to the classic Macallan style.

OTHERS TO TRY

ABERLOUR

Website www.aberlour.com

Founded 1826

Location Aberlour, Banffshire

Aberlour is France's best-selling single malt and a high proportion of ex-Sherry casks are used for its maturation. A'bunadh is a cask-strength version with full-on Sherry. The distillery specializes in connoisseurs' tours.

Tipple to try Aberlour A'bunadh

THE BALVENIE

Website www.thebalvenie.com

Founded 1825

Location Dufftown, Banffshire

The sister distillery to Glenfiddich prides itself on its handcrafted single malts which are offered in a wide range of varying expressions. The distillery operates its own floor maltings and may be toured by appointment.

Tipple to try The Balvenie Signature –12-year-old

BENRIACH

Website www.benriachdistillery.co.uk

Founded 1897

Location Longmorn, Elgin, Morayshire

Despite being closed twice during its history, BenRiach is now a thriving distillery with the charismatic Billy Walker in charge. There have been some exceptional releases produced in the last decade.

Tipple to try BenRiach Curiositas

BENROMACH

Website www.benromach.com

Founded 1898

Location Invererne Road, Forres, Morayshire

Benromach is the smallest working distillery on Speyside and is owned by legendary Elgin-based independent bottler Gordon & MacPhail. Benromach single malt has a smoky style reminiscent of the Speysides of old.

Tipple to try Benromach Traditional

CRAGGANMORE

Website www.discovering-distilleries.com

Founded 1869

Location Ballindalloch, Morayshire

Marketed as one of Diageo's Classic Malts. The distillery was established by John Smith close to a railway line for easy transportation of raw materials and casks of whisky. Smith was so fat that he could only travel in the guard's van!

Tipple to try Cragganmore – 12-year-old

GLEN MORAY

Website www.glenmoray.com

Founded 1897

Location Bruceland Road, Elgin, Morayshire

Part of the Speyside Malt Whisky Trail, this Elgin distillery started life as a brewery. It was converted to whisky-making during the Victorian blended whisky 'boom' period. It is now owned by the French firm La Martiniquaise.

Tipple to try Glen Moray – 12-year-old

LOWLANDS

The Lowlands region of malt whisky production takes in mainland Scotland below the theoretical 'Highland Line' from the Firth of Tay in the east to the Firth of Clyde in the west. Stylistically, Lowlands are traditionally the 'lightest' and most delicate of all Scotch single malts.

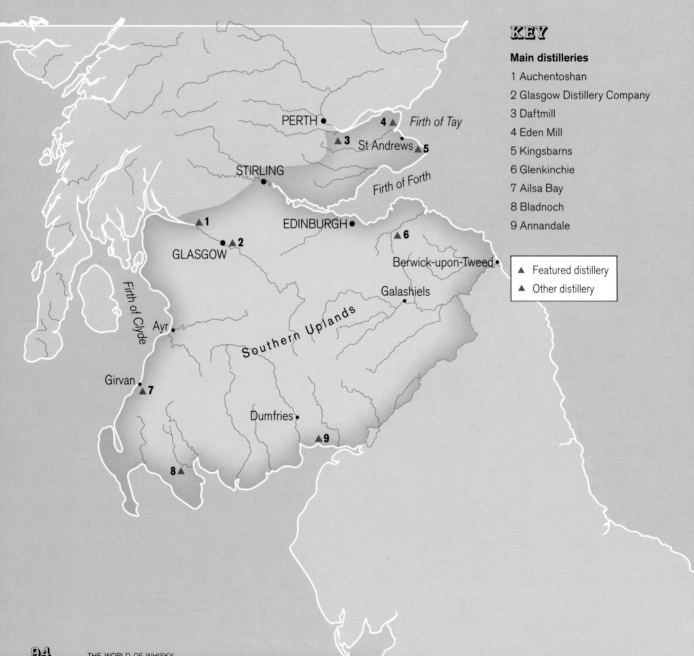

KEY

Main distilleries

1 Auchentoshan

2 Glasgow Distillery Company

3 Daftmill

4 Eden Mill

5 Kingsbarns

6 Glenkinchie

7 Ailsa Bay

8 Bladnoch

9 Annandale

▲ Featured distillery

▲ Other distillery

AUCHENTOSHAN

Website www.auchentoshan.com
Founded 1822
Location Dalmuir, Glasgow

At one time, the Lowland area was a powerhouse of single malt Scotch whisky production. In 1797 there were no fewer than 31 Lowland distilleries in operation, and together they produced 82% of the total of legally made whisky distilled in Scotland that year, even though there were almost twice as many Highland distilleries.

Time has not been kind to the Lowlanders, however, and the relatively recent closures of three historic distilleries – St Magdalene in Linlithgow (1983), Littlemill at Bowling (1992), not far from Auchentoshan, and Rosebank at Falkirk (1993) – robbed the region of more of its diversity and heritage.

However, the survivors appear to be in good health, most notably Auchentoshan, which is the closest surviving malt distillery to Glasgow, just a dozen miles from the city centre, and as such is sometimes known as 'The Glasgow Malt'. Given its comparatively delicate, light, quite subtle character, the whisky could be said to contrast with the essential character of Glaswegians as they are often perceived, rather than complement them!

Auchentoshan is the last survivor of the great Lowland tradition of practising triple distillation, which involves the use of an intermediate still between wash and spirit still, with the result being a subtle style of single malt. It's clearly a popular style, since sales have been increasing in recent years, as the range has been added to.

Auchentoshan was first licensed in 1822, though there is a good chance that distilling was taking place on the site quite a few years earlier. Between 1903 and 1969, Auchentoshan was owned by Glasgow brewers, first Machlachlans, and latterly by Tennent's. The plant is now in the hands of Morrison Bowmore Distillers Ltd, which also has Bowmore on Islay and the under-rated Glengarioch distillery in Aberdeenshire.

If you're in the Glasgow area, Auchentoshan is is definitely worth a visit.

TASTING NOTES

Auchentoshan – 12-year-old – 40% abv

Nose Very distinct aromas of dried coconut, unblanched almonds and cherry drops. It is light but has plenty of individuality.

Palate Ripe pears, more almond notes and perhaps the deftest hint of Sherry wood.

Finish Lingering fruit notes, with a hint of woody oak creeping in at the death.

BLADNOCH

Website **www.bladnoch.co.uk**
Founded **1817**
Location **Bladnoch, Wigtown**

Bladnoch is an old-established distillery which has endured mixed fortunes over the years, changing hands on a number of occasions and being silent for several periods. Its luck finally appeared to have run out in 1993, when owner United Distillers closed the distillery, with no intention of allowing whisky-making to take place there again.

However, the company reckoned without the persuasive powers of Northern Irish businessman Raymond Armstrong. The construction company boss came across Bladnoch Distillery while holidaying in the area and decided that he liked the idea of keeping the visitor centre – which for some strange reason remained open, although the distillery itself was closed – and converting much of the rest of the site into apartments. He talked United Distillers into selling him Bladnoch, but there was a covenant in place forbidding distilling ever to resume there.

At first this was not a problem for Armstrong, but gradually he came to prefer the idea of reviving whisky-making at Bladnoch to property development. It took a great deal of talking by the silver-tongued Ulsterman to get the covenant revised, so that up to 100,000 litres (26,400 gallons) of spirit could be produced each year. Most of the equipment had been stripped out, except for the pair of stills and the washbacks, and the deal included no maturing spirit. Undeterred, however,

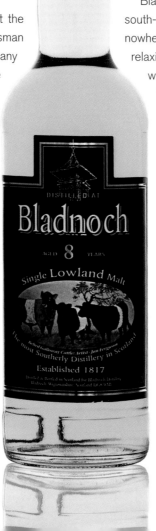

Armstrong set about re-equipping the distillery, and spirit flowed from the pair of stills again in 2000. Modest quantities are now distilled annually, and a variety of bottlings are available, including peated expressions. Most notable is the 8-year-old using spirit made during Armstrong's time in charge.

Bladnoch is in a pretty and tranquil corner of south-west Scotland, but it's really on the way to nowhere, so be prepared to spend a bit of time relaxing in the area, taking in the soft coastline with its views of Ireland and Scotland's official 'Book Town' of Wigtown.

The distillery welcome is always warm, and it plays host to a wide variety of community events, including musical performances and readings, while from time to time a 'Whisky School' is staged, where you can go along to learn how to make your own whisky!

TASTING NOTES

Bladnoch – 8-year-old – 46% abv
Nose Lemongrass, vanilla, cereal and malt on the nose.
Palate Smooth, with soft malt, nuts and cream-soda notes.
Finish Medium in length, with spice to the end.

GLENKINCHIE

Website **www.discovering-distilleries.com**
Founded **1837**
Location **Pencaitland, East Lothian**

Glenkinchie stands in arable countryside a few miles south-east of Edinburgh. Although it is not a particularly pretty distillery compared to some of its competitors, and it is owned by the world's largest whisky distiller, Diageo, there's still a feeling of a connection here between the land that grows the barley and the distillery that makes the whisky – until not that many years ago the distillery boasted its own farm, and the distillery manager's herd of Aberdeen Angus cattle were his pride and joy. Glenkinchie is also notable for having the largest wash still in Scotland.

The distillery was established in 1825 by a local farming family at a time when the Lowland region was the very heart of large-scale Scotch whisky production – a far cry from today, when only five distilleries are in operation.

Glenkinchie was one of six distilleries to be part of the original 1988 Classic Malts line-up, and its subsequent popularity and availability as a single malt, coupled with its location not far from Edinburgh, has long ensured a steady stream of visitors. Indeed, its location near the capital may even have saved Glenkinchie from closure, since when the Classic Malts were introduced, Rosebank was the obvious alternative to represent the Lowlands, and having failed to be selected, the Falkirk Distillery subsequently fell silent. In addition to

the usual distillery tour and tasting, Glenkinchie has something a bit special for lovers of distilling heritage, namely the Museum of Malt Whisky Production, which even contains a superbly detailed model distillery.

The most widely available version of Glenkinchie is the 12-year-old, which replaced the original 10-year-old in 2007. However, in common with quite a few other Diageo Classic Malts there is also a Distillers Edition expression, which has experienced a second period of maturation in former amontillado Sherry casks.

TASTING NOTES

Glenkinchie – 12-year-old – 43% abv

Nose Wet hay, toffee apples and honey. Sweet and approachable.

Palate Soft and buttery, with honey and caramel. Understated, but very drinkable.

Finish Relatively lengthy, with an earthy, herbal note.

OTHERS TO TRY

AILSA BAY

Website www.williamgrant.com

Founded 2007

Location Grangestone, Ayrshire

A large-scale malt distillery created in 2007 by William Grant & Sons Ltd within the company's existing Girvan grain-distilling complex. Ailsa Bay was designed to produce Speyside-style malt spirit for blending purposes and its eight stills are reminiscent of those at Grant's Balvenie Distillery. No single malt bottlings are expected, unless released for a special event or anniversary.

DAFTMILL

Website www.daftmill.com

Founded 2005

Location Daftmill, by Cupar, Fife

Daftmill was established by the Cuthbert family, who grow malting barley as part of their large-scale agricultural enterprise in Fife and offers a modern take on the farm-based distilleries of days gone by. Daftmill has a single pair of stills, and the Cuthberts have no plans to release a single malt bottling until around 2015.

ROSEBANK

Founded 1798 (now closed)

Location Falkirk, Stirlingshire

The Rosebank Distillery is now classed as one of the most iconic closed distilleries in Scotland. It ceased production in 1993 and part of the site has now been converted into accommodation, business premises and catering facilities. The remaining casks of whisky are becoming more difficult to find, but those that do get bottled frequently capture Rosebank whisky at its best – buttery, syrupy and zesty, with wonderful fruity/floral notes.

Tipple to try Rosebank 12-year-old – Flora & Fauna bottling – 43% abv

RIGHT: A distillery worker at Auchentoshan checking the temperature of the wort in a mash tun.

FACING PAGE: Nosing cask samples at the Bladnoch Distillery, one of only a handful of distilleries left in the Lowlands.

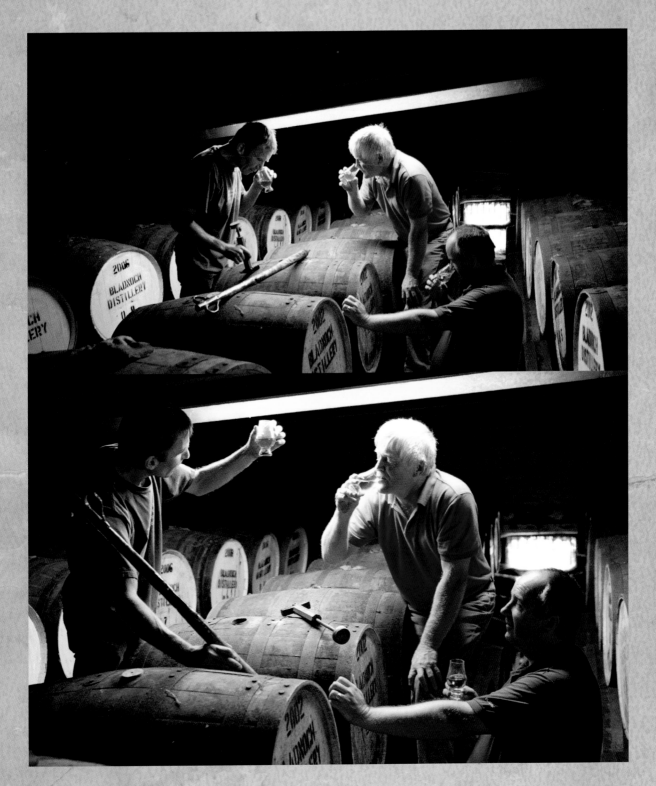

ISLAY

Islay is the southernmost island in the Inner Hebrides, and has a population of around 3200 people. It boasts 130 miles of coastline, dotted along which are seven of its eight working distilleries, with only Kilchoman located very slightly inland. The unique style of Islay single malts, traditionally seen as full-bodied and peaty, means that the island enjoys the status of its very own official whisky region.

KEY

Main distilleries

1 Bunnahabhain
2 Caol Ila
3 Kilchoman
4 Bruichladdich

5 Bowmore
6 Laphroaig
7 Lagavulin
8 Ardbeg

▲ Featured distillery

ARDBEG

Website www.ardbeg.com
Founded 1815
Location Port Ellen, Isle of Islay

The story of Ardbeg is heart-warming – a lost distillery comes back triumphantly from the dead, going on to repay the faith of all those people who took part in the revival and those who kept the peaty faith. Peaty indeed, for Ardbeg is the most routinely heavily peated of all the Islay single malts.

Closed down in 1996 by owners Allied Distillers Ltd, the historic distillery of Ardbeg was purchased the following year by The Glenmorangie Company Ltd, which saw potential in the run-down distillery on the southern shores of Islay and the whisky made there. In 2004 the French luxury goods group LVMH bought Glenmorangie along with Ardbeg and Glen Moray. Islay malts are now considered to be the 'sexiest' single malts in the world. It's difficult to appreciate that even as recently as the mid-1990s, the cult of peat had not really gathered momentum, and that Glenmorangie were taking quite a gamble sinking its profits into Ardbeg, but the investment has certainly come good.

As well as whisky, Ardbeg offers some of the island's best home cooking in its Old Kiln Café. If you can't pay a visit you can still become an online member of the 'Ardbeg Committee'. This keeps you up to date with Ardbeg and gives you a first chance to try new and sometimes Committee-exclusive bottlings.

Ardbeg has been fairly innovative when it comes to those bottlings, launching 'Very Young Ardbeg' as a way of showcasing the spirit being made under the Glenmorangie regime, and this at a time when age statements on single malts were seen as much more important than they are today. Further interim bottlings of the same 1997 whisky were released, culminating in the 10-year-old 'Renaissance' expression in 2008. Arbeg also has a fondness for extremes, both of whisky and language, producing the ultra-peaty Supernova in 2009, following on from the 2008 controversial Blasda, which confused many hard-core, peat-freak Ardbeg aficionados by only being peated to one-third of the normal Ardbeg level. Linguistic extremes come courtesy of the use of Gaelic names – try asking for a dram of Uigeadail or better still Airigh Nam Beist after a long stay in the bar.

TASTING NOTES

Ardbeg – 10-year-old – 46% abv

Nose Peat smoke, backed by zesty lemons and limes, a hint of milk chocolate and a touch of seaweed.

Palate Wonderfully warming peat, but refreshing notes of zesty citrus come flooding through: more lemons, limes and a hint of ginger.

Finish Salty notes linger on the palate to create a dry, peaty, medicinal finish.

BOWMORE

Website **www.bowmore.com**
Founded **1779**
Location **Bowmore, Isle of Islay**

Bowmore Distillery is situated close to the pier in the island capital of the same name. It's the oldest working distillery on Islay, and in terms of style offers a 'mid-way' between the full-on Ardbeg, Lagavulin and Laphroaig peat monsters of the southern shores and the less assertive charms of distilleries like Bunnahabhain and Bruichladdich.

A relatively high proportion of Islay distilleries operate floor maltings – three out of eight, in fact, though Kilchoman is a fairly recent addition to the fold. This is a high percentage when you consider that fewer than 2% of operational mainland distilleries retain floor maltings. On Islay, of course, malting tends to be about the influence of peat, and Bowmore uses a mix of its own 'home-made' malt and the balance from the mainland, all peated to a level of around 25ppm – a medium level of peating for an Islay whisky.

Since 1994, Bowmore, as part of Morrison Bowmore Distillers Ltd, has been owned by the Japanese distilling giant Suntory, which also operates Auchentoshan and Glengarioch in Scotland. The distillery's origins go back to the early years of the development of Bowmore as a specially planned settlement by island owner Daniel Campbell.

To this day, one of the original stone-built warehouses remains in use for the maturation of whisky, and it is thought to be the oldest working whisky warehouse in Scotland. At high tide, the building is

regularly soaked with seawater, and the marine environment plays a significant part in the character of the whisky as it ages.

Bowmore is keen to be seen as an environmentally friendly distillery, and a few years ago it gifted a former warehouse to the local community, converting it into a swimming pool heated by waste hot water from the distilling process. More recently, it has developed a method of dramatically reducing the amount of peat it uses in its maltings, without affecting the distinctive style of the whisky.

A wide variety of different single malt expressions are available, ranging in age from 12 to 40 years, and the whole of the production is now earmarked for single malts, rather than being used to contribute to blends.

TASTING NOTES

Bowmore – 12-year-old – 40% abv
Nose Floral and perfumed, with lots of sweet peat smoke, ripe oranges and a waft of brine.
Palate Earthy, with more seaside notes, smoke and contrasting violets, soft fruit and Sherry.
Finish Smoke, salt and citrus fruits. Lengthy.

BRUICHLADDICH

Website **www.bruichladdich.com**
Founded **1881**
Location **Bruichladdich, Isle of Islay**

Just like Ardbeg, Bruichladdich was a 'lost' distillery not so many years ago, deemed surplus to requirements by its owner Whyte & Mackay Ltd. And just like Ardbeg, it's impossible to think of Islay now without a vibrant, thriving, innovative Bruichladdich. The distillery is virtually a preserved Victorian whisky-making operation, but that didn't prevent The Bruichladdich Distillery Co Ltd from doing some fairly wild and wacky things during their ownership between 2000 and 2012. These included producing a quadruple-distilled 'rocket fuel' of a single malt, and making very heavily peated 'Octomore' spirit against the more recent trend for Bruichladdich to be lightly peated.

Supremo Mark Reynier and veteran distilling guru Jim McEwan also presided over the distillation of batches of 100% organic Islay-grown barley, the preparation of 'multi-vintage' expressions matured in a wide variety of cask types, the making of The Botanist Gin in a converted, redundant 'Lomond' still (nicknamed Ugly Betty because of her less than comely appearance), and generally living up to their self-proclaimed role as 'Progressive Hebridean Distillers.' Bruichladdich is a joy to visit, particularly for connoisseurs of traditional

distilling methods and equipment. On the website you can view the production processes in a series of webcams.

Given the sheer energy that Bruichladdich has put into its release programme, it has sometimes been difficult to decide what exactly the 'house' style of Bruichladdich is, but the release in 2011 of The Laddie 10-year-old provides a good benchmark from which to work. Bruichladdich was sold to Rémy Cointreau in 2012, since when there has been a degree of streamlining of the release programme, but aficionados of The Laddie need not worry that too much else is changing.

TASTING NOTES
Bruichladdich 'The Laddie' – 10-year-old – 46% abv
Nose A light and delicate nose giving off subtle tones of crème brûlée, fresh lemon cheesecake, dusted with icing sugar.
Palate Scottish tablet fudge with a creamy undertone, gingerbread and sweet tea are the headline flavours.
Finish Woody and spicy, vanilla and a return of the gingerbread.

KILCHOMAN

Website **www.kilchoman.com**

Founded **2005**

Location **Bruichladdich, Isle of Islay,**

Kilchoman is the newest and smallest of Islay's distilleries. It was developed due to the perseverance and faith of Anthony Wills and his family, who managed to realize their dream of building their own distillery. Wills is an Englishman with many years of experience in the wine trade and a brief foray into independent Scotch whisky bottling under his belt, but his wife's parents originate from Islay. While spending time there, Anthony began to consider creating a small-scale distillery on the island, taking advantage of the fact that the Islay single malt whisky 'brand' was achieving cult status.

Like Daftmill in Fife, Kilchoman represents a return to farm-based distilling. A quantity of the barley used is grown on Rockside Farm not far from the distillery. Kilchoman makes some of its own malt, buying in the rest from the Port Ellen Maltings that are owned by Diageo and serve a number of the island's distilleries. Kilchoman has its own small-scale bottling line, and with his 2011 '100% Islay' bottling, made exclusively from barley grown at Rockside and malted on site, Anthony Wills has fulfilled his original intention of running a 'barley to bottle' enterprise. The single pair of stills can only produce a maximum of

110,000 litres (29,000 gallons) of spirit per year, but even so there is a busy release programme, which has seen bottlings of whisky from a variety of cask types from the age of 3 upwards. Kilchoman sets out its stall to welcome visitors, and offers fare to rival that of Ardbeg's Old Kiln Café at the southern end of Islay. Kilchoman may be the new kid on the Islay distilling block, but after working so hard to establish it and receiving such a positive reception for its early releases, the Wills family and their distillery are definitely here to stay.

TASTING NOTES
Kilchoman 100% Islay – 50% abv

Nose Lemon and grapefruit, balanced by vanilla and honey, all with big peat notes and some liquorice.

Palate Oily, gently medicinal, with digestive biscuits, citrus fruits, brine and plenty of peat.

Finish Lengthy, fruity and floral, with peppery peat. From early on, Kilchoman showed a great deal of promise, and as it gets older it is clearly going to become a new Islay classic.

LAGAVULIN

Website **www.discovering-distilleries.com**
Founded **1816**
Location **Port Ellen, Isle of Islay**

One of the 'big three' southern Islay distilleries, offering plenty for 'peat-heads' to rave about, Lagavulin is one of the world's great whiskies, though it is outsold by Bowmore and Laphroaig. Like Caol Ila Distillery and the modern maltings of Port Ellen, Lagavulin belongs to Diageo, and it has traditionally contributed much of the peaty part of the famous White Horse blend.

When in the late 1980s Diageo's predecessor, United Distillers, decided to promote some of its single malts under the umbrella title of 'Classic Malts', a 16-year-old Lagavulin was chosen to represent the Islay region. However, at times this bottling has been hard to find, with available supplies of Lagavulin at that age sometimes lagging behind demand. Today, thanks to increased productivity at the distillery, that's no longer the case and the brand is relatively easy to source.

Like its shoreline neighbours of Ardbeg and Laphroaig, Lagavulin has several centuries of solid heritage behind it, and at various times, two other distilleries, Ardmore and later Malt Mill, shared its site. When Malt Mill closed in the early 1960s its two archaic little stills were removed to the main Lagavulin distillery, and the style of the Lagavulin stills today owes much to their design.

Malt is sourced from Diageo's nearby Port Ellen Maltings, which dates from the 1970s and supplies not only the company's own Islay plants of Lagavulin and Caol Ila, but also a number of other island distilleries. Some casks of Lagavulin mature in the traditional, stone warehouses of the closed Port Ellen Distillery, the remnants of which stand alongside the maltings.

In addition to the 16-year-old version of Lagavulin, there is a highly regarded Distillers Edition bottling, where secondary maturation has taken place in ex-Pedro Ximénez Sherry casks. These do a lovely job of complementing and enhancing the sweet, smoky notes of Lagavulin, delivering the ideal after-dinner Islay dram.

TASTING NOTES

Lagavulin – 16-year-old – 43% abv

Nose The peat in this dram is upfront, yet soft with freshly turned earth, carbolic soap, cereals, rich dark brown sugar and a surprising hint of Play-Doh.

Palate The smoke and peat manifest themselves as freshly toasted wholemeal bread. Wisps of burnt brown sugar, some green herbs and dark chocolate-covered Turkish Delight, followed by crème brûlée notes.

Finish A creamy finish which brings salty, delicate peat smoke and lingering fudge.

LAPHROAIG

Website www.laphroaig.com

Founded 1810

Location Port Ellen, Isle of Islay

Laphroaig is the world's best-selling Islay single malt, and enjoyed a cult following long before Islays in general became such objects of desire among serious-minded whisky-drinking folk. Its uncompromising style is not to everyone's taste, and it has been referred to as 'the Marmite of the whisky world', but its best-selling status and the fact that around half a million people from 150 countries have registered as 'Friends of Laphroaig' mean that it has more than its fair share of admirers. 'Friends' receive their own personal square foot of land at the distillery, which they may visit, and even stand upon, and they receive an annual rent payment in the form of a dram of the stuff itself.

The whisky industry has not been big on female emancipation until relatively recently, but Laphroaig was actually owned and run by a woman – the redoubtable Bessie Williamson – from 1954 until 1972.

Along with Bowmore and Kilchoman, Laphroaig operates its own traditional floor maltings, making around 15% of all the malt it uses, with the bulk of the rest coming from the nearby Port Ellen Maltings. The still house set-up is unusual in that it features three wash stills and four spirit stills, while most distilleries operate even numbers of both.

Peaty and medicinal, Laphroaig is undoubtedly one of the most individualistic of all Scotch whiskies, and a visit to the distillery has its individualistic aspects, too. In addition to the more usual experiences, the visitor can opt for the 'Hunter's Hike' – named after one-time owner Ian Hunter.

The 'Hunter's Hike' allows you to walk up to the Laphroaig water source and enjoy a dram there, to try your hand at cutting peat – harder than it looks – and then to get even more exercise by having a go at turning the malt on one of the malting floors. It's a great experience if you want to get really up close and personal with your whisky-making.

TASTING NOTES

Laphroaig – 10-year-old – 40% abv

Nose Huge wafts of peat smoke, bandages, TCP and liniment. Slight hints of ginger and vanilla.

Palate A fresh, fruity nature that goes from being tinned fruit salad (neat) to something more akin a homemade smoothie. The fire from the peat keeps this one lingering on and on.

Finish Lots of wood; spices and oak. A hint of hazelnut praline and loads of smoke.

OTHERS TO TRY

BUNNAHABHAIN

Website www.bunnahabhain.com

Founded 1881

Location Port Askaig, Isle of Islay

Bunnahabhain is one of the most remote of all Islay's distilleries, being located several miles down a very minor road near Port Askaig, in the north of the island. For many years, Bunnahabhain has been lightly peated in the manner of Bruichladdich, but batches of heavily peated spirit are also now being produced.

Tipple to try Bunnahabhain – 18-year-old

CAOL ILA

Website www.discovering-distilleries.com

Founded 1846

Location Port Askaig, Isle of Islay

The distillery you see today is modern in appearance and dates from a total reconstruction project, completed in 1974. Increased in capacity during 2012, Caol Ila has the largest potential output of any Islay distillery, and is a vital ingredient in many of owner Diageo's blends.

Tipple to try Caol Ila Moch

PORT ELLEN

Founded: 1825 (now closed)

Location: Port Ellen, Isle of Islay

In 1983 Port Ellen filled its last casks before the doors closed forever, sounding the death knell of what would subsequently become a celebrated and much talked about single malt whisky. Port Ellen had previously suffered extended periods of silence and because of the similarities in character with the Caol Ila distillery (owned by the same company) it was felt that the whisky, which at the time was classed as fairly unremarkable, was surplus to requirements. Little did the owners know that, over the next three decades, the remaining casks, some still slumbering away in Islay's many drafty coastal warehouses, would blossom into a whisky masterpiece.

Tipple to try Port Ellen 11th Release – 32-year- old –1978

BELOW: Bunnahabhain Distillery is one of Islay's most remote distilleries. Its sea-facing warehouses provide an ideal environment for maturing whisky.

CAMPBELTOWN

Campbeltown is by far the smallest malt whisky region in Scotland, since it consists of one remote fishing port on the Kintyre Peninsula of Argyll. It is also home to the fewest distilleries – just three in total. If its glory days have faded now, Campbeltown has certainly paid its dues and deserves its status as an individual region. It was referred to in Victorian times as 'Whisky City' because of the sheer number of its distilleries. Distilling has taken place on some 35 sites in the borough, and during the mid-1880s there were 21 working distilleries.

Campbeltown Harbour

Campbeltown Loch

Davaar Island

Campbeltown

Crosshill Loch

Beinn Ghuilean Mt

KEY

▲ Featured distillery

Main distilleries

1 Glen Scotia

2 Glengyle

3 Springbank

GLENGYLE

Website **www.kilkerran.com**

Founded **2004**

Location **Campbeltown, Argyll**

Glengyle is another distillery that has spent a very long period in 'silence' – the Scotch whisky world's equivalent term to a disused theatre being 'dark.' The original distillery was established in 1872, but fell victim to the economic slump of the years between the two world wars, when so many other Campbeltown distilleries closed down, and Glengyle was distilled for the last time in 1925.

Or so it seemed. But then along came Hedley Wright, owner of Springbank Distillery, a relation of Glengyle founder William Mitchell and a passionate advocate of Campbeltown as a distilling region in its own right. He purchased the Glengyle site in 2000, and determined to return it to its former glory: a little brother for Springbank, if you like. All the distilling kit had long gone but a pair of stills from the closed Ben Wyvis Distillery in Invergordon was sourced and suitably altered to produce the style of whisky desired. Ben Wyvis also supplied the spirit safe and spirit-receiving vessels. The Boby mill used to grind the malt into grist prior to mashing was another cast-off, in this case sourced from the Craigellachie Distillery on Speyside. Four brand-new larch washbacks were constructed to order. Thus, Glengyle combines a pleasing mixture of rejuvenated and bespoke equipment.

Malt is supplied from the malting floors of nearby Springbank, whose staff also operate Glengyle when whisky-making

takes place. In 2004 the initial spirit flowed from what was effectively the first 'new' Campbeltown distillery in 125 years.

Because 'Glengyle' was already registered as a whisky brand, owned by Loch Lomond Distillers, which also operates Campbeltown's Glen Scotia distillery, Hedley Wright settled on 'Kilkerran' as the name for his single malt. Kilkerran is derived from the Gaelic 'Ceann Loch Cille Chiarain', which is the name of the original settlement where St Kerran had his religious cell and where Campbeltown now stands. A limited release of 3-year-old Kilkerran was launched in 2007, and a number of bottlings under the 'Work in Progress' label have appeared since then.

TASTING NOTES

Kilkerran Work in Progress 3, June 2011 – 46% abv

Nose Toffee, vanilla, honey, cinnamon, apples, pears and a whiff of gentle peat smoke.

Palate Full and quite oily, milk chocolate, honey, ginger, malt and pipe tobacco.

Finish Citrus fruits, pepper and pine.

GLEN SCOTIA

Website www.glenscotia-distillery.co.uk
Founded 1832
Location Campbeltown, Argyll

Glen Scotia is one of those distilleries that just won't die. Even while Campbeltown's other distilleries were being demolished or converted into bus garages and creameries, the distillery on High Street somehow survived intact to the present day. That's not to say, of course, that its history isn't filled with periods of closure and changes of ownership, and only hefty doses of good fortune have led to its survival.

One of the many proprietors of Glen Scotia was Duncan MacCallum, who owned the distillery between 1924 and 1930, two years after it fell silent. The story goes that MacCallum was defrauded of the then enormous sum of £40,000 ($64,400) by a group of confidence tricksters, and he subsequently drowned himself in Cross Hill Loch in December 1932. His ghost is said to appear in the old distillery maltings from time to time.

Campbeltown's demise as a distilling centre came about for a variety of reasons, including the period of US Prohibition from 1920 to 1933, as well as a change in the style of whisky favoured by blenders from the big, robust malts of Campbeltown to the more sophisticated and less intense whiskies of Speyside. By 1925 only 12 distilleries were still working, and by 1935 only Glen Scotia and Springbank were making whisky. Owned since the mid-1990s by the same firm that operates

Loch Lomond malt and grain distillery, Glen Scotia looked decidedly down-at-heel until an on-going programme of refurbishment and general investment began in 2008, with the old washbacks being replaced by new stainless steel ones and the installation of a new system to treat the leftovers of distilling, known as pot ale. There are even plans to re-open the second warehouse, which has lain dormant for some time now, and to offer new releases of the actual single malt to complement the physical work to enhance and upgrade the distillery.

TThe investment in Glen Scotia's fabric was matched by the release in 2012 of an entirely new range of single malts – ranging from 10 to 21 years old.

TASTING NOTES

Glen Scotia – 12-year-old – 40% abv
Nose A bit of an old-fashioned bruiser! Charcoal, engine oil, wood smoke, damp earth, with sweeter, spicy notes emerging.
Palate Peat smoke, stewed apples, raisins and oak.
Finish Long, smoky and sweet and slightly herbal.

SPRINGBANK

Website **www.springbankdistillers.com**
Founded **1828**
Location **Campbeltown, Argyll**

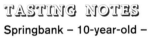

Springbank has been the keeper of the Campbeltown flame down the years, when Glen Scotia was almost unavailable as a single malt and Glengyle wasn't even a glint in Hedley Wright's eye. The distillery earned a reputation for quirkiness and old-fashioned, hands-on values, and the whisky made there has become loved by traditionalists and anyone who can appreciate a dram that is something out of the ordinary, in terms of style and sheer quality.

Springbank remains one of the last family-owned distilleries in Scotland, and the distillery itself is superbly idiosyncratic, continuing to malt its own barley on traditional malting floors and to bottle on site. The wash still is unique in being heated both by internal steam coils and direct-fired by oil. Three distinct types of spirit are produced, namely Springbank (distilled two and a half times), Longrow (heavily peated and distilled twice) and Hazelburn (unpeated and triple-distilled).

The first batches of heavily peated Longrow were distilled during the mid-1970s, when Hedley Wright decided to see if he could make a Campbeltown single malt that had the characteristics of an Islay. Remember, this was long, long before Islay single malts became the 'sexy' beasts they are today. As for Hazelburn, it was first produced in 1997 to give Springbank another stylistic string to its bow.

Having taken a break from distilling during 2008 and 2009, when fuel and barley costs were notably high, Springbank is once again very much alive and kicking, contrary to the opinions of conspiracy theorists at the time, who had the distillery dead and buried along with so many of its long-lost rivals. Springbank looks sure to go on forever! It is an open secret that the distillery does not hold large stocks of old whiskies, so don't expect to see 40- and 50-year-old limited-edition releases any time soon.

There are a number of cask-finished Springbank and Longrow whiskies to look out for, offering interesting takes on the usual 'house' styles.

TASTING NOTES

Springbank – 10-year-old – 46% abv

Nose Lemon, apples, oranges and earthy peat on the nose, not to mention a whiff of brine.

Palate Oily, peaty, with black pepper and a sprinkling of nutmeg.

Finish Lengthy, with peat, spicy oak and sea salt.

ISLANDS

The Islands include a vast geographical area, from Arran in the south-west to Orkney in the north. They embrace some of the wildest and most beautiful parts of Scotland. Each island has its own unique identity and character, just as every island distillery and the whisky it produces is also a one-off. Islay is recognized as its own region due to its huge influence and number of distilleries.

Isle of Mull — Calgary, Tobermory, Sound of Mull, Craignure, Lochbuie, Carsaig, Firth of Lorn

Isle of Skye — Uig, Dunvegan, Portree, Sound of Raasay, Talisker, Carbost, Cuillin Hills, Broadford, Kyle of Lochalsh, Armadale

Orkney Islands — North Ronaldsay, Westray, Sanday, Rousay, Stronsay, Stromness, Kirkwall, Scapa, Highland Park, Scapa Flow, Eloy, South Ronaldsay, Pentland Firth

Isle of Jura — Ardlussa, Tarbert, Lagg, Paps of Jura, Feolin Ferry, Jura, Craighouse, Islay, Sound of Jura

Isle of Lewis — Càrlabhagh, Stornoway, Abhainn Dearg, Tarbert, The Minch

Scotland map — Cape Wrath, Pentland Firth, Orkney Islands, Isle of Lewis, Wick, The Minch, Ullapool, North Uist, North West Highlands, South Uist, Loch Ness, Grampian Mountains, Aberdeen, Rhum, Inner Hebrides, Coll, Isle of Skye, Tiree, Isle of Mull, Oban, Dundee, North Sea, Atlantic Ocean, Jura, Firth of Forth, Islay, GLASGOW, EDINBURGH, Kintyre, Arran, Firth of Clyde, Ayr, Southern Uplands, Mull of Kintyre, Dumfries

Isle of Arran — Sound of Bute, Lochranza, Arran, Kintyre, Kilbrannan Sound, Firth of Clyde, Machrie, Brodick, Lamlash, Blackwaterfoot, Whiting Bay

▲ Featured distillery

NORTHERN IRELAND

ENGLAND

ARRAN

Website **www.arranwhisky.com**
Founded **1993**
Location **Lochranza, Isle of Arran**

Arran Distillery was one of the first of a new generation of relatively small-scale, independent Scotch whisky distilleries. It was established by former Chivas Brothers' senior executive Harold Currie, who had long harboured an ambition to return whisky-making to Arran. The island had once boasted many illicit distilleries, while the last legal one at Lagg had closed in 1837.

Since Arran's new distillery began production, ownership has passed from the Currie family, though Isle of Arran Distillers Ltd remains proudly independent. As with any new distillery venture, the early years can be fairly lean ones in terms of cash flow, and the Arran team used cask finishing as a way of developing a wider product range and gaining more attention.

Now that the distillery has built up reserves of maturing stock and a solid reputation for the quality of its spirit, it is concentrating on developing an 'aged' range, with 10- and 14-year-olds now available. Special 'finishes' remain part and parcel of the Arran portfolio, with Amarone, Port and Sauternes being permanent fixtures. There are also regular releases of limited editions, single casks and a variant without an age statement by the name of Arran Original, not to mention a peated version called Machrie Moor. A modest amount of peated spirit is now made each year to service future demand for peated expressions of the single malt.

As island distilleries go, Arran is one of the more accessible, with frequent one-hour ferry sailings from the Ayrshire port of Ardrossan, some 30 miles south-west of Glasgow, to Brodick on Arran. An alternative if you happen to be distillery-spotting in the Campbeltown area during the summer months is to take the short, seasonal ferry trip from Claonaig on the Kintyre Peninsula to Lochranza on Arran, conveniently close to the distillery.

Arran Distillery was built with the requirements of visitors in mind, and tourist income is a significant element of the operation. Accordingly, access to the actual production areas is very good and visitors are well catered for in terms of refreshments and shopping opportunities. All this and the widely varying scenery of the Isle of Arran, too!

TASTING NOTES

Arran – 10-year-old – 46% abv
Nose Grassy and herbal, soft fruit and allspice.
Palate Malty and sweet, biscuity, more spice, sliced cooking apples.
Finish Malty and mildly citric.

HIGHLAND PARK

Website **www.highlandpark.co.uk**

Founded **1798**

Location **Kirkwall, Orkney**

Quite simply, Highland Park is one of the world's great whiskies, produced in a fascinating and historic distillery and located in a very special part of the world. The Orkney Islands, with their strong Norse heritage, are a place apart, and Highland Park single malt stands out from the crowd just like the Orcadian landscape.

The distillery dates back to the late 18th century and was built on the site of a smuggling bothy operated by Magnus Eunson, a celebrated Orkney character who was a butcher, church officer and smuggler. Eunson allegedly stored illicit whisky beneath a church pulpit, on one occasion moving it to his house when he feared a raid by excise officers.

When the excisemen arrived at the house they found Eunson and his family solemnly gathered around what looked like a bier but was actually the offending casks of whisky, covered with a white cloth. Eunson told the officers there had been a death, and someone muttered the word 'smallpox', after which the excisemen decided not to stay too much longer!

Highland Park continues to run its own floor maltings, burning Orkney's unique style of peat in the kiln, which

undoubtedly contributes to the singular character of the whisky. Around 20% of the distillery's malt requirements are made 'in house,' while the rest is unpeated and shipped in from a mainland supplier.

All the spirit destined for single-malt bottling is matured in ex-Sherry casks, and the Highland Park team reckons that the maturation regime is another factor in the whisky's favour, since temperature variations on Orkney are less extreme than in most of Scotland – and a whole lot less extreme than Kentucky. You can buy Highland Park in a wide variety of ages, from 12 up to 50 years and if at all possible, go to the distillery and buy it in the stylish shop there!

TASTING NOTES

Highland Park– 12-year-old – 40% abv

Nose A well-balanced, delicate aroma, with fresh vanilla, white chocolate and freshly diced apple, followed by heather honey.

Palate Silky with summer fruits, sweet apple pie with vanilla custard.

Finish Lingering traces of vanilla and apple on the drying palate.

JURA

Website **www.isleofjura.com**

Founded **1810**

Location **Craighouse, Isle of Jura**

For many years, Jura single malt lived in the shadow of its arguably more glamorous and more macho Islay neighbours, but in recent years owner Whyte & Mackay distillers has been spicing things up a bit at Jura, extending the range of whiskies and producing a good number of limited-edition bottlings, while the visitor centre underwent a major refit during 2011. Getting to Jura takes a bit of effort, so it's nice to receive a warm welcome in pleasant facilities when you arrive!

Apart from the distillery itself, located in the village of Craighouse, Jura offers superb wild scenery, highlighted by the three Paps of Jura: a trio of striking (and apparently breast-like) mountains, though maybe a dram or two of the local elixir makes the resemblance more obvious! The name Jura derives from the Gaelic for deer, and today the beasts outnumber humans by 30 to one. Jura is also where George Orwell escaped from city life to write his epic novel *Nineteen Eighty-Four*.

The original Jura distillery was established in 1810, but this closed in 1901, and it was not until 1960 that construction of the present plant began, with the first spirit flowing in 1963.

The distillery project was started by the old-established blender Charles Mackinlay & Co Ltd, but the firm was taken over by Scottish & Newcastle while building work was ongoing.

The intention was to provide much-needed jobs for the remote island community, and the new distillery distanced itself from the ones on Islay from the start by making an altogether more 'Highland' style of spirit, without peatiness or medicinal notes, though a few peated versions of Jura have now been released as well. Indeed, Jura Superstition, made with a percentage of peated malt, is a notably popular part of the permanent range, and in 2009 a second stronger, smokier, peated Jura appeared under the Prophecy label.

TASTING NOTES

Isle of Jura – 10-year-old – 40% abv

Nose Fruit salad without any cream, pine needles, a sprinkle of salt.

Palate Quite oily, with spices, malt and salt.

Finish Vanilla oak, medium in length.

SCAPA

Website www.scapamalt.com
Founded 1885
Location Kirkwall, Orkney

No matter what owner Chivas Brothers does, its Scapa distillery and the single malt whisky it produces will always live in the shadow of nearby Highland Park. It's not that Scapa whisky isn't good; it's just that Highland Park has established itself up there among the greats and has a fantastic story to tell as well as winning rather a lot of awards. But Scapa single malt isn't inferior; it's just different.

For a start, while Highland Park uses malt peated on its own malting floors and employs ex-Sherry wood for the maturation of all its single malts, Scapa imports unpeated malt and matures the spirit it distils almost exclusively in ex-Bourbon casks.

While Highland Park was busy making a single-malt name for itself, Scapa was quietly getting on with the business of supplying bulk malt spirit for blending, with the distillery being owned by major blenders Hiram Walker and Allied Domecq before coming into the hands of Chivas Brothers. It's only in the last few years that whisky enthusiasts have actually been able to find Scapa relatively easily. A 14-year-old bottling appeared in 2006, followed by a 16-year-old two years later.

When consumers got the chance to try Scapa, most were very impressed. Highland Park may be the Orkney star name, but Scapa is very far from being a bit-part player.

In addition to Highland Park and Scapa, Orkney used to boast a third distillery,

located in the historic port of Stromness. It operated from 1817 until 1928, and the whisky it produced was sold for many years as Man O'Hoy, after one of Orkney's most distinctive landmarks, the red sandstone sea stack off the island of Hoy. Later the whisky was marketed as Old Orkney, or 'OO'. Following closure in the economically unforgiving inter-war years, the distillery buildings were demolished during the 1940s, and ultimately replaced by local authority housing. For many years, one of the houses that occupy the site of Stromness distillery was home to celebrated Orcadian writer George Mackay Brown, who died in 1996, and today a blue plaque commemorates his association with the place.

TASTING NOTES

Scapa – 16-year-old – 40% abv
Nose Oranges, heather honey and vanilla – a pretty nose.
Palate Rich and flavoursome, with baked apple tart and a sprinkling of ginger.
Finish Long and gently drying, with just a hint of brine to remind you that it's made right beside the sea.

TALISKER

Website: **www.malts.com**
Founded: **1830**
Location: **Carbost, Isle of Skye**

You've got to make a real effort to get to Talisker Distillery, which is located in the remote north-west of the Isle of Skye, yet remarkably this is the most visited of all the distilleries owned by Diageo. Bearing in mind that Diageo owns Glenkinchie near Edinburgh and Dalwhinnie alongside the main A9 Perth-to-Inverness road, that's quite something. It is testament to the lure of a beautiful, rugged island, but also to the respect and affection whisky-lovers feel for this individualistic single malt.

The 'Lava of the Cuillins', as it's sometimes known, is distilled in what may seem a disappointingly factory-like distillery, but it is set in the stunning landscape of the shores of Loch Harport, and in the shadow of the Cuillin Hills. The distillery was altogether more attractive before 1960, when someone accidentally left a valve open on one of the stills, with the result that much of the production plant was burnt to the ground.

Undaunted, the owners rebuilt the distillery, complete with precise replicas of the five idiosyncratic stills, so that the character of the whisky would remain the same. Distillers are very particular about that sort of thing.

Today you can routinely buy Talisker at 10 and 18 years of age, along with Talisker 57° North (a cask-strength expression with no age statement, the name of which reflects the latitude of the

distillery itself), and a Distillers Edition, finished in amoroso Sherry casks for extra sherried depth and rich complexity. Every year Diageo issues limited editions of a few rare and unusual variants of some of its single malts as special releases, and 25- and 30-year-old Taliskers have become firm favourites among those.

If you make the long and complex journey to Talisker Distillery, as so many do, your efforts may be rewarded by the purchase of a bottle of 12-year-old cask-strength single malt, only available there. With the exception of such cask-strength bottlings, Talisker is always presented at the decidedly quirky strength of 45.8% abv, but then Talisker is a quirky malt, a whisky not quite like any other.

TASTING NOTES

Talisker – 10-year-old – 45.8% abv
Nose A massive mix of hot chilli, carbolic soap, malt and cracked black pepper.
Palate Big-bodied, lots of nutty smoke, big dashes of black pepper and chocolate ginger.
Finish Long, smoky, with dried fruit and chilli peppers. Unforgettable.

TOBERMORY

Website www.tobermorymalt.com
Founded 1798
Location Tobermory, Isle of Mull

The port of Tobermory on the Isle of Mull became well known a few years ago as the colourful setting for children's television programme *Balamory*, but for whisky-lovers the main attraction is the historic distillery, which stands at the heart of the small town beside Tobermory Bay.

The distillery may date from the late 18th century, but its heritage has been chequered, to say the least: the plant was actually closed for more years than it has been open. It even had the role of a power station and a canteen for sailors at various times.

However, current owner Burn Stewart Distillers has given Tobermory stability and an altogether enhanced profile and reputation, most notably by reformulating the single malt at a strength of 46.3% and by not chill-filtering it. That particular process ensures that whisky doesn't go cloudy at low temperatures, but the price you pay for clarity is a loss of texture and significant aromas and flavour elements.

Today Tobermory makes two entirely different single malts. Half the annual production is unpeated spirit, which carries the Tobermory name when matured and bottled, while the other half consists of heavily peated spirit that is marketed

as Ledaig – the original name of the distillery and Gaelic for 'safe haven'.

Ledaig was first produced in 1996, as a way of returning whisky made at Tobermory to something like its original style, and the initial intention was simply to use it as a component in various Burn Stewart blends. However, as it began to mature, the owner decided that it had something worthy of single malt bottling, and it was launched as a 10-year-old in 2007.

A previous owner had sold off the imposing stone-built distillery warehouse when in financial straits some years ago, so most of the spirit made at Tobermory is matured on the mainland in Burn Stewart's Deanston Distillery in Perthshire.

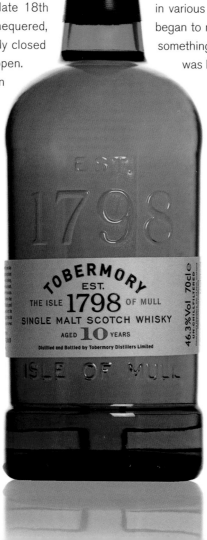

TASTING NOTES

Tobermory – 10-year-old – 46.3% abv

Nose Barley, nuts and ginger – buttery and approachable.
Palate Light and sweet, with honey, malt and cinnamon.
Finish Spicy and citric.

OTHERS TO TRY

ABHAINN DEARG

Website www.abhainndearg.co.uk

Founded 2008

Location Carnish, Isle of Lewis

Abhainn Dearg, meaning 'Red River' in Gaelic, is the newest of Scotland's island distilleries and the only licensed one in the Outer Hebrides. It is located on the site of a former salmon hatchery on the Atlantic coast and boasts the most idiosyncratic-looking pair of stills in all of Scotland – reminiscent of old-fashioned, domestic hot water tanks, with necks like elongated witches' hats!

Abhainn Dearg began production in September 2008, meaning that its spirit legally became Scotch whisky in 2011. To celebrate that milestone 2011 bottles of 3-year-old Abhainn Dearg Single Malt Special Edition were released.

Once those 2011 bottles have been sold, no more whisky will be bottled until it is five years of age, and owner Mark Tayburn, a Stornoway businessman, expects a general release of Abhainn Dearg to happen when his whisky is aged between 7 and 10 years old. In addition to the youthful single malt, there is the 'Spirit of Lewis', which is new spirit filled into ex-Pedro Ximénez Sherry casks for a three-month period of maturation.

Tipple to try Abhainn Dearg Single Malt Special Edition

BELOW: Abhainn Dearg, on the western coast of the Isle of Lewis in the Outer Hebrides, is the newest of Scotland's island distilleries.

BLENDING SCOTCH WHISKY

ABOVE: Richard Paterson, Whyte and Mackay's master blender, using his 'nose' to blend the recreation of Mackinlay's Rare Old Highland Malt Whisky.

Although a great deal of attention is paid to single malts, the fact remains that some 90% of all Scotch whisky sold around the world is actually blended, and many international markets have virtually no interest in malts. The modern Scotch whisky industry was founded on sales of blends, and blends continue to make the bulk of profits for major players such as Diageo and Pernod Ricard.

There is an all too prevalent view that blends are somehow inferior to single malts, and that the latter are classier and more exclusive, but this is a gross simplification of the facts. At their best, blends created with integrity and from fine component whiskies are at least the equal of single malts. Blends are not inferior to malts; they are simply different drinks.

The art of blending is one of the most skilful aspects of whisky production, and the best blenders are very highly regarded. They work almost exclusively by nose, rarely actually tasting any of the whiskies they are evaluating. Blending is sometimes likened to conducting an orchestra – each instrument is impressive in its own right, but when combined under skilful direction, the sum is greater than the parts.

The average blended whisky comprises malts from up to 30 different distilleries, along with two or three grain whiskies, and the blender will choose these to produce a whisky in the required style and to sell at a specified 'price point'. The more expensive blends usually contain a higher proportion of malt to grain and an increased percentage of older whiskies.

Once selected, casks of the various malt and grain whiskies are disgorged into a large blending vat, where compressed air mixes the contents. The newly created blend may then be casked for several months to allow the components to 'marry', though some blenders prefer to keep the marriage of malts and the marriage of grains separate until bottling, while some producers don't marry their blends at all.

Before bottling, the blend is usually reduced with water to market strength. Caramel (E105a) may be added to enhance the colour and ensure consistency, and chill-filtration normally takes place so that the whisky will not become cloudy if water is added by the consumer.

Despite the fact that blended whisky accounts for over over 90% of total Scotch whisky sales, blended Scotch whisky is a relative newcomer. It was really only developed during the second half of the 19th century. The discovery that mixing a number of malts with a proportion of grain whisky produced a very drinkable, consistent product coincided with the devastation wreaked on French vineyards by the phylloxera vine louse during the 1860s, which in turn soon led to a shortage of Cognac, which was a hugely popular spirit at the time.

However, there was no shortage of eager entrepreneurs ready to leap to the aid of thirsty men all over the British Empire and beyond, who suddenly had nothing to drink with their soda. Blended Scotch whisky was the solution, and it soon took the world by storm, creating fortunes for many of those involved in the blending business and establishing brand names that continue to dominate global markets to this day.

BEST-SELLING BLENDS

BALLANTINE'S

Ballantine's is the world's second best-selling blend after Diageo's Johnnie Walker, and is owned by Diageo's great blended Scotch rival, Pernod Ricard. Ballantine's origins go back to 1827, when farmer's son George Ballantine established a grocery business in Edinburgh. At the heart of today's Ballantine's blend is single malt from the Speyside distilleries of Glenburgie and Miltonduff, and stylistically Ballantine's is complex, elegant and refined. It is available in expressions up to 30 years of age.

BELL'S ORIGINAL

Arthur Bell was born in Perth and, after learning the wine and spirit business with T. H. Sandeman in his home city, he set up in partnership with James Roy in 1851, going on to specialize in blending Scotch whiskies. Bell's, which counts Blair Athol as its 'heart malt', is now part of the Diageo empire. It is the eighth best-selling blend in the world, and the current UK leader. Bell's Original is fresh yet full-bodied, with a smoky, Islay note.

BLACK BOTTLE

Black Bottle was the creation of Aberdeen-based Graham brothers, Charles, David and Gordon. They started out as tea blenders but soon turned their attention to blending whiskies instead, creating Black Bottle in 1879. Now under the ownership of Burn Stewart Distillers Ltd, their Islay malt of Bunnahabhain plays a major part in Black Bottle, which also contains whisky from all Islay's operational distilleries, giving it a distinctive, peaty style all its own.

CHIVAS REGAL

Chivas Regal was first marketed in 1909 by the Aberdeen firm of Chivas Brothers Ltd, which like so many 19th-century blending companies started out as part of a grocery business. Chivas Regal has developed into what is arguably the world's best-known premium blended Scotch whisky. Chivas Regal carries age statements ranging from 12 to 25 years and is owned by Chivas Brothers, which showcases its brand in their Strathisla distillery on Speyside. Chivas Regal is a classic 'Speyside' blend: smooth, malty and with good body.

CUTTY SARK

Unlike many of the world's best-selling blended Scotches that were established during the late 19th century, Cutty Sark was a product of the 1920s, being specifically formulated for the US market and intended as the ideal base for cocktails. The blend was developed by the venerable London wine and spirit merchants Berry Bros & Rudd, and took its name from the famous record-breaking tea clipper, now preserved in Greenwich, London. Cutty Sark is light in colour and body, easy-drinking and best served long.

DEWAR'S WHITE LABEL

John Dewar was a grocer and wine and spirits merchant of Perth who began to specialize in whisky. Under his sons John and Tommy, sales of Dewar's blends expanded dramatically, and Aberfeldy Distillery was constructed to supply malt for them. Dewar's White Label dates from 1899 and now has the distinction of being the best-selling blended Scotch in the USA. It is relatively light, fruity and sweet, with just a faint wisp of smoke.

THE FAMOUS GROUSE

Like Bell's and Dewar's, The Famous Grouse was created in Perth by Matthew Gloag, who established a grocery and wine business there in 1820. The Grouse blended whisky brand was introduced during the 1890s, and was subsequently re-branded as The Famous Grouse as it had become a firm favourite with the shooting set of rural Perthshire. Now owned by The Edrington Group Ltd, The Famous Grouse is Scotland's best-selling blend. It is balanced and succulent in character, with good mouth-feel and overall presence.

GRANT'S FAMILY RESERVE

William Grant, the founder of the Glenfiddich Distillery, first began to blend whiskies in 1898. The result was Stand Fast, which was first presented in a distinctive triangular bottle presented in a distinctive triangular bottle during 1957. The Stand Fast name gave way to Family Reserve, which is now the fourth best-selling blend in the world. At its heart are malt whiskies from the company's own Glenfiddich, Balvenie, Kininvie and Ailsa Bay distilleries, along with Girvan grain spirit. The result is an elegant and well-mannered blend, fruity and floral, with a hint of smoke.

J&B RARE

J&B is the world's third-best-selling blend after Johnnie Walker and Ballantine's, and gives Diageo a second very powerful string to its bow alongside the Walker 'family'. The brand was established by the London society wine and spirits merchant Justerini & Brooks in the years after the ending of Prohibition in the USA and, like its great rival of the time Cutty Sark, it was a light blend, intended primarily for mixing. Speyside whiskies lie at its heart, and character-wise, J&B Rare is fragrant, sweet, delicate and balanced.

JOHNNIE WALKER

The world's best-selling blended Scotch whisky has its origins in Kilmarnock, where young John Walker established a licensed grocery business in 1820. However, it was really during the second half of the nineteenth century that the whisky side of the operation began to flourish, with Johnnie Walker coming to be characterized by its square bottle and 'striding man' logo. Today, the Johnnie Walker range has expanded from Red Label and Black label to embrace a range of more exclusive expressions. The overall Johnnie Walker house style is full-bodied, sweet, robust and slightly peaty.

TEACHER'S HIGHLAND CREAM

Teacher's Highland Cream was first marketed by William Teacher in 1884, and has been associated with Ardmore distillery on Speyside ever since it was built by the Teacher family in order to supply malt for blending purposes in 1899. The peaty Ardmore spirit is at the heart of Teacher's, which is very rare among blends in that a specified malt content of 45% appears on the label. The brand now belongs to Beam Global Spirits & Wine Inc, and stylistically speaking Teacher's is a big, old-fashioned blend, full-bodied, smoky and malty.

WHYTE & MACKAY SPECIAL

Whyte & Mackay is forever associated with the city of Glasgow, where the company's roots date back to 1844, even though the firm is now owned by Philippines-based brandy producer Emperador. Malt from Whyte & Mackay's Dalmore, Fettercairn, Jura and Tamnavulin distilleries is present in the blend, along with grain spirit from the company's own Invergordon grain distillery. As well as the 'Special' bottling, Whyte & Mackay is available with a variety of age statements, right up to a 40-year old bottling. 'Special' is a big, characterful, malty blend. In short, very Glaswegian!

ALL HAIL THE 'ROCK 'N' ROLL' BLENDERS

Over the last ten years, blended whiskies have been unfairly viewed in a few quarters as 'inferior' products to single malts, but there are some contemporary blending companies right at the cutting edge of bringing the unique flavour of blended whisky to a brand-new audience. Here, we profile two of them: Master of Malt and Compass Box.

MASTER OF MALT

In 2011 English whisky retailer Master of Malt (www.masterofmalt.com) took the rather unusual step of giving the general whisky-drinking public the opportunity to put together their very own personalized blended whisky. The company packaged up Blend Your Own kits, containing small samples of malt and grain whiskies from the main whisky-making regions of Scotland. Once satisfied with your blending skills, you send the recipe back to the company, which re-creates it on a larger scale and, hey presto, a case of bespoke blended whisky, complete with your very own label arrives on your doorstep!

Although the idea is unlikely to trouble the likes of blending giants Johnnie Walker, Ballantine or Chivas Regal for market share, it provides the whisky-drinker with a unique understanding of just how differently flavoured whiskies work in harmony together in a blend – and how complicated it is to create a consistent, world-class recipe every time. Here's to the would-be whisky blenders of the future.

BELOW: The Master of Malt home blending kit, containing 12 x 3cl samplers.

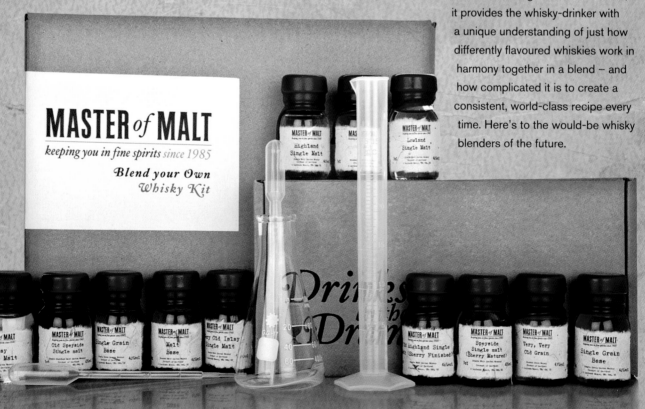

with glass demijohns and other vessels holding new experiments which will eventually see the light of day – and the inside of our whisky glasses. Recently, Glaser aimed to enter the record books for hosting the largest number of whisky tastings held in one day, frantically travelling across the UK by car to eight tastings and a number of thirsty whisky fanatics.

The company is also no stranger to brushing with the Scotch Whisky Association [SWA] on the odd occasion, in its pursuit of bringing blended whisky into the 21st century. Its Spice Tree blend pioneered a technique of secondary maturation widely used in the French wine industry, whereby additional oak staves are placed inside oak casks, giving an intense secondary maturation to the whisky. The whisky was eventually 'outlawed' by the SWA as it was ultimately deemed to breach several (perhaps outdated) rules, and Glaser and his team were forced to come up with innovative ways to continue producing this excellent, small-batch blended whisky.

The rebellious streak in Compass Box struck once again on 22 November 2011, when Glaser put together the last legal 'Vatted Malt' in front of a small gathering on London's Westminster Bridge next to Big Ben. Seconds later, after midnight had chimed, a new UK law came into place banning the term, replacing it with the even more confusing and hotly debated 'Blended Malt Whisky'. The Last Vatted Malt contains 100% malt whisky, delivering a perfect balance of rich, spicy, sherried notes from a Speyside distillery and some wafts of wonderful smokiness from a very old Islay whisky.

LEFT Poster for Orangerie which is made from smooth, sweet Scotch whisky infused with the hand-zested peel of Navalina oranges.

BELOW: Flaming Heart, made from a blend of Scotch whiskies.

COMPASS BOX

Compass Box, a London-based artisanal whisky company run by master blender John Glaser, has approached blending whisky from a distinctly modern, flavour-based angle. Its strikingly presented bottlings, such as Flaming Heart, The Peat Monster, Asyla and Spice Tree, each use a simple but highly complex blend of Scotch single malts of a certain style to bring out bold and characterful notes, perfect for using in cocktails or drinking straight up. The Compass Box mantra is 'above all, share and enjoy', to demonstrate the sociable aspects of whisky to a new, younger audience of whisky-drinkers.

Based in Chiswick, southwest London, Compass Box's office-cum-laboratory is filled

IRELAND

At one time Irish whiskey was more popular in England than Scotch, but for much of the 20th century and into the 21st century, Irish was very much a poor relation of Scotch whisky, looking on enviously as blends like Johnnie Walker, Ballantine's and Grant's took the drinking world by storm. The breakaway of the Irish Free State from Britain in 1922 meant that Irish distillers lost the lucrative Empire markets. Irish distillers tended to stick with pure pot still whiskey rather than opting for lighter style blends as their Scotch competitors had done, and Irish whiskey came to have a similar status to rye whiskey in the USA: it was little more than an historic and stylistic curiosity. For a long time, there was much less diversity of style and choice of brands compared to Scotch, too.

True, Jameson bucked the trend somewhat. The actual whiskey was always well respected and the company threw a huge marketing budget behind the brand, but it was pretty much alone in doing so. Then suddenly, a few years ago Irish whiskey became sexy, much like Islay single malts. As consumers began to explore more widely due to the greater availabilty of whiskies from around the world, they began to discover Irish whiskies. At the same time, increasing competition among the Irish distillers (now Pernod Ricard, Diageo, Cooley and the producers of Tullamore Dew) led to new expressions of Irish whiskey, more marketing spend and ultimately a greater emphasis on pure pot still Irish whiskey (as shown by Midleton).

Irish whiskey began to experience extraordinary growth, with an overall increase of 11.5% during 2010, while in the same year sales across the US – the biggest market for Irish whiskey – rose by a remarkable 20.8%. In 2011 Jameson alone sold almost four million cases. Distillers and bottlers rushed to expand their portfolios and add new expressions to old-established names that were suddenly once again on everyone's lips. After so many years as an also-ran, Irish whiskey is happily and gloriously one of the favourites.

IRELAND'S DISTILLERIES

▲ Featured distillery
▲ Other distillery

North Channel

Donegal Bay

Bushmills
Coleraine

LONDONDERRY

NORTHERN IRELAND

Larne

Omagh
Cookstown
Antrim
Lough Neagh
BELFAST

Belfast Lough

Lower Lough Erne
Enniskillen

Sligo
Armagh

Echlinville

Lough Allen
Upper Lough Erne

Dundalk

Cooley

Lough Mask
Lough Corrib

Lough Ree

Drogheda

Irish Sea

Galway

Galway Bay

Kilbeggan

DUBLIN
Tullamore Dew • Tullamore
Teeling
Dún Laoghaire

REPUBLIC OF IRELAND

Lough Derg

Atlantic Ocean

Wicklow

Limerick

Kilkenny

Dingle

Dingle Bay

Wexford
Rosslare

Waterford

St George's Channel

Cork • Midleton

Celtic Sea

BUSHMILLS

Website **www.bushmills.com**

Founded **1784**

Location **Bushmills, County Antrim, Northern Ireland**

'Old Bushmills', as it is known, is the only surviving distillery in Northern Ireland. There are claims that the distillery was founded as long ago as 1608, but this is misleading as this was the year in which King James I of England issued a licence to distil in this area of County Antrim.

The company name, 'Old Bushmills Distillery', was first registered during the 1790s, and from 1972 until 2005 it was part of the Irish Distillers Group, itself owned by Pernod Ricard. In 2005 Diageo acquired Bushmills from Pernod Ricard, which continues to own Midleton Distillery south of the border, in County Cork. Bushmills ranks third in the Irish whiskey sales league table behind Jameson and Tullamore Dew.

Pitting Diageo against its arch-rival Pernod Ricard in the Irish whiskey arena, which had previously suffered from a serious lack of internal competition, helped rejuvenate the sector. Diageo has invested £10 million ($16 billion) in Bushmills, which now operates ten copper pot stills and can produce up to 4.5 million litres (1 million gallons) of spirit per year. The stills are relatively small, with long, slender necks, and their design, coupled with triple distillation, produces a smooth, light style of spirit.

As with most Irish whiskies, triple-distillation is practised, with unpeated and

lightly peated malt used to produce a range of Irish single-malt whiskeys and two blended whiskeys. The principal range comprises the blends Original and Black Bush (with a higher malt content and more Sherry wood maturation influence than Original), and 10-, 16- and 21-year-old single malts. The 16-year-old single malt is 'finished' in Port casks for several months, while the 21-year-old spends a final two years in ex-Madeira casks.

Bushmills Distillery enjoys a superb location close to the Giant's Causeway on the Antrim coast, and is very well geared up to receive visitors, with over 100,000 people passing through its doors each year.

TASTING NOTES

Bushmills Original – 40% abv

Nose Very approachable, light, fruity and spicy, grassy and nutty, with vanilla and honey.

Palate Sweet and clean, with cereal notes and soft fruit.

Finish Short and spicy, with a fresh oak feel. A drink for any time of the day – or night!

COOLEY

Website **www.cooleywhiskey.com**
Founded **1987**
Location **Riverstown, County Louth, Ireland**

Until 2012 the independent Cooley enterprise was the maverick of Irish distilling. It was established in 1987 by entrepreneur John Teeling and other investors in the former state-owned Ceimici Teoranta Distillery near Dundalk. The distillery had previously manufactured industrial alcohol and neutral spirit in column stills. When it opened, Cooley was the first new whiskey distillery in Ireland for more than 100 years, and it broke the monopoly on whiskey-making in Ireland previously enjoyed by the Irish Distillers Group.

John Teeling rejected the Irish tradition of triple-distilling his whiskey and instead opted for the Scotch model of double distillation in copper pot stills, in this case a pair that had previously seen service in the Old Comber Distillery near Newtownards in County Down. He also made grain whiskey for blending in the existing column stills.

After some difficult years, the owners began to reap the benefits of their courage and vision; sales of Cooley brands grew and awards were won. In 2012 the US-based Beam Inc, owner of the Jim Beam Bourbon brand and of the Teacher's blend in Scotland, bought Cooley for $95 million

(£152 million). Cooley may have lost its coveted independent status, but in Beam the Irish whiskey sector gained another major player to compete against Diageo, Pernod Ricard and Tullamore Dew brand owner William Grant & Sons Ltd.

TASTING NOTES

Connemara – 12-year-old –
40% abv

Nose A smouldering turf fire, with someone toasting marshmallows over it. More subtle lemongrass and young oak in the background.

Palate Soft fruits, almonds and black pepper, with peat smoke and oak.

Finish Spices, vanilla and sweet peat. A 'modern' Irish classic!

KILBEGGAN

Website **www.kilbegganwhiskey.com**

Founded **1757**

Location **Kilbeggan, County Westmeath**

Kilbeggan is the oldest distillery in the world to operate on its original site and to have been licensed continuously. Sometimes known as Brusna, the distillery was first leased by members of the Locke family in 1843, and remained in their hands until a few years before its closure in 1953. Lack of funds for investment over the years meant that at the time of its closure Kilbeggan was something of a museum piece, still equipped with just pot stills, never having succumbed to the fashion for a Coffey still and the lure of blending.

The distillery later became the site of a car dealership before being acquired by the local community in 1982. It was then restored to something like its former glory and functioned as a distilling museum.

In 1988 John Teeling of Cooley acquired most of the Kilbeggan site and began to use it to mature stocks of Cooley whiskey as well as the Kilbeggan blend and Locke's blend and malt. Although the original pot stills had long gone, three pots from the closed Tullamore Distillery were subsequently transported to Kilbeggan, and Teeling began to muse on the possibility of restoring whiskey-making to Kilbeggan.

Accordingly, on 19 March 2007, the 250th anniversary of the distillery's establishment and 54 years to the day since its closure, spirit flowed at Kilbeggan

once again. However, the spirit in question was produced not in the vast Tullamore trio of stills, but in a small 'boutique' still, also acquired from Tullamore and reputedly the oldest working still in the world. In 2009 a second still was installed, and the result was the production of Kilbeggan Distillery Reserve malt whiskey, along with a wide variety of experimental distillations for which the small-scale plant is ideally suited.

Kilbeggan used to receive many visitors when it was merely a distillery museum, but it has gained new relevance and impetus since whiskey-making started up again on the site, and a visit is warmly recommended.

TASTING NOTES

Kilbeggan Distillery Reserve – 40% abv

Nose Highly individualistic. Oily and herbal, with tarragon, warm leather, paper gum, and even violets.

Palate Delicate, yet far from fragile, with gentle leather and developing fruity spices.

Finish Medium length and drying.

MIDLETON

Website **www.jamesonwhiskey.com**
Founded **1825**
Location **Midleton, County Cork**

There are two Midleton distilleries. The site that produces Jameson Irish Whiskey is called the Midleton Distillery and is based in Cork. The heritage centre based in Dublin was the site of Jameson production but now serves as a museum. Old Midleton dates from 1825 and was established in a converted mill by three Murphy brothers, with the distillery being merged with four others in the area in 1867 to form the Cork Distilleries Company. Production was soon centred on Midleton, and that pattern was to be repeated after the Cork Distilleries Company merged with John Power & Son and John Jameson & Son of Dublin to form Irish Distillers in 1966.

Today, Old Midleton Distillery is home to the Jameson Experience, a hugely popular visitor facility, which serves as a second 'brand home' for Jameson, the world's leading Irish whiskey. The major Irish distilleries always used to be noted for the large size of their stills compared with those of their Scotch rivals, and visitors can see the three original stills, including one installed in 1949, with a capacity of 141,000 litres (31,000 gallons), making it the largest pot still in the world.

Meanwhile, in July 1975, the distillery staff famously clocked off one Friday afternoon from the old Midleton site and clocked on again on Monday morning in its state-of-the-art and hugely versatile replacement. 'New' Midleton contains three pot and three column stills, configured to produce a bewildering range of whiskeys, including classic blends like Jameson, Paddy and Powers, as well as pot still whiskeys such as Redbreast and Green Spot. Capacity is 19 million litres (4 million gallons) per annum, but in 2012 owner Irish Distillers Ltd – a Pernod Ricard subsidiary – announced a major expansion project for Midleton, designed to increase its output to reflect rising sales of Jameson in particular, and featuring a new stillhouse, which will be home to six pot stills. This ties in with Irish Distillers' major investment in what it terms 'single pot still' whiskey, the original Irish whiskey that was produced before blended Irish became all the rage. In recent years, the company has developed new variants on the single pot still theme, including Powers John's Lane Release and Midleton Barry Crockett Legacy, named after Midleton's long-standing master distiller.

TASTING NOTES
Jameson Original – 40% abv
Nose An interesting combination of floral, orange, toffee, Sherry and spice notes.
Palate Initially citric, along with classic Irish oiliness; more profound notes of Sherry develop, along with fudge, vanilla and spice.
Finish Long, warming and spicy, remaining oily to the very end.

TULLAMORE DEW

Website **www.tullamoredew.com**

Founded **1829**

Location **Tullamore Dew Heritage Centre, County Offaly**

Tullamore distillery was established in 1829 by Michael Moloney, probably on the site of an earlier plant, and it stood beside the Grand Canal in County Offaly, at the heart of Ireland's barley-growing Midlands' countryside.

In the 1880s Daniel Edmond Williams took over the running of the distillery. He encouraged his employer to expand the plant, and Tullamore 'Dew,' an acronym of his initials, was launched. The marketing slogan 'Give every man his Dew' was soon famous throughout Ireland and beyond, with sales booming in Britain and even as far afield as Australia.

In 1903 a recipe for a traditional Irish liqueur made from whiskey, heather honey and herbs was fortuitously sourced from an Austrian refugee, and Irish Mist was launched to great success. Such was its impact that in 1953 the firm changed its name to the Irish Mist Liqueur Company Ltd. However, demand for Tullamore whiskey was now being outstripped by supply, and the decision was taken to close the distillery in

1954 and concentrate on the production and marketing of Irish Mist.

In 2010 William Grant & Sons Ltd purchased the Tullamore Dew brand, for which the actual whiskey was produced under contract by Irish Distillers at Midleton, along with the existing Tullamore Dew Heritage Centre, located in a former bonded warehouse on the Tullamore distillery site, dating from 1897.

Grant revamped the visitor centre, and then in 2012 announced plans to return whiskey-making to Tullamore, with a £28 million ($44 million) project to build a new distillery on the outskirts of the town. Yet more evidence of how dynamic the Irish whiskey sector has become.

TASTING NOTES

Tullamore Dew – 40% abv

Nose Delicate, floral, undemanding, with pineapple and milky coffee.

Palate Gentle and fruity, with characteristic Irish whiskey oiliness.

Finish Fudge and peaches – gently drying.

OTHERS TO TRY

GREEN SPOT

Website www.singlepotstill.com

Location **Midleton, County Cork**

Green Spot is made at the Midleton Distillery and comprises whiskeys aged from 7 to 12 years, some 25% of which have been matured in ex-Sherry casks. Only a limited number of bottles are produced each year, making Green Spot one of the more elusive Irish whiskeys on the market.

Tipple to try Green Spot – Pure Pot Still Irish Whiskey – 40% abv

GREENORE

Website www.greenorewhiskey.com

Location **Riverstown, County Louth**

The only single Irish grain whiskey in the world, Greenore is produced by Cooley Distillery from maize, and while this grain whiskey is used for blending, an amount is set aside and matured for eight years in first-fill ex-Bourbon casks prior to bottling on a stand-alone basis. There are also 6-, 8-, 15- and 8-year-old expressions.

Tipple to try Greenore – 8-Year-Old Single Grain Irish Whiskey – 40% abv

REDBREAST

Website www.singlepotstill.com

Location **Midleton, County Cork**

The Redbreast brand dates back to the early 20th century, and is distilled in Midleton Distillery. Maturation takes place principally in ex-Sherry casks, along with some ex-Bourbon casks. As well as the 12-year-old version there are now cask strength and 15-year-old expressions available.

Tipple to try Redbreast – 12-Year-Old Pure Pot Still Irish Whiskey – 40% abv

IRISH COFFEE

Although this book is about whisky, an honourable mention has to be given to Irish coffee, a drink which actually did quite a lot to keep Irish whiskey in the public eye during the spirit's more barren years.

Irish coffee was born during World War II, when transatlantic seaplanes landed at Foynes, close to today's Shannon Airport. One wild, wet night during the winter of 1942, Jim Sheridan, the barman at the Shannon House Hotel Jim Sheridan bucked up a group of travellers whose flight to Canada had been forced to turn back due to storms, by adding a splash of whiskey and a dollop of fresh cream to the coffee he served them. When a passenger asked, 'Is this Brazilian coffee?' Sheridan reputedly replied 'No, this is Irish Coffee!' and a legend was born.

JAPAN

Despite having a provenance that dates back over 90 years, the last decade has seen a huge surge in interest in Japanese whisky, capturing the attention of whisky-lovers around the world as well as remaining as popular as ever in the domestic market. Since its widespread availability across Europe and the US, many of the key brands of Japanese whisky (which we discuss in greater detail in the pages overleaf), including both single malts and blended whiskies, have won numerous awards for their complex balance of flavours, also popularizing new trends in how to serve whisky.

Japanese whisky has many similarities to Scotch; indeed, the raw materials that go into making Japanese whisky, from the malted barley to the main types of oak cask used, remain the same. In fact, it was Japan's admiration for the whisky produced in Scotland that eventually led to the first domestic whisky distillery being built nearly a century ago, largely based on techniques and manufacturing processes learned in Scotland by one man, Masataka Taketsuru. However, a few subtle differences in the production process (from the style of still shape through to the differing climate the whisky is matured in, as well as a unique strain of oak cask only used in Japan) help to give Japanese whisky a flavour of its own.

CHINA

RUSSIAN FEDERATION

La Perouse Strait

Sea of Okhotsk

NORTH KOREA

Sea of Japan

Hokkaido

Otaru
• Sapporo
▲ **Yoichi**

• Hakodate

• Aomori

SOUTH KOREA

Oki Islands

• Akita

Ou Mountains

▲ **Miyagikyo**
• Sendai

Sado

• Niigata • Fukushima

Honshu

• Iwaki

Nagano •
Karuizawa ▲

Hakushu ▲

Mars Shinshu ▲

Tsushima

Korea Strait

• Hiroshima

Eigashima ▲

Biwa Lake

• Kyoto
Yamazaki ▲
• Kobe
Osaka

Mount Fuji
△

Hanyu ▲

Chichibu ▲
TOKYO
• Yokohama

Fuji-Gotemba ▲

• Nagoya

• Shizuoka

Nampo Shoto

Kii Mountains

• Kitakyushu
• Fukuoka

Shikoku

Kyushu

Kumamoto

Nagasaki •

Kyushu Highlands

Pacific Ocean

• Kagoshima

East China Sea

JAPAN'S DISTILLERIES

▲	Featured distillery
▲	Other distillery

JAPAN'S WHISKY CULTURE

As well as producing some subtle, sublime and occasionally highly complex single malts, Japan is also home to some of the most well-regarded blended whiskies in the world.

From a flavour perspective, you could argue that Japanese whisky occupies a fairly distinct world somewhere in between Scotch whisky and American whiskey. It has a malty character, much in the tradition of Scotch single malt, but in addition a wealth of other sweeter, perfumed and spicy flavours jump out of the glass. This is largely because of the use of ex-Bourbon and ex-Sherry casks, and particularly Mizunara oak (*Quercus mongolica*), a unique strain of the oak tree indigenous to East Asian countries including Japan, Korea and eastern Mongolia.

Although there are definite similarities between some Japanese whiskies and their Scotch counterparts matured in the same types of wooden cask, Mizunara oak imparts some distinct cedar, sandalwood and coconut notes to the whisky, to such an extent that many whisky connoisseurs suggest they can pick up the aroma of Japanese incense.

The Japanese have been successfully distilling whisky commercially since the early 1920s. The first whisky produced in Japan was called White Label. It was made by the Yamazaki Distillery and was accompanied by a bold advertising campaign urging consumers to: 'Wake Up! The time has gone when you have to appreciate imported goods. Now, for the first time, superb domestic whiskies are available in Japan.'

The thirst for Japanese whisky has developed at a huge pace, and today Japan is home to eight working distilleries, ranging from the powerhouse brand names owned by Suntory and Nikka to smaller, artisan-sized whisky producers.

BLENDED WHISKY

Both the current major players, Suntory and Nikka, produce a huge portfolio of different bottlings, although many of them will never see the light of day outside Japan.

Japanese blended whisky is produced in an almost identical way to blended Scotch whiskies, using malt and grain whisky from the various distilleries across the country. Unlike Scottish blends (which contain whisky from many distilleries, some owned by rival companies), most Japanese distilleries possess a number of differently shaped spot stills, which produce a wide range of whisky styles, allowing each company to have a comprehensive 'palate of flavours' to blend with.

SUNTORY

Suntory's range of Hibiki blended whiskies is particularly noteworthy. The buttery, floral and highly fruity 12-year-old gains much of its unique profile from an additional maturation time in casks that have previously held Japanese Ume plum wine. Older expressions include the rich and robust 17-year-old, which showcases woody, spicy and dried-fruit characteristics, and a truly majestic 21-year-old – voted the 'World's Best Blended Whisky' at the World Whisky Awards in 2010. Kakubin is the leading Japanese blended whisky by far. Produced by Suntory since 1937, its light, fresh and easy-drinking style goes well with Japanese food.

NIKKA

The Nikka Company also produces a handful of expertly blended whiskies. All Malt is a whisky blended from only malted barley, partly distilled in pot

ABOVE: Tokyo has a strong bar culture and some of the best ones have highly innovative ways of serving whisky, including your very own personal blend.

ABOVE: Whisky is a popular drink in Japanese bars.

ABOVE RIGHT: The Japanese have a culture of drinking blended whisky (heavily watered down) as a refreshing apéritif or throughout a meal. The Japanese highball (or hi-ball) drink is hugely popular in bars and restaurants and is often served in mugs.

stills and a traditional Coffey grain still. From the Barrel weighs in at a whopping 51.4% abv, but is surprisingly drinkable, even with such a high level of alcohol.

WHISKY AND FOOD PAIRING

Whisky and food pairing in Japan differs greatly from that in Europe and North America. In Japan it is commonplace to open a bottle of blended whisky at the start of a meal, as we would with a wine in the West, to share among friends. The whisky is not usually enjoyed neat, but heavily diluted as part of either a *mizuwari* (whisky poured over ice into

a tall glass and topped up with crystal clear Japanese mineral water) or as a highball, which substitutes the still water for soda. There's even a Japanese version of the traditional hot whisky toddy called an *oyuwari* ('mixed with hot water').

BAR CULTURE

Scotch and Japanese malts are, of course, hugely popular with enthusiasts and connoisseurs alike but Japanese blended whisky used in a highball is popular with younger drinkers.

Numerous twists on the simple premise of 'whisky and soda' have now cropped up in the multitude of Tokyo's

buzzy bars, including adding a piece of lemon zest, using tonic and soda water, and adding green tea liqueur. In some larger pubs and outlets 'highball towers' have become a fairly common sight: a whisky and soda mix, dispensed from a gun, or pump, just as you would see a pint of lager pulled! The result is a fresh, thirst-quenching and, most importantly, fun, sociable drink. Japanese blended whisky is also used in another popular Japanese cocktail, the sonic, whereby tonic water and a twist of fresh lemon are added to the whisky.

One possible explanation for the popularity of the whisky highball is an almost fanatical fascination with ice. In many of the more stylish Japanese whisky and cocktail bars, which are numbered in their thousands across Tokyo, bar owners go to the furthest and chilliest of extremes rather than just using regular cubed ice. Huge blocks of the purest, glass-like ice are chipped into smaller blocks and fashioned into all manner of impressive ice sculptures, sometimes individually tailored for each drink served. Diamonds, gems and, more prominently, ice balls (which are remarkably smooth, considering how difficult a material ice is to work with) are all hand-carved using a variety of tools, including razor-sharp knives and multi-pronged ice picks.

The clear message here is – don't try this at home without proper tuition!!

ABOVE: The Japanese bartender's tools for fashioning a perfect ice ball. Ice carving takes years to perfect and is a highly intricate skill.

CHICHIBU AND HANYU

Website **www.one-drinks.com**

Founded **2007**

Location **Chichibu, Saitama Prefecture**

The story behind Chichibu, Japan's newest distillery, stems from a moment of triumph crossed with a very close brush with disaster. Behind the distillery's continuing success lies the determination of one man, Ichiro Akuto. Akuto-san is the descendant of a successful family of sake producers dating back to the 17th century, and grandson of the man who established the Hanyu Distillery, which had been producing single malt whisky since the early 1980s but closed its doors permanently in 2004. With the prospect of seeing 400 potentially priceless casks of excellent whisky disposed of into cheap blended whiskies or worse, Akuto-san stepped in to produce a last-minute buyout, thus starting his own distilling empire. Bottled under the name Ichiro's Malt, the original whiskies were labelled with a range of playing cards, each representing different ages and cask type. These whiskies differ hugely in flavour profile, reflecting the different nature of the values and suits of playing cards, thanks to the varying types of cask used and lengths of maturation.

With very few casks of Hanyu left, Ichiro Akuto embarked on his next endeavour: the Chichibu Distillery, based about 80km (50 miles) north-west of Tokyo. The distillery follows a distinctly home-grown theme: Japanese oak has been used to construct the washbacks, and future whisky production will include local barley, grown in fields close to the distillery site. The First was released in 2011 as a 3-year old and demonstrates a level of complexity far beyond its tender years.

TASTING NOTES

Chichibu The First – 3-year-old – 61.8% abv

Nose Rich honey, honeysuckle, white pepper and milk chocolate.

Palate: Lemon grass notes, fresh lime coconut milk and vanilla.

Finish Dried apricot notes and vanilla linger develop leaving a long lasting impression.

Ichiro's Malt
CHICHIBU
Japanese Single Malt Whisky
THE FIRST
Distilled 2008   Bottled 2011

秩父

Bottle #   1 / 7400

EIGASHIMA

Website www. ei-sake.jp
Founded 1984
Location Akashi, Hyogo Prefecture

Technically, Eigashima (also called The White Oak Distillery) is one of Japan's newest – in the sense that whisky has intermittently been produced at the distillery since 1984, when the concept of distilling Japanese whisky on a micro level was particularly popular. However, mounting production costs and the huge rise in popularity of *shochu* (a Japanese spirit made from barley, rice or sweet potatoes) forced the distillery to produce whisky only for extremely short periods, often using the spirit to bulk out Japanese blended whiskies.

In 2007, Eigashima released its very first single malt, an 8-year-old bottled under the Akashi White Oak Single Malt label, and interest in the distillery is growing steadily, with bottles of a blended whisky available for the first time outside Japan. As with many of the lesser-known Japanese distilleries, whisky produced by Eigashima is still fairly hard to locate outside the country, but the (now rebranded) Akashi blend has been specially produced for the European market, as well as 5-year-old and 12-year-old single malts, which are released in very small quantities.

One of the most remarkable facts about Eigashima is that, rather controversially, the owner has traced its heritage back to

1888, and whisky production at the distillery back to around 1919 – a good four years before the foundation of Yamazaki, widely acknowledged as the first Japanese whisky distillery. While it's unlikely that history will be rewritten, the future looks bright for this promising distillery, considering the renewed excitement in the Japanese whisky category as a whole.

TASTING NOTES

Akashi – White Oak Blended Whisky – 40% abv

Nose Light floral and cereal notes, candyfloss and creamed fondant. A dash of water reveals some sweetened tea notes, icing sugar and a little touch of dry ginger.

Palate Sweet, with vanilla cream and lemon zest notes. Rather than being a whisky to sip neat, it works nicely over ice, with a dash of chilled water.

Finish Short, with some lingering creamy notes.

HAKUSHU

Website: www.suntory.com/whisky/en/hakushu
Founded: 1973
Location: Hakushu, Yamanashi Prefecture

At over 600m (2000ft) above sea level, the Hakushu Distillery is one of the highest operational distilleries in Japan, and it is quite possible that such an exceptionally high altitude plays a major part in the development of the spirit's character. Hakushu is to all intents and purposes a younger sibling to big brother Yamazaki (as both distilleries are owned by Japanese brewing and distilling giant, Suntory) and it well known among Japanese whisky connoisseurs for its wonderfully balanced and malty qualities.

The softness and low mineral content of Hakushu's water source plays almost as much importance as the altitude, with the distillery drawing its reserves from the foot of Mt Kaikomagatake in Kai Province.

But a visit to Hakushu is not just about tasting the majestic whiskies it produces. The land on which the distillery is built is also home to a breathtakingly beautiful bird sanctuary and nature reserve, lined with Japanese maple trees. Visit the distillery at lunchtime and you may find on offer a number of tasty treats freshly smoked in the outdooor smokery.

The whiskies range from a lightly smoky and fragranced expression called Distiller's Reserve through to the more complex 18- and 25-year-old bottlings, of which a proportion

of the spirit will have been matured in Japanese Mizunara oak casks, which impart a subtle cedar/woody spice to the developing whisky. As with many Japanese whiskies, there is an underlying character that marks them out as the purveyors of unique flavour profiles, and The Hakushu is no exception. The younger expressions of Hakushu work extremely well when used in a refreshing highball or *mizuwari*, or in a sonic, another long-style Japanese cocktail. The sonic incorporates a helping of tonic water and a twist of fresh lemon zest, which highlights the lighter more zesty notes in the whisky. *Kampai!*

TASTING NOTES

The Hakushu – 12-year-old – 43.5% abv

Nose Distinctly fresh, with light green tea, orchard fruit and a wisp of aromatic smoke.

Palate Ripe red apples, some sweetened cereal notes and more delicate smoke. Adding water gives the whisky a slightly mineral-like quality, with an additional note of fudge.

Finish Soft, lingering fruit notes of plums and pears.

KARUIZAWA

Website **www.one-drinks.com**
Founded **1955**
Location **Mount Asama, Nagano Prefecture**

This is a truly mountainous whisky – in more ways than one. When considering a whisky from Karuizawa, the words 'bold', 'intense' and 'complex' immediately spring to mind. Undoubtedly this much-fabled distillery, based high in the Japanese alps, has produced some of the most charismatic and well-received Japanese single malts in the past few decades. Whether the distillery's location close to an active volcano had more than just a symbolic influence on the type of whisky produced is unclear. But the bold, richly flavoured and resinous bottlings from the early 1970s and '80s demonstrated a very different style of Japanese whisky from other lighter-style Japanese whiskies on the market, perhaps more closely mirroring the Scotch whiskies produced in the Speyside region. Made from imported and highly prized 'Golden Promise' barley from Berwick-upon-Tweed on the Scottish–English border, the whisky was heavily influenced by ex-Sherry casks and matured for decades.

Karuizawa ceased production in 2000 and closed permanently in 2011. The remaining casks were recently purchased by the respected British Number One Drinks Company, and are being stored at the Chichibu Distillery. Fortunately the world can once again enjoy this unique whisky.

The microclimate that surrounds the distillery, and its high humidity (an average of 80% compared to other regions of Japan and Scotland), meant that the maturing whisky rarely lost any alcoholic strength, the water evaporating much faster from the slumbering casks. As a result, the whisky that made it to the European shores was bottled at a cask strength of around 62% abv, packing a huge punch. Japanese whiskies seldom come bigger than this. The great news for lovers of this big, bold and highly characterful whisky, with huge mossy, earthy Sherry notes, rich, sweet, vanilla tones and lashings of spice thrown in for good measure, is that future casks (with some dating back to the 1960s and '70s) are currently being selected for vintage single-cask releases by Number One.

TASTING NOTES

Karuizawa 1971– 64.1% abv

Nose Powerful, earthy, forest floor notes; pine, moss, rich dark Sherry and polished wooden floors.

Palate Rich dried fruits, aged Sherry and spicy, tannic notes. The palate is explosive at first, but with a little water it reveals subtle layers of sweet syrup, backed up with meaty undertones.

Finish Lengthy, brooding and complex.

MIYAGIKYO

Website **www.nikka.com**
Founded **1969**
Location **Sendai, Miyagi Prefecture**

In the years following the founding of the Nikka Whisky Company in the early 1930s and the founding of its first distillery, Yoichi by Taketsuru-san, the popularity of Japanese whisky in the domestic market developed at a swift pace. By the mid-1960s Taketsuru-san was looking for a second site on which to build a new distillery. In 1969 Miyagikyo, which lies close to the city of Sendai, began production, aiming to produce a differing but complementary style of whisky to that of Yoichi. Miyagikyo draws its water from the confluence of two rivers, which seems suitably fitting, given the importance Taketsuru placed on providing his previously successful distilleries with an abundance of crystal-clear water.

The style of Miyagikyo whisky differs hugely from the richer, smokier style of Yoichi. It offers a much lighter and more refreshing fruity/floral character. Part of this style can be attributed to the still shape used, which incorporates a 'boil ball' style bulge of copper underneath the traditional straight sides. This helps purify the spirit vapours through a process known as spirit reflux.

Nikka also produces a number of popular blended whiskies that are partly produced in Miyagikyo's Coffey grain still, which was installed in the late 1990s. In the past Miyagikyo

whisky has been difficult to find outside Japan, but thanks to its popularity and to numerous top international awards it is now much easier. As a result, Japanese whisky enthusiasts can now find a 10- 12- and 15-year-old Miyagikyo in the shops – and if they're very lucky, a few particularly rare and absolutely exquisite single-cask bottlings, including both a 1988 and 1990 release.

TASTING NOTES

Miyagikyo – 15-year-old – 45% abv

Nose Very light and delicate notes of fresh flowers, orange and lemon zest and sweet vanilla. A dash of water reveals a slight anise note alongside a distinct nuttiness.

Palate Ripe apricots, more vanilla and a citrus tang sit alongside some sweet-buttery cereal. Neat, this has wonderfully thick, oily mouthfeel. A dash of water opens up the flavours, giving more pronounced orchard fruit (peach and crisp apple) and golden syrup.

Finish: Fresh, with notes of vanilla, caramel and green apple.

YAMAZAKI

Website **www.suntory.com/yamazaki**
Founded **1923**
Location **Osaka Prefecture**

Because of its widespread availability Yamazaki is the perfect place to start your journey into Japanese single malts. Yamazaki is also considered to be the founding father of Japanese whisky. Save for the love of a good Scottish woman, the history of Japanese whisky might have been very different, indeed. Established in 1923 by a successful wine importer Shinjiro Torii, Yamazaki can lay claim to be the first, and essentially the original, Japanese malt whisky distillery.

The distillery sits on the outskirts of Kyoto in the highly wooded area above the Kansai plain. It was here that a true whisky revolution began when Torii employed Masataka Taketsuru, an organic chemist who had learned the art of whisky distillation while studying in Scotland. Taketsuru drew on his experiences of working at the Hazelburn Distillery in Campbeltown. There, he met and married Jessie 'Rita' Cowan and eagerly travelled back to Japan with her – despite both their parents' displeasure – intent on producing the first Japanese malt whisky.

The Yamazaki Distillery takes its water supply from a confluence of three rivers: the Katsura, Kizu and Uji, priding itself on the fact that one of the great masters of the Japanese tea ceremony, Sen no Rikyu, also situated his tea house nearby many years before.

The house style of Yamazaki is wide-ranging, from the light, fruity and floral 12-year-old to the robust, rich and full-bodied 18-year-old, owing to the differently shaped stills used and the combination of maturation and climate. The distillery claims that the misty, humid atmosphere surrounding the warehouses makes for an ideal location for maturing its whisky, helping halt the loss of moisture from the casks. There is also a range of superbly balanced blended whiskies, including the Hibiki bottlings.

The distillery has won widespread acclaim among critics and whisky judges for its range of expressions, including the 18-year-old and a very rare 1984 vintage release.

TASTING NOTES
The Yamazaki – 12-year-old – 43% abv

Nose Light, floral, fruity notes, with delicate apple, pear and lemon zest.
Palate Sweet and zesty, with a delicate hint of spice.
Finish Lingering cereal notes and woody spices.

YOICHI

Website: **www.nikka.com**
Founded: **1934**
Location: **Yoichi, Hokkaido Prefecture**

Masataka Taketsuru helped to establish Yamazaki in the 1920s. In the early 1930s he left to set up the Nikka Whisky Company, and its first distillery, Yoichi, now produces one of Japan's most successful and popular single malts. Yoichi is situated in the south-west of Hokkaido Island, which was originally where Taketsuru-san envisaged the site of a whisky distillery, due to the geographical and climatic similarities to Campbeltown in Scotland, where he had first learned to make whisky. Perhaps the allure of the traditional local *Soran* folk song, which is native to Hokkaido reminded him of the Scottish ceilidh nights?

Yoichi has since become a powerhouse in the world of Japanese distillation, and little has stood in the way of the distillery's attention to detail and tradition. Despite its large size (producing 5 million litres/1 million gallons of spirit a year), the distillery still retains a few traditional production techniques: it is one of the only distilleries in the world to continue with coal-firing of the spirit stills. As a result, Yoichi produces a Japanese single malt unlike any of its contemporaries.

The house style focuses on rich, fruity flavours and festive spices, with a complex set of aromas and a deft helping of peat smoke. Older examples of Yoichi give more balance

and complexity, with notes of vintage oak and a less prominent peatiness. The 15-year-old has a deeply peaty heart, but is rounded off with wonderful dried fruit and a woody spiciness. A 20-year-old cask-strength expression gives a distinct briny note, with richer notes of crème caramel and cedar on the palate.

In harsher winters, the distillery is often shrouded in a thick blanket of snow, not only making it a striking place to visit, but giving it an even greater resemblance to the Scottish distilleries that influenced Taketsuru all those years ago. Yoichi is steadily developing a devoted following outside Japan, with more expressions being found in specialist retailers across Europe.

TASTING NOTES

Yoichi – 12-year-old – 45% abv
Nose Rich toffee and sweet cereal notes, followed by a hint of sweet, aromatic peat smoke.

Palate An abundance of summer fruits, including ripe plums and damsons, with smoke and a rich marmalade note developing. Water opens up the fruity flavours and helps bring out a slightly floral element in the smoke.

Finish Lingering smoke and dried-fruit notes.

OTHERS TO TRY

KARUIZAWA

Website www.one-drinks.com

A newly released marriage of selected casks filled in 1999 and 2000 from the now closed Karuizawa distillery (see page 143), Asama is rich in Sherry-influenced flavours, such as dried figs, dark chocolate, orange zest and rich caramel, with a drying, oaky finish.

Tipple to try Karuizawa Asama – 46% abv

NIKKA

Website: www.nikka.com

Here are three different Nikka whiskies to try:

This first one is produced at Nikka's Miyagikyo distillery (see page 144) in Sendai, made predominantly from corn in the distillery's column still, based on the original designs that Irishman Aeneas Coffey patented back in 1830. Grain whiskies traditionally exhibit lighter, more vibrant characteristics, and this Japanese example contains very detailed notes of vanilla custard, fresh floral notes and freshly cut green apples.

Tipple to try Nikka Coffey Grain – 45% abv

This second whisky from Nikka proudly took the title of Best Blended Malt Whisky at the 2012 World Whiskies Awards. Taken from matured stocks of both Yoichi and Miyagikyo single malts, it is an elegant whisky, rich with notes of resin, cedar, dried fruit and a subtle waft of smoke on the nose, with a rich, unctuous palate of bonfire toffee, stewed orchard fruit and floral peat smoke.

Tipple to try Nikka Taketsuru – 17-Year-Old Pure Malt Whisky – 43% abv

The third Nikka whisky to try is one of a trio of Nikka's Pure Malt releases, which also include a Red Label and White Label. This whisky is a blend of malt whisky from both the Yoichi and Miyagikyo distilleries. It is subtly peated, with notes of sweet malted bread, golden syrup and caramel, making it reminiscent of a slightly smoky blended Scotch whisky such as Johnnie Walker.

Tipple to try Nikka 'Black' Pure Malt Whisky – 43% abv

NONJATTA

For more information on Japanese whisky, especially lost classic bottlings, distillery tours and a more in-depth history, look no further than the brilliant website/blog Nonjatta – nonjatta.blogspot.com. It is run by Japanese whisky expert Stefan Van Eycken and is, by far, the most informative online guide to Japanese whisky. It is also worth checking out *Drinking Japan*, written by journalist and whisky enthusiast Chris Bunting. The book has entries on some of the country's best bars, as well as being the first wide-ranging survey in English of the history and current state of Japanese drinks, covering not only the well-known rice brew, sake, but other much less explored traditions like *shochu*, *awamori*, beer, wine and Japanese whisky.

UNITED STATES

For such a vast country as the US, whiskey-making has long been concentrated in a remarkably small area. Historically, distilling took place down the East Coast in Maryland, Pennsylvania and Virginia, but for much of the 20th century – apart, of course, from the years of Prohibition (1920–1933), when the liquor industry across the entire US was disrupted – and until the explosive growth of the craft-distilling industry during the last 20 years or so, virtually all of the nation's distillation was focused on the states of Kentucky and Tennessee. Bourbon has long had to compete with Scotch whisky, and increasingly with white spirits such as vodka in its home country, but Americans, and a growing international audience, seem to have rediscovered pride in their native whiskeys, and overall, the health of whiskey-making in the US seems pretty good. There is certainly a greater variety of products now to sample and savour.

KENTUCKY AND TENNESSEE

Kentucky and Tennessee became the main whiskey-making states because they provided the optimum conditions for the production of good whiskey (both growing conditions for the grain and climate conditions for the subsequent maturation).

The limestone soil of Kentucky grows fine crops of corn (maize), and Tennessee and most of the principal distilling states of the US, past and present, partly overlie the same limestone shelf. Limestone also produces high-quality spring water with a significant calcium content, which helps enzyme action during the fermentation process of whiskey-making. In warmer and more humid climates like those of Kentucky and

Tennessee, maturation takes place more quickly than in Scotland, say. There is a greater level of evaporation than with Scotch, but the alcoholic strength stays higher.

The term 'Tennessee whiskey' rather than Bourbon is used by both Jack Daniel's and George Dickel distilleries – its production differs slightly to Bourbon in that the newly made spirit is filtered through layers of maple charcoal (known as the 'Lincoln County Process') before being bottled. Although only two major distilleries survive in Tennessee today, around a century ago as many as 700 were operating. As with neighbouring Kentucky, the whiskey industry was decimated by Prohibition, which was imposed in Tennessee almost a decade earlier than it was adopted nationally, coming into force in 1910.

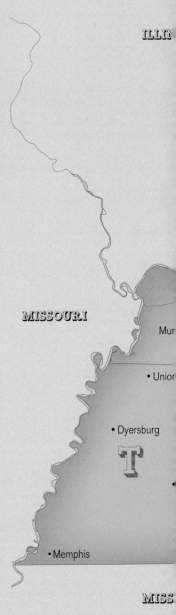

ILLIN

MISSOURI

Mur

• Union

• Dyersburg

T

• Memphis

MISS

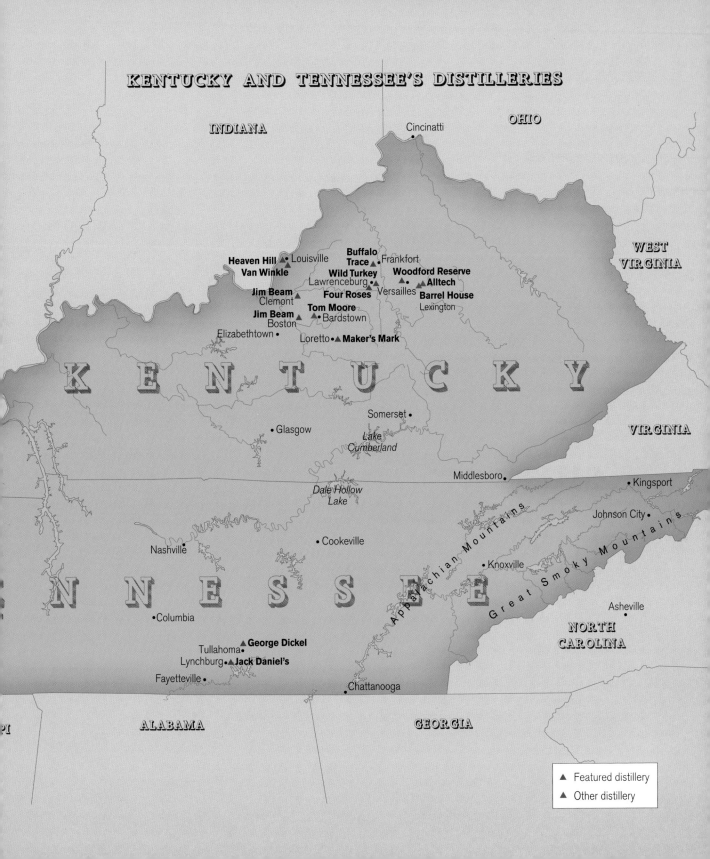

KENTUCKY AND TENNESSEE'S DISTILLERIES

INDIANA

OHIO

Cincinatti

WEST
VIRGINIA

Heaven Hill ▲• Louisville
Van Winkle

**Buffalo
Trace** ▲• Frankfort

Wild Turkey
Lawrenceburg •
Woodford Reserve ▲
Alltech ▲

Jim Beam ▲
Clemont

Four Roses ▲
Versailles

Barrel House ▲
Jim Beam ▲
Boston

Tom Moore ▲
• Bardstown

Lexington

Elizabethtown •

Loretto •▲ **Maker's Mark**

K E N T U C K Y

Somerset •

• Glasgow

*Lake
Cumberland*

VIRGINIA

Middlesboro •

• Kingsport

*Dale Hollow
Lake*

Johnson City •

• Cookeville

Nashville •

Appalachian Mountains

Knoxville •

Great Smoky Mountains

T E N N E S S E E

Asheville •

• Columbia

NORTH
CAROLINA

Tullahoma • ▲ **George Dickel**
Lynchburg ▲ **Jack Daniel's**

Fayetteville •

• Chattanooga

ALABAMA

GEORGIA

▲ Featured distillery

▲ Other distillery

Today, there are 11 full-scale, commercial distilleries in Kentucky, and two in Tennessee. Many of those in Kentucky are part of the Kentucky Bourbon Trail and welcome visitors, while both Tennessee distilleries encourage public access.

WHISKEY STYLES

The dominant style of American whiskey has long been Bourbon, made with a 'mash bill' in which corn predominates, along with various permutations of other grains such as rye, wheat and malted barley. However, in recent years there has been a welcome, if modest, resurgence in the fortunes of what is for many drinkers the 'true' spirit of America – rye whiskey. Rye is made with a mash bill mainly made from rye grain, along with corn and malted barley.

CRAFT DISTILLATION

Many of the major distillers wish to be seen as craftsmen, no matter what size their operation is, or how well known their brand. The actual 'craft' involved has evolved spectacularly over the last decade, and a new set of players with fresh ideas has come to town.

Looking back some 100–150 years ago, as in Scotland, there were literally hundreds of distillers across the US, each turning their hand to making something predominantly handcrafted. Prohibition pretty much destroyed many of the more artisanal distilleries, and it has taken until now for craft distillation, which operates outside the auspices of the rules that traditionally govern American Bourbon and Tennessee whiskey, to be vibrant once again.

Since the 1980s craft distilleries all over the US have been producing variations on the traditional themes, and many full-scale traditional distilleries in Kentucky and Tennessee are beginning to release increasingly interesting limited editions and experimental bottlings outside the standard 'Bourbon box,' as well as 'small batch' whiskeys bottled from the vatting of a small number of particularly fine casks of spirit, and considered the equivalent in prestige and quality to Scotch single malts

There are now over 300 craft distilleries in the US, and the only limiting factor is the imagination of the distiller (and budget, of course). Cereals such as quinoa, millet, blue corn, einkorn and the wonderfully named Job's Tears are at the distiller's disposal, each bringing a different taste to the mash and the eventual flavour of the spirit. Similarly, the limitations placed on maturation have been removed, giving rise to some bizarre and wonderful ideas – from infusing the finished whiskey with a variety of aromatic wood smokes to 'agitating' the slumbering spirit continuously with loud rap music!

For more information on craft distilleries, check out the American Distilling Institute website www.distilling.com

ABOVE: A raid on a speakeasy in 1926 by enforcement officers.

PROHIBITION — JUDGMENT DAY FOR THE BOURBON BUSINESS

For US whiskey- and wine-lovers, one particular date in the country's history stands out. On a chilly Tuesday, 28 October 1919, the Volstead Act, a popular name for the National Prohibition Enforcement Act, prohibited the 'manufacture, sale, or transportation of intoxicating liquors' in the USA.

This led to impending doom for distillery-owners all over the country, who, facing financial ruin, saw their maturing casks destroyed and their distilling equipment dismantled and in some cases melted down. Some owners, like the Beam family, had to diversify into running a bus factory; others managed to register their spirit as the bearer of medicinal properties.

In Chicago, one man saw the Prohibition era as a huge opportunity for the taking. Alphonse Gabriel 'Al' Capone began a prolific bootlegging operation, bringing in imported booze from the Canadian border under the noses of the authorities, and financing the production of illegal moonshine corn whiskey (so named because it was usually produced by 'moonshine' so the distillers could go undetected), which was distributed across a network of speakeasies and nightclubs around the city. From his plush seat at the Green Mill Jazz Club, Capone reaped the benefits from his various operations across the USA, and it is estimated that bootlegging from the sale of illegal booze was making him around $100 million (£62 million) a year – not bad for a man who was reported to have 'Used Furniture Dealer' printed on his business cards.

On the one hand Prohibition may have drained the lifeblood from the Bourbon producers, whose once-popular brand names ceased to exist, but on the other it no doubt unified those who managed to stay afloat until the law was repealed in early December 1933.

BUFFALO TRACE

Website **www.buffalotrace.com**
Founded **c. 1773**
Location **Frankfort, Kentucky**

When is a distillery not really a distillery? Answer: when it's a number of them. Whereas the Buffalo Trace Distillery can lay claim to being one of the longest-serving distilleries in Kentucky (even during Prohibition it continued to make Bourbon for 'medicinal' purposes), its namesake Bourbon is a relatively new introduction, and the distillery produces a large number of some of the best-known and most respected whiskeys in America.

The distillery's history reads like a *Who's Who* of distilling legends: the Blantons once owned the site; some years later it was E. H. Taylor Jr. and George T. Stagg, who constructed the first warehouse climate-control system, helping to revolutionize the technique of maturation consistency. The name George T. Stagg lives on through one of Buffalo Trace's subsidiary bottlings – a limited-edition Bourbon, bottled at the terrifying strength of 70% abv!

Buffalo Trace also produces the distinctive flavours of Sazerac and Thomas H. Handy rye whiskeys, as well as a number of single-barrel recipes. But the brand has begun to set its sights on delivering a number of hugely innovative whiskeys under the tenure of current master distiller Harlen Wheatley. Since being introduced in 1987, the Buffalo Trace Experimental series now numbers over 1500 unusual barrels, ranging from whiskey made from different mash-bill recipes (including rice and oats) to a huge variety of cask types, including a collection of exotic wine casks and rum, all with different levels of toast and char. But despite all this innovation his experiments are still rooted in his knowledge of traditional Bourbon and the flavours of the classic expressions of Buffalo Trace, which he knows so well, so it gives him an ability to know when he's gone too far in a different direction.

TASTING NOTES

Buffalo Trace – Kentucky Straight Bourbon – 40% abv
Nose Sweet vanilla notes with an aroma of candyfloss, brown sugar, cereal notes and some woody spices.
Palate Malty and sweet, with notes of burnt sugar and vanilla. Some dried fruitiness (apricots and raisins) develops, with cloves and cinnamon also appearing.
Finish Lasting impressions of liquorice and root beer.

FOUR ROSES

Website **www.fourroses.us**
Founded **1888**
Location **Lawrenceburg, Kentucky**

According to legend, Paul Jones Jr, the founder of Four Roses, became infatuated with a local southern beauty and nervously asked for her hand in marriage. The girl replied with deft ambiguity: should she be wearing a floral corsage to the local dance the answer would be yes. Of course, the answer was yes and her floral acceptance became the iconic branding on the Bourbon's label. Or so goes the story. One thing, however, is clear: Four Roses, once the most popular Bourbon in the USA, then savagely mistreated, is now back with a vengeance.

After years of producing an inferior spirit, the distillery has rebuilt its reputation, and under the watchful eye of master distiller and international ambassador Jim Rutledge, some exceptional whiskies have been released. Whereas much of the Kentucky Bourbon scene is built on recipes that rarely change, Four Roses has experimented and pushed the boundaries – particularly in the fermentation department.

Yeast plays a much bigger part in developing the range of flavours exhibited in the Four Roses bottlings than many of the other major players – from the standard Yellow Label, through to the exclusive and sought-after single-barrel releases. Rutledge has over ten different recipes, each using different strains of yeast and a varying mash bill, one using a high percentage of rye for added spiciness. The range of spirits means Rutledge has a broad palate of flavour from which to construct the ultimate Bourbon.

TASTING NOTES

Four Roses Small Batch – Kentucky Straight Bourbon Whiskey – 45% abv

Nose Bittersweet vanilla notes combine with freshly cut honeysuckle, coconut and dried apricots. With a dash of water, more earthy and powerful dark, leafy tobacco notes appear, with some woody spice lurking in the background.

Palate Sweet and spicy, with Virginia tobacco notes, a big kick of vanilla fudge and some zingy liquorice notes.

Finish: A very weighty finish, with the floral notes right at the death.

GEORGE DICKEL

Website **www.dickel.com**

Founded **1877**

Location **Normandy, Tennessee**

Together with Jack Daniel's, George Dickel is the only full-scale commercial distillery in the state of Tennessee, though half a dozen 'micros' are now up and running.

George A. Dickel was a German immigrant to the USA who worked for some years in Nashville as a liquor dealer, buying whiskey from various distilleries before creating his own small distillery in Cascade Hollow, a few miles from Tullahoma. Or so goes the 'official' version of the Dickel story. Another version claims that Dickel never actually owned the distillery, and merely had the exclusive rights to bottle the whiskey at the time when his brother-in-law owned a majority share in the Cascade distillery.

Whatever the truth, the Scotch spelling of 'whisky' has long been used, because Dickel insisted that the spirit he made was as smooth as the finest Scotch, but when Prohibition struck Tennessee in 1910, almost a decade earlier than it came into force nationwide, distilling was transferred to Kentucky. The company was bought in 1937 by Schenley Industries, with production being transferred to that firm's Ancient Age Distillery. In 1958 Schenley decided that George Dickel should return to its Tennessee roots, and a brand-new distillery was built close to the old Cascade Hollow site. Since then, a series of mergers and acquisitions brought Dickel into the Diageo portfolio.

Like 'Jack,' George Dickel uses the Lincoln County Process of charcoal filtration to create a smoother 'sippin' whiskey,' and is classified under the official category of Tennessee Whiskey. Unlike Jack Daniel's, George Dickel whiskey is chilled before entering the charcoal mellowing vats. According to the distillers, this is because George Dickel noticed that whiskey made during the winter was smoother than that distilled in summer. They claim that chilling filters out the oils and fatty acids inherent in most whiskies.

There are a few expressions of George Dickel available – Cascade Hollow, No 8, No 12 and Barrel Select, all with differing flavour profiles.

TASTING NOTES

George Dickel No 12 – 45% abv

Nose Herbal and spicy, with vanilla, honey and lemon notes.

Palate Initially full and sweet, with more honey, plus ginger and cinnamon, gradually becoming more citric, with lemon and lime.

Finish Toffee, soft, a subtle char and discrete smoky maple notes.

HEAVEN HILL

Website **www.heaven-hill.com**
Founded **1935**
Location **Louisville, Kentucky**

The original Heaven Hill distillery closed long before the five Shapira brothers came along in the 1930s. The new company, Heaven Hill Distilleries Inc, was founded in 1935 by the brothers who built a new distillery south of Bardstown in 1935. Their descendants continue to own and run the company to this day and it is the largest US independent producer of distilled spiritis.

Many distilleries around the world feature incidents of fire in their histories, but one of the most memorable of recent times occurred at the Heaven Hill distillery in 1996, when much of the production plant and a number of warehouses were seriously damaged in a spectacular blaze.

Jim Beam and Brown-Forman distillers came to the rescue by producing spirit for Heaven Hill in the short term. It was then decided not to rebuild on the fire-ravaged site but instead to purchase the Bernheim Distillery in Louisville.

Although production of the Heaven Hill portfolio of whiskeys occurs at Bernheim, maturation and bottling functions continue to be centred on the old Heaven Hill distillery site. Close by is the Bourbon

Heritage Centre, which is situated among the 'rickhouses,' where the world's second-largest stock of Bourbon (600,000 barrels) matures.

Heaven Hill turns out a wide variety of brands, both for itself and for external customers, but the company's best-known brands include Evan Williams and Elijah Craig Bourbons (introduced in 1986). The Reverend Elijah Craig was a Baptist minister, widely regarded as the 'father of Bourbon', having reputedly pioneered the use of charred barrels to store and mature his whiskey. Among its diverse output, Heaven Hill also produces Bernheim Original Straight Wheat Whiskey, Pikesville Rye and Rittenhouse Rye

TASTING NOTES
Elijah Craig – 12-year-old Kentucky Straight Bourbon Whiskey – 47% abv
Nose: Mature and alluring, with caramel, honey, spice and vanilla.
Palate: Rounded and full-bodied, mellow, with more caramel, spicy rye and slight maple smoke.
Finish: Vanilla, liquorice sticks and soft oak.

JACK DANIEL'S

Website **www.jackdaniels.com**

Founded **1875**

Location **Lynchburg, Tennessee**

Jack Daniel's Tennessee whiskey is one of the most recognizable brand names in the world, and a titanic force when it comes to whiskey-making of any kind.

The distillery suffered badly during the Tennessee Prohibition of 1910 and again during the nationwide Prohibition of 1920–1933, but it survived. Today the distillery – famous for its simple, homely image – is a distillation giant, producing 20 million litres (4.3 million gallons) of spirit every year. The distillery has become an award-winning tourist attraction, with fans flocking from across the globe for a taste – but with an unexpected and bizarre twist. Moore County, where the distillery lies, is still a dry county and the law has only just changed to allow whiskey-sampling on the distillery tour.

The range starts with the standard Old No 7 Tennessee whiskey. There are also Single Barrel releases and Gentleman Jack, a premium version, which is filtered twice through charcoal (once before bottling and once after). These are classified as Tennessee Whiskey, and although there are huge similarities in flavour and aroma, and most of the key production elements are similar to those of a

Bourbon whiskey, Tennessee Whiskey uses the 'Lincoln County Process'. Although not unique to Jack Daniel's (it is also practised by fellow Tennessee distiller George Dickel), the newly made spirit is effectively filtered very slowly in large vats, through around 3m (10ft) of burnt sugar-maple charcoal, before being matured in new, white, American oak barrels. This hugely expensive process is said to contribute a smoother element, but one thing's for sure: despite the additional cost, it has become ingrained in the fabric of Jack Daniel's, and we suspect that no one would be willing to mess with such a phenomenal success story or the enduring legacy of the great man himself.

TASTING NOTES

Jack Daniel's Single Barrel – 45% abv

Nose Sweet notes hit first, then corn, vanilla, charred oak, a touch of smoke and bonfire toffee.

Palate A big, mouthfilling whiskey on the first sip, then notes of malted cereal, more bonfire toffee, vanilla and some spicy tobacco flavours.

Finish Lengthy, with lingering touches of vanilla, lemon zest and drying oak notes.

156 THE WORLD OF WHISKY

JIM BEAM

Website www.jimbeam.com
Founded 1795
Location Clermont, Kentucky

In 1795 Jacob Boehm sold his first barrel of whiskey, so may be taken as the date in which 'Jim Beam' – the world's best-selling Bourbon brand – was established. Jacob Boehm was a German-born miller and farmer who arrived in Kentucky towards the end of the 18th century and established a corn mill and small distillery in Nelson County.

The family name became anglicized over time to 'Beam,' and there really was a Jim Beam, born in 1864 who lived to the age of 83. Five years before his death the name 'Jim Beam' appeared on the bottle label for the first time, and much is made by the company of the continuing family involvement – since current Master Distiller Fred Noe is a great-grandson of Jim and a seventh-generation Beam family member.

However, Jim Beam is no longer family-owned, having belonged since 1967 to what was then American Brands, now operating under the Beam Inc banner. The company has two Jim Beam distilleries: Clermont, in Bullitt County, which was established soon after the repeal of Prohibition in 1933; and nearby Boston distillery, built in 1953. Between them, the two plants can turn out some 40 million litres (9 million gallons) per year.

There are several variants of Jim Beam, with the best-selling being the 4-year-old 'white label' expression.

Recent innovations have included Jim Beam Red Stag, flavoured with black cherry, and Jim Beam Devil's Cut. The latter is made from spirit extracted from deep within the barrels after they have been emptied, mixed with their 6-year-old Bourbon.

Since the 1990s Jim Beam has also produced four highly regarded 'small batch' Bourbons – Baker's, Basil Hayden's, Booker's and Knob Creek. These are Bourbon from a limited number of barrels that have been given choice positions in the company's warehouses, and have also been allowed to mature for longer than most bottlings.

Until 2012, the Beam distilleries were out of bounds to the public, though the Jim Beam American Outpost at Clermont served as an excellent visitor centre. Now, however, tours of the actual production areas at Clermont are on offer, in addition to the chance to visit the Outpost and nearby Beam family homestead.

TASTING NOTES

Jim Beam 4-year-old Kentucky Bourbon Straight Whiskey – 40% abv
Nose Floral notes, plus vanilla.
Palate Sweet, with vanilla, but becoming drier and more oaky.
Finish Furniture polish and malt.

MAKER'S MARK

Website **www.makersmark.com**
Founded **1953**
Location **Loretto, Kentucky**

The actual Maker's Mark Distillery dates from 1805 and was originally known as Burk's Distillery. It stands beside Hardin Creek, near Loretto in Marion County. During the past 50 years or so it has been closely linked to the Samuels family. It all began in 1780 when a Robert Samuels moved to Kentucky, where he soon commenced whiskey-making. The story of Maker's Mark, however, begins in the mid-1950s, when Robert Samuels' great-great-great grandson, Taylor Williams Samuels Sr, acquired the old Burk's Distillery site, at that point known as Happy Hollow Distillery, and proceeded to renovate its somewhat dilapidated structures.

Samuels renamed the distillery Star Hill, and although he possessed the old family recipe for Bourbon, he saw the opportunity to create a new and mellower style, and to that end he burnt the existing recipe.

He then set about developing a replacement, seeking advice from the sage Stitzel-Weller distiller Julian 'Pappy' Van Winkle, before going on to experiment by baking bread from various grains in the family kitchen. The recipe he settled on comprised locally grown corn (maize) and malted barley, coupled with red winter wheat, rather than the traditional rye. The Scottish spelling of 'whisky' was employed for the new product, in recognition of Samuels' Scottish ancestry.

When it came to choosing a name for this smoother, softer Bourbon, Samuels' wife, Margie, suggested Maker's Mark. She was a keen collector of pewter, each piece of which was hallmarked, suggesting that the producer was sufficiently proud of his creation to give it the 'maker's mark'. Margie Samuels was also responsible for the signature red wax seal, created on each bottle by hand-dipping.

Although the Samuels family continues to have a close involvement with Maker's Mark, the distillery and brand were acquired in 1981 by Hiram Walker & Sons, subsequently becoming part of Allied Domecq. Since 2005, Maker's Mark has been owned by Fortune Brands Inc, now Beam Inc, which is also responsible for Jim Beam.

TASTING NOTES

Maker's Mark Kentucky Straight Bourbon Whisky – 45% abv
Nose Complex and relatively subtle, with vanilla and spice.
Palate Honey and rich, spicy fruit notes. Well rounded.
Finish Lengthy, with liquorice and coffee notes.

VAN WINKLE

Website **www.oldripvanwinkle.com**
Founded **1972**
Location **Louisville, Kentucky**

The Van Winkle family has a distinguished Bourbon pedigree dating back to the 1890s, when Julian 'Pappy' Van Winkle acted as a salesman for the Louisville liquor company of W L Weller & Sons. He later became president of the Stitzel-Weller Distillery, which first distilled during 1935.

Pappy's son, also Julian, ran the distillery until its sale in 1972, at which point he established the Old Rip Van Winkle label, using Stitzel-Weller-distilled whiskey. The third generation, in the form of Julian Van Winkle, joined the new company five years later, taking over after the death of his father in 1981. Since 2001 a fourth generation has been represented in the business, through Julian Van Winkle III's son, Preston.

Pappy Van Winkle's original wheated Bourbon recipe is still used, with the inclusion of wheat rather than the less expensive rye, as this is supposed to give the whiskeys a smoother, sweeter flavour during the extended maturation period favoured by Van Winkle. The youngest Van Winkle whiskeys are a minimum of 10 years old, and the current expressions were distilled at a number of distilleries, subsequently being matured at the Van Winkle's now silent Old Hoffman Distillery in Anderson County. However, since 2002 the Van Winkle whiskeys have been produced under licence at Heaven Hill Distillery, with Heaven Hill also undertaking

their bottling and distribution. The range includes a 12-year-old rye whiskey, alongside 15-, 20- and 23-year old 'Family Reserve' Bourbons, the latter being highly revered by Bourbon connoisseurs.

TASTING NOTES

Van Winkle Special Reserve –12-year-old – 45% abv

Nose Caramel and molasses, soft and mellow.

Palate Honey and rich, spicy fruit notes. Well-rounded.

Finish Lengthy, with liquorice and coffee. A very classy older Bourbon.

WILD TURKEY

Website www.wildturkey.com

Founded 1869

Location Lawrenceburg, Kentucky

As with a great number of successful distilleries, Wild Turkey started life in relatively humble surroundings. Austin Nichols founded his grocery store, which specialized in tea, coffee and whiskey, 14 years before the actual distillery was established on Wild Turkey Hill in 1869. Under the tenure of the Ripy brothers, the distillery flourished, later in the century receiving the honour of being one of over 400 whiskies to be selected to represent Kentucky at the World's Fair in Chicago in 1893. It was no doubt a great success, showcasing why Kentucky had steadily risen to the top step of America's finest whiskey-producing states. But as with many of the great names, the stills fell silent during the dark days of Prohibition, although unlike others the distillery managed to hang on by a thread.

The story goes that the name 'Wild Turkey' wasn't fully adopted until around 1940, when the Bourbon proved popular with a number of guests on a turkey hunt organized by one of the distillery executives. A year later, the same hunting party met and demanded he bring along more of 'that wild turkey Bourbon'. The rest is history, and under the tenure of master distiller Jimmy Russell, who has been with Wild Turkey since 1954, the 'Kickin' Chicken' as Russell likes to call it (due to the high proof of their most popular bottling), has been enjoyed on the rocks, in mint juleps and drunk neat across the whole of the USA.

Continuing with the avian theme, Wild Turkey has recently launched its Rare Breed Society, giving Bourbon fans the chance to try special bottlings as well as read Jimmy Russell's impassioned thoughts on his beloved whiskey. This is definitely a full-bodied whiskey, with lots of sassiness and bite. Try it as part of a classic mint julep, with a dash of water or over ice.

TASTING NOTES

Wild Turkey 101 Straight Bourbon Whiskey – 8-year-old – 50.5% abv

Nose A huge hit of vanilla and caramel, with some cherry sherbet notes and a lovely perfumed aroma. The high strength means that the alcohol notes are powerful at first and water brings a softness and mellows the fruit notes and vanilla aromas.

Palate Rich, dark chocolate, some woody dryness, brandy butter and some spicy aniseed notes. Very mouth-coating. With water, the palate becomes lighter, with citrus notes, sweetened vanilla ice cream and a touch of hickory/woody spice.

Finish: Lingering notes of butter and aromatic spices.

WOODFORD RESERVE

Website **www.woodfordreserve.com**
Founded **1812**
Location **Versailles, Kentucky**

The site on which the distillery stands is one of the oldest in Kentucky and home to something not really seen in the manufacture of Bourbon – copper pot stills. The distillery was called Old Oscar Pepper Distillery but was renamed Woodford Reserve in 2003, after previously being mothballed for several decades.

Despite the extensive use of copper pot stills in the production of single malt Scotch whisky, the relatively inefficient use of the pot still (compared with the more streamlined column still, widely used in Bourbon production) is what gives Woodford Reserve many of its unique characteristics. Other factors are the highly calcified water source, which flows through thick layers of limestone rock, and the lengthy fermentation process: the sour mash is left to ferment for up to seven days, leading to a much fuller-flavoured beer, which is then triple-distilled in the pot stills.

Like the distillery's 19th-century forefathers, Oscar Pepper and James Crow, who are widely regarded as pioneering numerous Bourbon production techniques used today, Woodford Reserve is still a keen innovator, and its Masters Collection aims to challenge conventional Bourbon wisdom by experimenting with unusual mash bills and additional maturation in casks made of maple wood and ex-Californian Chardonnay casks. The Bourbon has become very popular as a key cocktail ingredient, and the Woodford Reserve website boasts nearly 25 original cocktail recipes. And if that's not enough, Woodford Reserve also offers a lucky few the chance to create their own two-barrel batch of the Bourbon, complete with personalized labels.

TASTING NOTES

**Woodford Reserve
Distiller's Select Kentucky
Straight Bourbon
Whiskey – 43.2% abv**

Nose A pleasing malty cereal note develops first, followed by earthy notes, freshly turned soil, charred oak and rich vanilla.

Palate Smooth and very velvety mouthfeel, with sweet vanilla, dark chocolate, sweetened black coffee and honey.

Finish Touches of mint, lingering notes of chocolate.

CANADA

WASHINGTON

• Seattle Spokane • ▲ Dry Fly

MONTANA

▲ Ellensburg

Helena •

Rocky Mountains

Portland • ▲ McMenamins/
Rogue/ ▲   Edgefield
Clear Creek   Troutdale

▲ Roughstock ▲ Yellowstone
Bozeman   Billings

OREGON

NEBRASKA

Great Salt
Lake • ▲ High West
Salt Lake City •

Charbay   Stillwater
St Helena ▲ ▲ Petaluma
Anchor Distilling ▲
San Francisco •

UTAH

Stranahan's • Denver
▲

COLORADO

KANSAS

▲ St George
Alameda

CALIFORNIA

Los Angeles • ▲ St James

San Diego • ▲ Ballast Point

Phoenix •

Oklahoma

TEXAS

San Ant

Pacific Ocean

▲ Featured distillery
▲ Other distillery

MEXICO

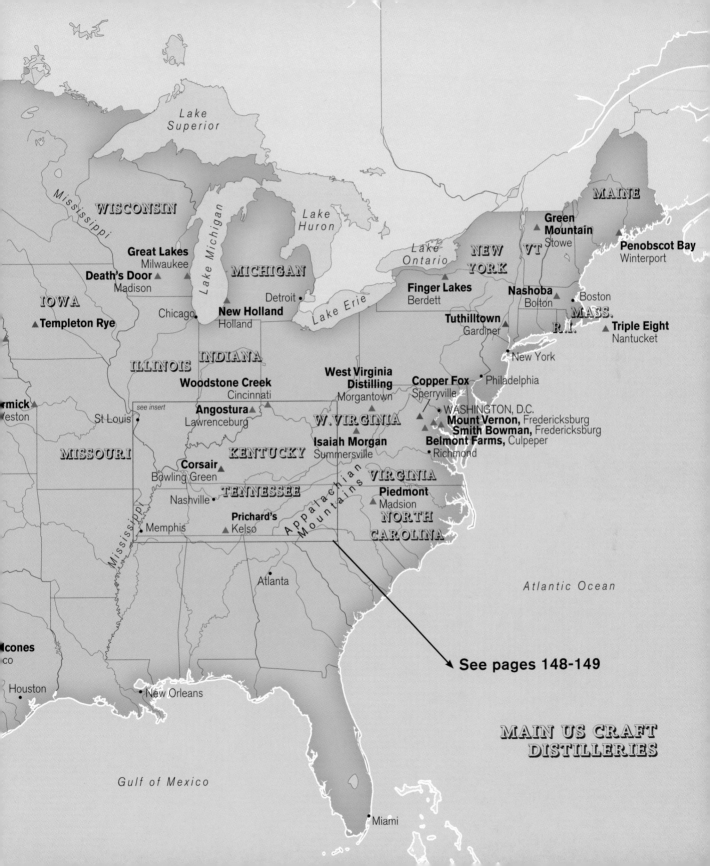

Lake Superior

Mississippi

WISCONSIN

Lake Michigan

Lake Huron

MICHIGAN

Detroit

Chicago

New Holland
Holland

Lake Erie

Lake Ontario

NEW YORK

VT

MAINE

Green Mountain
Stowe

Penobscot Bay
Winterport

Great Lakes
Milwaukee ▲

Death's Door ▲
Madison

IOWA

▲ **Templeton Rye**

Finger Lakes
Berdett

Nashoba
Bolton

• Boston

MASS.

Tuthilltown
Gardiner

R.I.

Triple Eight ▲
Nantucket

ILLINOIS

INDIANA

Woodstone Creek
Cincinnati

West Virginia Distilling
Morgantown

Copper Fox
Sperryville

• Philadelphia

New York

see insert

• St Louis

Angostura ▲
Lawrenceburg

W. VIRGINIA

• WASHINGTON, D.C.

Mount Vernon, Fredericksburg
Smith Bowman, Fredericksburg
Belmont Farms, Culpeper

▲mick
▲ston

MISSOURI

KENTUCKY

Isaiah Morgan
Summersville

• Richmond

Corsair ▲
Bowling Green

VIRGINIA

Piedmont
Madsion ▲

TENNESSEE

Nashville •

Mississippi

Appalachian Mountains

NORTH CAROLINA

Prichard's
Memphis •   ▲ Kelso

Atlanta •

Atlantic Ocean

▲cones
▲co

Houston •

See pages 148-149

• New Orleans

Gulf of Mexico

Miami •

MAIN US CRAFT DISTILLERIES

BALCONES

Website **www.balconesdistilling.com**
Founded **2008**
Location **Waco, Texas**

When Chip Tate, master distiller at Balcones, decided to build a distillery, he really took the whole theme of 'handcrafted' to heart. Indeed, Chip, whose background lies in brewing, decided to go the whole hog and not only produce a portfolio of highly innovative whiskeys, but build much of the actual distilling equipment.

Balcones is built on the simple premise that you can't make exceptional whiskey without nailing the fermentation process and, through his many experiments, Chip and his team have opened up a whole new window on what can be categorized as whiskey. Balcones was one of the first distilleries successfully to ferment and distil a sour mash made from atole, a roasted variety of blue corn, which Chip describes as being like 'brewing a thick porridge'. Balcones has also pioneered a spirit using a local recipe, which probably can't be called a whiskey, but certainly ranks up there with the best of them in the flavour department. Balcones 'Rumble' uses distilled Texas wildflower honey, turbinado sugar (unrefined and usually from Hawaii) and spirit derived from the mission fig, matured in American oak casks. Hot on the heels of Rumble, Balcones released another innovative product called

Brimstone, which infuses the corn-based whiskey with smoke from wild Texas scrub oak. It is fascinating to see how a small distillery with limited resources can develop such uniquely flavoured whiskeys and create a portfolio of interesting and innovative releases. Balcones is one of a growing number of US-based craft distilleries to buck the trend and ruffle a few feathers with its maverick approach to whiskey-making. Balcones is now generating plenty of attention across the Atlantic, and European palates can begin to see what all the fuss is about.

TASTING NOTES

Balcones Baby Blue – Corn Whisky – 46% abv

Nose Sweet, nutty notes, milk chocolate-covered peanuts, burnt caramel and a hint of coffee beans. Water reveals some toasted cereal notes and an additional sweetcorn note.

Palate Rich in the mouth, with very sweet – then spicy – liquorice notes and milky coffee.

Finish Lingering sweetness with a touch of poached pear at the death.

COPPER FOX

Website **www.copperfox.biz**
Founded **2000**
Location **Sperryville, Virginia**

Copper Fox Distillery is owned and run by Rick Wasmund, and stands at the foot of Virginia's Blue Ridge Mountains. Wasmund spent a highly influential period in 2000 learning about distilling while based in Scotland. He then proceeded to buy an existing Virginia distillery, where he developed Copper Fox Whisky, launched in 2003. According to Wasmund it was the first applewood chip-aged whisky in the world, and we're sure that it was.

Wasmund built his current distillery in 2005. It boasts its own maltings, where barley is malted in the traditional Scottish manner and then dried using apple, cherry and oak wood. It is distilled in a double pot still in one-barrel batches and matured using Wasmund's innovative 'chip and barrel aging process': hand-chipped and toasted fruitwood chips are added to the spirit in cask, with the result that maturation is speeded up dramatically. Indeed, Rick Wasmund bottles his single malt after just four months in the cask, releasing batches of between 250 and 1500 bottles, with a monthly production figure of around 2500 bottles.

In 2006 the first batch of Wasmund's Single Malt Whisky – note the Scottish spelling – hit the shelves, and rapidly developed an enthusiastic following for its unique US take on old-established Scotch whisky-making practices. Copper Fox also turns out a rye whiskey, made from two parts Virginia-grown rye and one part malted barley, along with entirely unaged single malt and rye whiskeys.

Copper Fox has also introduced the innovative Wasmund's Barrel Kit, which comprises a 2-litre charred American white oak barrel and two bottles of either single malt spirit or rye spirit. Purchasers can fill the barrel, drink the contents and then refill it ad infinitum, noting the subtle differences from one fill to the next, due to the ongoing interaction between oak and spirit.

TASTING NOTES

Wasmund's Single Malt Whisky – 48% abv

Nose Floral, with honey, vanilla, watermelon, freshly sawn wood and new leather. Individualistic!

Palate Nicely balanced sweet and dry flavours, floral and herbal, with nuts, cinnamon, pepper and vanilla.

Finish Medium in length, warming and drying.

CORSAIR

Website **www.corsairartisan.com**
Founded **2007**
Location **Kentucky (with an additional site in Tennessee)**

It's probably fair to say that Corsair represents everything one would expect from a craft distiller: passion, ingenuity, resourcefulness, innovation and certainly an element of wackiness alongside so much more. Since opening in 2007, the owner Darek Bell has painstakingly assembled an array of unusual-looking yet traditional distillation equipment (including a 100-year-old copper pot still), allowing him to get right under the skin of just about every element of making whiskey.

His recipes range from the sublime to the ridiculous, including whiskeys based on classic craft beers, barrel-aged gin, milk chocolate stout whiskey (using heavily toasted chocolate rye malt) and a plethora of smoked whiskeys, using cherry, cedar, pimento and even seaweed! But alongside the more ostentatious flavours and aromas, Corsair has created some solid recipes, based on the classics, including a 100% rye whiskey and a triple-smoked single malt whiskey, matured in American white oak casks. Bell has also documented his journey in a fascinating book (*Alt Whiskeys* www.altwhiskeys.com), where he lifts the lid on many of his wonderful creations – it makes for a highly entertaining read. It's highly

unusual for a distiller to give so many insights into his secret recipes, but Bell and his team seem to delight in instilling other enthusiasts with ideas and great taste.

Taking the craft-distilling movement by the scruff of the neck, Corsair has paved the way in how these small-time distilleries can be reactionary and revolutionary with flavour and production innovation. In fact, such is the lack of convention on show at Corsair, it's a wonder that Bell hasn't just ripped up the rulebook, thrown it into one of his mash tuns and begun to make yet another unusual whiskey with the pages.

TASTING NOTES

Corsair 100% Rye Whiskey – 46% abv

Nose Intensely spicy, with peppery, meaty pastrami notes, a touch of vanilla and roasted peanuts.

Palate The pepper and spice continues onto the palate, with a woody, cinnamon note.

Finish Hot, with lingering white pepper.

ROUGHSTOCK MONTANA

Website **www.montanawhiskey.com**
Founded **2008**
Location **Bozeman, Montana**

Roughstock Distillery is the first legal whiskey-making operation in the state of Montana, and is owned and operated by husband-and-wife team Bryan and Kari Schultz – fourth-generation Montana folk.

This is a craft distillery, located at the base of the Bridger Mountain Range in the stunning scenery of south-western Montana. It uses locally grown grains and boasts a 260-gallon (1180-litre) copper pot still, fabricated for the Schultz family by legendary Louisville still-maker Vedome Copper and Brass Works. In 2011 the distillery moved to new, larger premises, and a second copper still, along with additional Oregon fir fermenters, was installed to meet demand for the distillery's products.

Roughstock employs the slogan 'The First Best Whiskey in the Last Best Place', and each bottle is hand-numbered and dated. The range embraces a number of varying styles, including Rough Stock Montana Malt Whiskey, the distillery's first whiskey and still its flagship product. It's made with malted barley, double-distilled in the pot still and matured in lightly charred virgin American white oak barrels. Other whiskeys are Spring Wheat, Sweet Corn and Straight Rye.

Bryan and Kari Schultz use both 225-litre (50-gallon) barrels made from new American oak and quarter casks for maturation, while French oak casks and some that previously held fortified wine have also been filled and are being monitored to see just how they suit the whiskey. Aging takes place to the sound of Johnny Cash, which is apparently the spirit's favourite country music!

Tours of the distillery have been described as half-day volunteer 'bottling parties', where visitors are put to work filling and labelling bottles before receiving their reward in the tasting room. Anyone planning a visit should note that these 'working tours' are only offered on three Saturdays per month.

TASTING NOTES:
Roughstock Montana Whiskey – 45% abv
Nose Brittle toffee, vanilla and tinned pears.
Palate More toffee and pears, baked apple and custard, with youngish oak.
Finish Vanilla, milk chocolate and oak. Something like half Scotch, half Bourbon.

ST GEORGE

Website **www.stgeorgespirits.com**
Founded **1982**
Location **Alameda, California**

Not to be confused with the English St George's Distillery, St George can proudly proclaim that it undoubtedly preempted the explosion of American craft distillers, enjoying three decades of success, distilling eaux de vie, vodka, gin and more recently a fine malt whiskey. Despite the capacious surroundings of the distillery building (a converted navy hangar in California), the St George team, led by Jorg Rupf and his master distillers, have refined the process of whiskey-making. In 2012 they released their 12th single malt whiskey, which is made from a mixture of regular malted barley, as well as a proportion of roasted barley, alongside a small amount smoked over both beechwood and alder. The current batch of whiskey comes from a variety of casks, including ex-Bourbon, Port pipes, French oak and a touch of Sherry cask for good measure, and St George firmly adheres to the mantra of 'positive inconsistency' – meaning that this batch will taste different to anything else it has released previously. Leading the craft-distillation movement has kept the distillery busy and, over the last 25 years or more, the distillery has honed on what makes a great recipe, as well as

experimenting in a number of different spirit fields. In fact, the distillery's innovative range of vodkas has sparked excitement among Europe's bartending community, especially when the key ingredients feature flavours such as chipotle pepper, Budda's Hand citron (look them up!) and spiced pears.

St George has also released a bottling comprising a blend of different Bourbon casks from across Kentucky under the 'Breaking & Entering' label. Clearly, thievery never tasted so good.

TASTING NOTES

St George Single Malt Whiskey – 11th Release – 43% abv

Nose Youthful, with some nice zesty notes, coupled with fresh vanilla, cut grass and fresh red fruit. Given time in the glass, a subtle maltiness begins to develop and some oaky dryness.

Palate A touch of menthol, followed by more vanilla, a dash of woody spice and orange zest. Water brings out the spices and a touch of sweet wine and fresh apricot.

Finish Short, with some drying oak notes in the background.

STRANAHAN'S COLORADO

Website **www.stranahans.com**
Founded **2004**
Location **Denver, Colorado**

When Jess Graber and George Stranahan established the Denver distillery in 2004, it was the first licensed distillery in Colorado. Today, there are more than 20 distillers operating in the state, which just goes to show the speed with which the micro-distilling movement has grown in the USA.

The partnership between Graber and Stranahan began in unique circumstances, with volunteer fire-fighter Jess Graber being called to help put out a blaze in a barn owned by liquor connoisseur George Stranahan. The two discovered a mutual love of good whiskey and set about developing a recipe for what they claim is 'The smoothest, most flavourful whiskey in the world', using the purity of their mountain surroundings to their advantage.

Originally, wash was purchased from local breweries and distilled by the Stranahan's team, but then in 2009 a disused brewery in Denver was acquired, complete with equipment, and the whiskey-making business was transferred to that location. Since 2010 Stranahan's has been owned by the New York-based Proximo Spirits Company.

Around 80% of the barley bought by Stranahan's is grown in Colorado, and double-distillation takes place in a custom-made combination pot (Scotch-style) and column (Bourbon-style) still, though additional distilling capacity has subsequently been added to the original set-up.

The spirit is matured for a minimum of two years in charred, American white oak barrels prior to bottling, and as many as 20 casks, which have been maturing for between two and five years, are 'married' to create each batch of whiskey.

Other cask types are also filled on an occasional basis – in 2011 a new whiskey called Solitude was released, having been aged in American white oak, European oak Port 'pipes,' and finally, Hungarian oak casks that had formerly held Chardonnay wine. This was the tenth release in Stranahan's signature 'Snowflake' series of new oak and wine cask-aged whiskies.

TASTING NOTES

Stranahan's Colorado Whiskey – 47% abv

Nose Spicy, creamy and reminiscent of Bourbon, with caramel and liquorice.

Palate A little oily, fruity and spicy, with honey and lively oak.

Finish Relatively short, more lively oak.

TUTHILLTOWN

Website **www.tuthilltown.com**
Founded **2003**
Location **Gardiner, New York**

Tuthilltown Spirits, established by Ralph Erenzo and Brian Lee, is based in a converted granary in Gardiner, New York. It opened for business in 2005 and now produces a range of products, led by Hudson Baby Bourbon. This is the first Bourbon to be made in New York State and the first legal pot-distilled whiskey to be distilled in the state since Prohibition.

In 2010 the young company caught the eye of the Scottish distiller, William Grant & Sons Ltd, keen to take a stake in the burgeoning US craft-distilling arena. Accordingly, Grant acquired the operation's Hudson whiskey range. Having the well-established sales, marketing and distribution operation of such a major-league distiller behind the Hudson line-up, means that the whiskeys now have far greater international availability.

The Tuthilltown team first started making corn whiskey, filling it into small casks to speed up maturation, and this evolved into Hudson Baby Bourbon, which remains the distillery's leading expression. From an initial 225 litres (50 gallons) per week, production has risen to around 3400 litres (750 gallons). In addition to Baby Bourbon, the range includes Hudson Manhattan Rye, Hudson

Single Malt Whiskey, Hudson New York Corn Whiskey and Hudson Four Grain Bourbon.

Erenzo and Lee like to do things their own way and are experimenting with different grains such as spelt, oats and rice, and the Tuthilltown warehouses resonate to the sound of loud drum-and-bass music, intended to aid the aging process – they call it sonic maturation!

TASTING NOTES

Hudson Baby Bourbon Whiskey – 46% abv

Nose Vanilla, pepper, slightly herbal, toasted cereal, a big hit of cloves, and spearmint with thyme.

Palate Smooth and quaffable, with lively spices, caramel and corn, then a herbal note.

Finish Lengthy, drying, herbal, with light oak char.

HUDSON
BABY BOURBON
WHISKEY

375 ml   46% alc/vol
Made with 100% New York Corn
Aged under 4 yrs in American Oak
Handmade and Bottled by:
Tuthilltown Spirits, Gardiner, New York

OTHERS TO TRY

BULLEIT BOURBON

Website www.bulleitbourbon.com

Introduced 1999

Location Lawrenceburg, Kentucky

Despite its recent emergence on the global Bourbon markets, Bulleit has already made a huge impression, favoured for its high rye content (which is around 30% of the mash bill) and mixability in a variety of cocktails. The recipe stems from Augustus Bulleit, a 19th-century bar owner who disappeared under mysterious circumstances when transporting barrels of Bourbon between Kentucky and New Orleans. The recipe was revived and revisited by his great-great grandson Tom Bulleit in 1987 and is now distilled at the Four Roses Distillery.

Tipple to try Bulleit Bourbon – 40% abv

KNOB CREEK

Website www.knobcreek.com

Introduced 1992

Location Clermont, Kentucky

Knob Creek is the Kentucky town where Abraham Lincoln's father, Thomas, owned a farm and worked at the local distillery. Knob Creek is one of four brands in Jim Beam's Small Batch Bourbon Collection, featuring whiskeys produced in limited quantities and aged for between six and nine years. In the case of Knob Creek, the maturation period is nine years. The mash bill includes a relatively high proportion of rye grain.

Tipple to try Knob Creek – Kentucky Straight Bourbon – 50% abv

PIKESVILLE RYE

Website www.heavenhill.com

Founded c.1890

Location Louisville, Kentucky

The Pikesville brand of rye whisky was first produced by the Winand brothers at a distillery based in the town of Scott's Level in Maryland. However, Prohibition all but finished it off and the brand was sold in 1936 to a company that contracted the production out to a distiller in Baltimore. In the early 1980s it was sold again, this time to Heaven Hill Distillery, and with the current rise in popularity of rye whiskey, this distinctly spicy whiskey has found new fans, favouring it as part of a Manhattan or a classic Sazerac cocktail.

Tipple to try Pikesville Straight Rye Whiskey – 40% abv

TEMPLETON RYE

Website www.templetonrye.com

Introduced 2006

Location Templeton, Iowa

The town of Templeton in Iowa was noted as a centre of illicit whiskey production during the Prohibition era, with its high-quality rye spirit allegedly becoming gangster Al Capone's whiskey of choice! In 2001 locally born businessman Scott Bush set out to recreate Templeton Rye, using a recipe originally devised by the Kerkhoff family. Templeton Rye was launched in 2006, and contains an exceptionally high proportion of rye grain in its mash bill.

Tipple to try Templeton – Small Batch Rye Whiskey – 40% abv

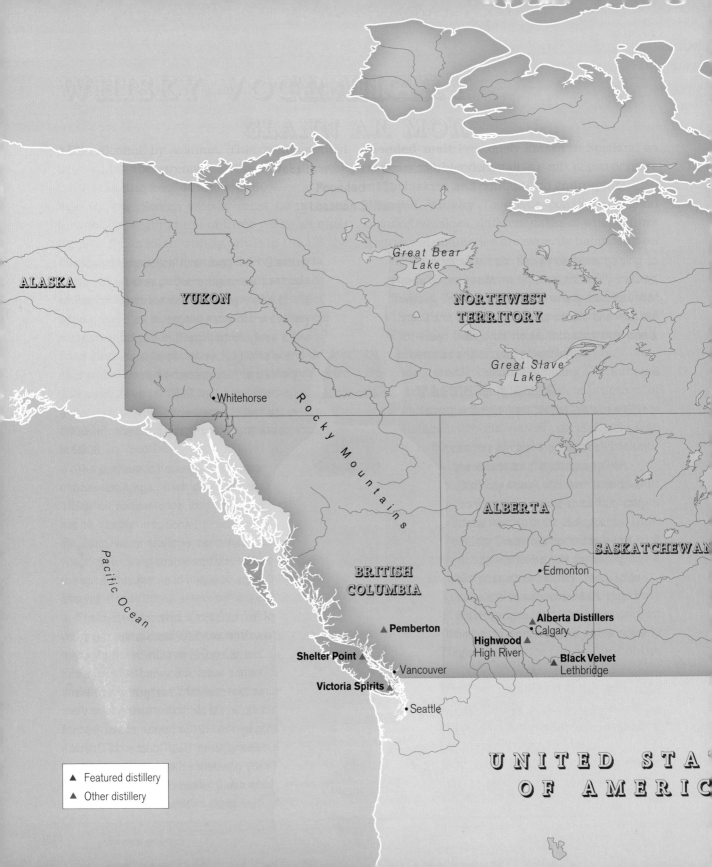

CANADA'S MAIN
DISTILLERIES

Labrador Sea

Baffin Island

Iqaluit•

Hudson Strait

Hudson Bay

Churchill•

MANITOBA

*Lake
Winnipeg*

QUEBEC

NEWFOUNDLAND & LABRADOR

ONTARIO

Winnipeg•

Thunder
Bay•

*Lake
Superior*

Gulf
of
St Lawrence

NEW
BRUNSWICK

Charlottetown•

Glenora
Glenville

Sault Ste Marie•

Québec•

Gibson's Seagram

Fredericton•

Saint John•

*Nova
Scotia*

Atlantic Ocean

OTTAWA•

▲**Valleyfield**

•Montreal

*Lake
Huron*

Canadian Mist
Collingwood

**Still
Waters**

Prescott

•Kingston

Halifax•

Toronto▲

Lake Ontario

Hiram Walker
Windsor

*Lake
Michigan*

London•

▲*Niagara Falls*

Kittling Ridge/Forty Creek
Grimsby

Detroit•▲

*Lake
Erie*

Chicago•

CANADA

Unlike most of its American counterparts across the US border, Canadian whisky uses the Scotch spelling, without the 'e'. Whisky is currently made at some 13 distilleries throughout this vast country, with the bulk being produced by large-scale companies in relatively industrial-style distilleries. The US craft-distilling bug has started to bite in Canada, albeit to a modest extent.

Canadian whisky is usually made from a blend of different grains, notably barley, corn, rye and wheat, with the greater emphasis now on corn. Stylistically it tends to be light, smooth and mellow. The legal definition of blended Canadian whisky rather strangely allows for a percentage of the total to consist of another liquid, which sometimes may be Kentucky Bourbon or even non-alcoholic flavouring. Historically, Canadian whisky is associated particularly with rye, and the terms 'Canadian whisky' and 'rye whisky' are usually taken to refer to the same product in Canada. Distillation occurs in column stills and a minimum maturation period of three years is specified by law.

The commercial Canadian distilling industry really developed during the 19th century, with English, Dutch and German influences, as well as some from across the border in the USA. During the period of US Prohibition (1920–33), Canadian whisky was routinely and illegally 'run' into the USA, and Hiram Walker's distillery at Windsor, Ontario, was conveniently located directly across the Detroit River from Detroit, Michigan. Americans clearly got a taste for Canadian whisky during Prohibition, as it remains notably popular there today, accounting for a significant share of the overall distilled spirits market.

FORTY CREEK

Website **www.fortycreekwhisky.com**
Founded **1992**
Location **Grimsby, Ontario**

The world of Canadian whisky is dominated by multinational players like Diageo, Pernod Ricard and Beam Inc, so independent, small-scale, innovative operations like Glenora and Kittling Ridge Distillery add a welcome touch of diversity to the independent sector.

Kittling Ridge Winery & Distillery was set up in 1992 by winemaker John Hall in a former eaux-de-vie distillery. Located between the backdrop of the Niagara Escarpment and the southern shores of Lake Ontario, at the gateway to Niagara Wine Country, the winery and distillery name is taken from the ridge that creates excellent local growing conditions for vines.

For inspiration John Hall looked to his winemaking background rather than to Canadian whisky-making tradition, installing a 500-litre (110-gallon) copper still and distilling malted barley, corn and rye separately, instead of making up one 'mash bill' of different grains in the more traditional North American manner.

Each spirit type is then matured in casks considered appropriate to its style. Corn, for example, is filled into heavily charred barrels and, in the spirit of innovation, John Hall has even produced his own 'sherry' to fill into casks ultimately used to mature whisky. After maturation of between six and ten years the various types of spirit are blended together

before spending some time 'marrying' in real ex-Sherry casks. They are then bottled as Forty Creek Whisky. Kittling Ridge offers a number of Forty Creek expressions, including Barrel Select and Double Barrel Reserve.

Visitors are welcome at Kittling Ridge during the summer months where they can see wine- and whisky-making, and sample and purchase a wide range of products.

TASTING NOTES

Forty Creek Premium Barrel Select Whisky – 40% abv

Nose Rich, spicy, floral, with spice, walnuts, vanilla and raisins.

Palate Smooth and spicy, with milk chocolate, blackcurrants.

Finish More spice, soft oak.

GIMLI

Website **www.crownroyal.com**
Founded **1968**
Location **Gimli, Manitoba**

Owned by Diageo, Gimli Distillery is located on the western shore of Lake Winnipeg in Manitoba. It is home to Crown Royal, the best-selling Canadian whisky and one of Diageo's flagship North American brands.

Crown Royal was created in 1939, when King George VI and Queen Elizabeth made the first royal tour of Canada by any reigning monarch. To mark the occasion, Samuel Bronfman, president of the mighty Seagram Company, at one time the world's largest distiller of alcoholic beverages, decided to produce a high-quality whisky, which was presented in a crown-shaped bottle, 'dressed' in a royal purple-coloured bag.

Crown Royal was only available in Canada until 1964, but now enjoys international sales. It was produced in Seagram's vast Waterloo Distillery in Ontario until that facility closed in 1992. The Waterloo Distillery had been established in 1857 and was closely associated with Joseph Seagram before the Bronfmans took control in 1928.

Here are a few figures just so you can appreciate the scale of the operation: daily production of Crown Royal uses 10,000 bushels of grain and requires 3.4 million litres

(0.7 million gallons) of water. The whisky is aged in two million barrels, stored in 46 warehouses, over 5 acres of land. The whisky is subsequently blended and bottled in Amherstburg, Ontario.

Gimli produces six versions of Crown Royal, headed by the original De Luxe expression, described by the distiller as having 'a blend of 50 distinct, full-bodied whiskies matured in white oak barrels. Crown Royal has a taste profile defined by smoothness, enhanced by a rich, lingering finish'.

TASTING NOTES

Crown Royal De Luxe – 40% abv

Nose Pears, honey, milk chocolate, summer flowers and ginger.

Palate Cake mixture, vanilla, honey, more spice and some oak notes.

Finish Medium in length, slightly earthy, a little wood.

GLENORA

Website **www.glenoradistillery.com**
Founded **1990**
Location **Glenville, Nova Scotia**

Glenora was the first malt whisky distillery in Canada, and features a pair of Scottish-made copper pot stills. Indeed, the whole establishment is consciously Scottish in appearance, but then Glenora is located in Inverness County, and Nova Scotia is a translation of 'New Scotland'. During the 18th and 19th centuries, this region of Canada was heavily settled by Scottish migrants, so having a Scottish-style distillery seems entirely appropriate.

The Scottish influence has not been without problems, however, since Glenora has fought a long battle with the Scotch Whisky Association over use of the name 'Glen Breton', first applied to a 10-year-old single malt in 2000. The Scotch Whisky Association claims that the 'Glen' prefix is likely to cause confusion among would-be consumers, who might imagine they were buying Scotch. Only if they didn't see the large wording 'Canada's Only Single Malt Whisky' on the label.

Glen Breton Rare 10-year-old is the core bottling, but a novel variant is a 10-year-old which has spent four months being 'finished' in a cask that had formerly held icewine. This was the first single malt to be matured in an ex-icewine cask, and a variety of older expressions have followed the initial 2006 10-year-old 'ice' bottling.

The distillery site also has a pub and a number of chalets, while guided tours are available during the summer months. Not too many Canadian distilleries are visitor-friendly, so make the most of a trip to Glenora if at all possible.

TASTING NOTES

Glen Breton Rare – 10-year-old – 43% abv

Nose Orange, spice, milk chocolate, honey and vanilla, with suggestions of maple and cherries.

Palate Hazelnut and fresh fruits, plus maple and cherry carry over from the nose.

Finish Lengthy, silky, with cooked apple and finally ginger.

HIRAM WALKER

Website **www.canadianclub.com**
Founded **1858**
Location **Windsor, Ontario**

Massachusetts-born entrepreneur Hiram Walker established a distillery near Windsor, Ontario, in 1858, naming the settlement that grew up to serve it 'Walkerville'. The principal product of the distillery was initially called Club Whisky, but was changed to Canadian Club in 1882.

Canadian Club was reputedly drunk by Queen Victoria and Prince Albert, but it was also associated with altogether more unsavoury characters, as it was the principal brand of Canadian whisky smuggled into the US during Prohibition by mobster Al Capone and associates.

The Hiram Walker Distillery was largely rebuilt during 1955, and is Canada's biggest and oldest whisky-making plant. The giant drinks company Pernod Ricard bought it in 2005. With the Canadian Club brand now in the ownership of Beam Inc, Canadian Club is produced under licence by Pernod Ricard, which also distils Gibson's Finest and Wiser's whiskies on the site.

Along with Crown Royal, Canadian Club is the best-known Canadian whisky brand in the world, with global sales in more than 150 countries. There are six different expressions available, ranging from the 6-year-old Premium up to a 30-year-old.

Although visitors are not allowed into the distillery itself, they are more than welcome at the Brand Heritage Center, a striking, turn-of-the-19th-century Italianate structure which houses an impressive collection of fine art. Here the story of Canadian Club and its production is interpreted on film and in tasting sessions.

TASTING NOTES

Canadian Club Whisky – 6-year-old – 40% abv

Nose Cut grass, barley sugar, sweet corn, a hint of aniseed.

Palate Sweet and smooth, with gentle ginger, malt and floral notes.

Finish Floral and medium-sweet. Highly drinkable, but begging to be the base for a cocktail – and actually the whisky used in the first Manhattan!

OTHERS TO TRY

BLACK VELVET

Website www.blackvelvetwhisky.com

Introduced 1951

Location Lethbridge, Alberta

Black Velvet is owned by Constellation Brands Inc and now sells two million cases per year across some 55 countries, making it the second-best-selling Canadian whisky behind Crown Royal. [

Tipple to try Black Velvet Deluxe – 40% abv

GIBSON'S

Website www.gibsonsfinest.ca

Gibson's has its origins in a brand of Pennsylvania rye whiskey, with the name being salvaged after Prohibition by the Canadian distiller, Lewis Rosenstiel, who applied to a new Canadian whiskey, distilled in Quebec. Today Gibson's is owned by distiller William Grant & Sons Ltd of Scotland, and the 12-year-old is produced at the Hiram Walker Distillery.

Tipple to try Gibson's Finest – 12-year-old – 40% abv

SEAGRAM'S

Introduced 1913

Website www.diageo.com

Seagram's in one of the best-known names in Canadian whisky, and indeed, global distilling circles. Seagram's VO was formulated in 1913 for the wedding of the daughter of founder Joseph Seagram, whose distillery was located at Waterloo in Ontario. Seagram's VO is now in the hands of Diageo which makes it at its Valleyfield, Quebec distillery.

Tipple to try Seagram's VO – 40% abv

WISER'S

Website www.wisers.ca

Location Windsor, Ontario

John Philip 'J P' Wiser began to distil in Ontario during 1857, and the modern line-up of Wiser's whiskies is part of the Pernod Ricard portfolio, being produced in that company's Hiram Walker Distillery in Ontario. In addition to the principal Deluxe bottling, there are also 18-year-old and small batch variants.

Tipple to try Wiser's Deluxe – 40% abv

VISITING CANADIAN DISTILLERIES

As well as Glenora (see page 177), Kittling Ridge/Forty Creek (see page 175) and the Canadian Club Brand Heritage Center (see page 178), visitors are also welcome at three other fairly new micro-distilleries, all located in British Columbia:

* Pemberton Distillery
(www.pembertondistillery.ca)
* Shelter Point Distillery
(www.shelterpointdistillery.com)
* Victoria Spirits
(www.victoriaspirits.com)

ICELAND

Norwegian Sea

SWEDEN

Box ▲

NORWAY

Mackmyra ▲

Faeroe Islands

OSLO •

Shetland Islands

Atlantic Ocean

North Sea

DENMARK

Braunstein ▲
Stauning ▲ Copenhagen • ▲ **Hven**

• Hamburg

Lakes ▲ ▲ **Tirril**

UNITED KINGDOM

NETH.

BERLIN

P

Dublin •

IRELAND

• Amsterdam

GERMANY

St George's ▲

Cotswolds ▲

Adnams ▲

London •

Zuidam ▲

BELGIUM

Pradlo ▲ • PRAGUE

Penderyn ▲

The London Distillery Co.

Owl ▲

CZECH REPUBLIC

BRUSSELS

Hicks & Healey ▲

East London Liquor Co.

LUXEMBOURG

• Frankfurt

S

Glann ar Mor ▲

Guillon ▲

Blaue Maus ▲

Slyrs ▲

Warenghem ▲

The Bertrand ▲

PARIS •

Waldviertler ▲

Des Menhirs ▲

FRANCE

SWITZ.

Whisky Castle ▲

AUSTRIA

H

• LJUBLJANA

BERN •

Alps

SLOV. CROA

Bay of Biscay

BOS

• Bordeaux

Corsica

ITALY

MONTEN

• Toulouse

Pyrenees

• ROME

Destilerias y Crianzas Del Whisky

Segovia • ▲

• Barcelona

Sardinia

PORTUGAL

• MADRID

SPAIN

Balearic Islands

Sicily

LISBON •

• Granada

MALTA

M

MAIN DISTILLERIES
IN EUROPE

FINLAND

▲ Old Buck

Teerenpeli ▲
HELSINKI

• TALLINN

ESTONIA

Lake
Omega

Lake
Ladoga

RUSSIAN
FEDERATION

• RIGA

LATVIA

LITHUANIA

VILNIUS

• MINSK

BELORUS

ND

WARSAW

KIEV •

UKRAINE

AKIA

nhof

BARY

MOLDOVA

• CHISINAU

ROMANIA

BELGRADE

BUCHAREST

SERBIA

BULGARIA

O

SKOPJÉ

SOFIA

MACEDONIA

Black Sea

ISTANBUL

ANIA

▲ Tekel

GREECE

ANKARA

ATHENS

TURKEY

▲ Featured distillery

▲ Other distillery

NICOSIA •

CYPRUS

erranean
Sea   Crete

AUSTRIA
WALDVIERTLER ROGGENHOF

Website **www.roggenhof.at**
Founded **1995**
Location **Roggenreith, Austria**

Austria's first commercial distillery, Roggenhof is located in the Waldviertel ('Forest Quarter') area of the country – describing itself 'as mystical as the Scottish Highlands, as green as the Emerald Isles and as lonely as the Canadian woods'. It's surely no mistake, then, that owner and master distiller Johann Haider decided to build his distillery in such a highly wooded area of the country, especially when the spirit he produces is filled predominantly into casks made from fresh Manhartsberger summer oak, grown locally, which impart a distinct vanilla note to the whisky.

The distillery has created its own registered trade name for the whisky produced, and Waldviertler whisky is certainly unlike anything else produced within central Europe. Rye is the primary cereal. It is often toasted until it becomes a darker shade, imparting even more intense flavour compounds into the whisky, which is then matured for between three and 12 years, depending on the age and previous usage of the cask.

The distillery is also home to a tremendous visitors' centre, which aims to demonstrate the uniqueness of the spirit produced on site, compared with those produced in Scotland, Ireland and the USA. Unsurprisingly, around 75,000 people a year call by to see what all the fuss is about, proving that if you create something unusual, quirky and of extremely high quality, people will want to visit.

TASTING NOTES
Waldviertler Original Rye Whisky – 41% abv
Nose Spicy, with cigar notes, some cracked black pepper and a heavy vanilla note.
Palate Sweet and spicy, with pepper, cloves and more tobacco notes.
Finish Medium in length, with notes of oak and vanilla.

THE CZECH REPUBLIC
PRADLO

Website **www.stockspirits.com**
Founded **1989**
Location **West Czechoslovakia (now closed)**

The Pradlo Distillery was a nationalized company in Western Czechoslovakia, producing all manner of spirit-based products. During the 1980s, the distillery decided to start making single-malt whisky. A traditional hammer mill from 1928 was obtained and used to process the locally grown malted barley, and production started in earnest in 1989, with the spirit laid down in casks made exclusively from Czech oak. However, the distillery's shortcomings were written on the wall when, somewhat ironically, the Berlin Wall came down later that year, changing the landscape and the economic structure of the country forever. The project and the whisky were largely forgotten about and the casks remained slumbering away for over 20 years in Czech cellars – until the distillery's new owner, Stock Spirits, unearthed them.

The whisky was considered to be a treasure trove. It was bottled and named Hammerhead – in homage to the noisy hammer mill. Hammerhead is now available as a travel retail exclusive at many of the UK's airports, and a slew of recent awards give this unusual story a happy ending. It remains to be seen whether or not this brief flirtation with whisky distillation will ever return to the Czech Republic, but given the growing level of interest in whisky across Eastern Europe and the popularity of larger, better known brand names, it's hard to bet against someone having another attempt at making a domestic version of the spirit.

TASTING NOTES

Hammerhead – 1989 Czech Vintage Single Malt Whisky – 40.7% abv

Nose An initial note of scented furniture polish, some spiced notes of cloves, dry, oaky cask aromas and some slight rubber/hot tyre notes.

Palate A big, hard-hitting palate initially, with liquorice notes, dried fruit (ripe prunes) and some cedary cigar/tobacco notes, followed by some cream soda.

Finish Medium in length. The spice notes linger, with some residual dried fruit and a hint of burnt caramel.

ENGLAND
ADNAMS

Website **www.adnams.co.uk**
Founded **2010**
Location **Southwold, Suffolk**

When you have a reputation in the English brewing world such as that of Adnams, the idea of diversifying into the world of spirits is bound to be met with a mixture of caution and extreme excitement. Such was the case when, in 2008, the East Anglian brewery, which has been operating in Southwold since 1872, decided to expand into the production of a number of handcrafted and artisanal spirits. However, developing a new distillery on the site of an existing brewery has not been as simple as first thought.

Despite the obvious relationship between producing a great beer base and distilling a whisky, Adnams faced a stiff challenge from the licensing department at HM Customs & Excise, as apparently an archaic rule existed which prohibits brewers from becoming distillers on the same site, and which also requires a pot still to be no smaller than 16 hectolitres.

However, despite these issues, a licence to distil spirits was granted in 2010, and distillery equipment was assembled from across Europe, including some beautiful copper continuous stills, which can be used to produce just about any grain spirit from vodka to gin, and more importantly, whisky.

Technically speaking, the distillery has yet to release a 'whisky' but is midway through a number of very exciting innovations, which

include aging barley vodka, made using Adnams beer in both American and French oak barrels, and distilling wash made from different grains, such as rye and wheat, in addition to malted barley. The distillery has successfully experimented with distilling its already famous Broadside ale, first brewed over 40 years ago, creating 'The Spirit of Broadside' in the process. Despite the addition of hops and a rather short, 12-month aging period, this is the first real step toward what Adnams whisky will actually taste like. The distillery has also announced that the first whisky will be ready for bottling in November 2013, so time will tell as to whether one of the UK's most successful breweries has once again struck liquid gold.

TASTING NOTES

Adnams Copper House North Cove Oak Aged Vodka – 50% abv

Nose Sweet vanilla notes, reminiscent of a grain whisky, with white chocolate and notes of dried coconut.

Palate Clean, malty flavours, with a slightly dry, fruity note, some woody spices and aromatic, creamy vanilla flavours.

Finish Short, with a lingering malt note and drying oak.

ENGLAND
HICKS & HEALEY

Website **www.thecornishcyderfarm.co.uk**
Founded **2000**
Location **Truro, Cornwall**

Aside from some well-made ales and a plethora of deliciously tasty (but alarmingly potent) ciders, Cornwall hasn't stepped too far outside the box when it comes to developing something new in the world of drink – until recently, that is. In 2011 the first very limited edition Cornish whiskey (note the 'e', to distinguish it from other 'English' whiskies) hit the shelves, after quietly slumbering away in the cellars of the Cornish Cyder Farm in Penhallow, a stone's throw away from Newquay on the north coast. The first remarkable fact about this whisky is that it was bottled at seven years old, technically making it the oldest whisky to be matured in England.

The other remarkable fact is that Cornwall can lay claim to a heritage of (largely illicit) distillation dating back some 300 years, although there are no real records to substantiate it.

The new whiskey is a partnership between the St Austell Brewery and Healey's Cyder Farm, which developed from a conversation in 2000, concerning whether a newly installed 1200-litre (265-gallons) copper pot still at the Cyder Farm could be used to distil a whisky as well as its intended apple brandy. As the farm

also had three boreholes producing high-quality water, the next step was to persuade a local farm to grow some Maris Otter barley for the purpose of creating a wash, which is relatively well known in the brewing industry for its distinctive flavour. The resulting spirit was then filled into ex-Bourbon oak casks. The whiskey is made on a batch-by-batch basis and it is unclear when the next one will be available.

TASTING NOTES
Hicks & Healey – Single Malt Cornish Whiskey – 7-year-old cask 29 – 61.3% abv

Nose Spirity on the first nosing, with pine notes, a waft of coconut, wine corks and a slightly musty note, followed by cider vinegar, cinnamon and apple pie. Given time in the glass, the spicy, fruity apple pie notes develop.

Palate Hot and definitely needing a dash of water! Some initial spiced notes evaporating on the tongue, followed by cinnamon/clove and apple pie notes developing.

Finish Short and fruity, with lingering apple peel and lemon zest.

ENGLAND
ST GEORGE'S

Website **www.englishwhisky.co.uk**
Founded **2006**
Location **Roudham, Norfolk**

Perhaps it was fate that the Nelstrop family decided to build a distillery in the heart of their farming homeland, located close to the River Thet in Norfolk. With a 600-year-old heritage in growing and working with grain, this successful dynasty of farmers, led by James Nelstrop and his son Andrew, clearly has a major insight into the key building block of any malt whisky – namely barley. They believe that the best malted barley is grown in Norfolk and, with an abundance of it growing locally, coupled with the quality of Breckland water, the first English distillery for over 100 years took shape in January 2006, with the first spirit running from the copper stills in December 2006.

The distillery is now under the watchful eye of David Fitt, former brewer from the Greene King Brewery in neighbouring Bury St Edmunds. So far the distillery has produced over 1000 casks of both peated and unpeated single malt whisky. The character of the spirit is especially light, with a sweet, malty undertone, and St George's Distillery has been releasing its spirit as 'Chapters', giving enthusiasts a chance to document how the maturation process of different casks has an effect on the resulting whisky. Recent bottlings have included a commemorative release for the Queen's Diamond Jubilee in 2012, as well

as a rather interesting and experimental bottling which mixes Pedro Ximénez Sherry with a little of the distillery's single malt to create an unusual drink!

St George's also offers the option of purchasing a whole single cask of 3-year-old whisky in either 30- or 50-litre (3.5–11-gallon) casks. The distillery tour is worth doing, and for larger groups a special evening excursion around the still house can be arranged, including a sample of St George's latest bottlings.

TASTING NOTES

The English Whisky Co. Chapter 6 – English Single Malt Whisky – 3-year-old – 46% abv

Nose Immediate notes of sweet malty cereal, peanuts and turned earth.
Palate Sweet vanilla cream soda, light and fresh green apple.
Finish Short and malty, with lingering notes of orchard fruit.

FINLAND
TEERENPELI

Website **www.teerenpeli.com**
Founded **2002**
Location **Lahti, Finland**

Visiting the Teerenpeli Distillery in mid-January is an experience. Located in the sleepy town of Lahti, about an hour's train ride from Helsinki, it's easy to be dazzled by the brilliance of the thick snow which covers everything in its path, as well as the bracing nature of the air. Sub-zero temperatures are common across Finland, sometimes lasting until well into April – and with the crisp, clear air, the feel of a -18°C (-0.4°F) gust of wind against the skin is one way to wake up.

The location of the distillery comes as a surprise. It is housed in the basement of a local upmarket restaurant with a number of ski jumps in the background, and it is hard to spot the signs pointing down a nondescript staircase. But what lies beneath the unsuspecting diners is remarkable – the minute space is a hive of activity. Brewing and fermenting equipment, a perfectly proportioned, yet miniature, copper still and what must amount to at least 100 barrels are all laid out perfectly. Such precision is the work and dedication of Anssi Pyysing, a successful restaurateur and brewer who seized the opportunity to become

Finland's first commercial whisky distillery in 2002. The 1500-litre (330-gallon) copper still was manufactured by Forsyths in Scotland, the smallest ever produced by the highly regarded coppersmiths. Teerenpeli prides itself on the fact that every aspect of the whisky production is carried out on site, using 100% locally sourced ingredients. To date, the distillery has bottled several expressions, from 3-year-old up to the current (and oldest) release at 8 years old.

TASTING NOTES

Teerenpeli Single Malt Whisky – 8-year-old – 43% abv

Nose Spicy and rich, with liquorice, spiced apple and lemon sherbet. With time in the glass, a thick, creamy, vanilla ice cream note develops.

Palate Very clean and precise, with hints of charcoal first, then vanilla, green apple peel, malty cereal and slightly spirity notes.

Finish: Short, with zesty lemon and more of the green apple peel.

FRANCE
GLANN AR MOR

Website **www.glannarmor.com**
Founded **1999**
Location **Brittany**

The Celtic connection runs deep with Glann ar Mor, which is based on the northernmost peninsula of France, complete with stunning views of the surrounding isles. In fact, the name of the distillery means 'by the sea' in Breton, which gives a few clues as to the style of the resulting whisky and its distinctly maritime maturation. The distillery was established in 1999, but production on a more commercial scale began in earnest in 2005, with the first 3-year-old whisky released in 2008.

The distillery is housed within some old farm buildings, which date back to 1698. It operates on a truly artisanal nature, using traditional direct-fired stills and worm tub-style condensers, which give more copper contact with the spirit. This results in a heavier style of spirit.

The mild winter climate, coupled with warm summers, mean that the whisky, made from a mixture of unpeated and peated malted barley (the latter bottled under the Kornog label), tends to mature more quickly than casks that are housed further inland, resulting in a higher amount of alcohol loss or a greater 'angels' share'. As well as maturing the whisky in ex-Bourbon casks, Glann ar Mor is also part-matured in casks that have previously held Sauternes wine, helping to develop the sweet, malty notes in the fully matured whisky. The 3-year-old malt whisky bottled under the Glann an Mor label is unpeated and has lots ot lively, fresh fruit notes, including ripe pears, peaches and a touch of vanilla.

TASTING NOTES
Kornog – Single Malt Tourbé Whisky – 46% abv

Nose Has some of the medicinal characteristics of a young Islay malt. Distinctly smoky, with fresh pine-on-a-bonfire, coal dust and some fruity zesty notes nestling in the background.

Palate The smoke continues, with a rich bonfire toffee note developing alongside some peppery, woody spice notes and sweet orchard fruit.

Finish Lengthy, with the smoke becoming more medicinal as the palate dries out.

THE NETHERLANDS
ZUIDAM

Website **www.zuidam.eu**
Founded **1975**
Location **Baarle-Nassau, The Netherlands**

With the origins of Dutch gin (genever) distillation dating back to the 17th century, it's little wonder that the founders of many traditional gin distilleries have found time to make occasional forays into producing extremely high-quality whiskies from the various grains and cereals they have lying around. In fact, there are many similarities between the flavour profile of Dutch whisky and the style of whiskey produced in America, largely due to the huge influence of rye and corn, both of which impart highly unique flavours into a whisky.

Like American whiskey, traditional *oude* or old Dutch genever is made from a fermented mash of grains, which is then distilled up to five times, the final time with aromatic botanicals, mainly juniper berries, from which genever takes its name.

The Zuidam Distillery, which lies about 60km (37 miles) northeast of Antwerp, has been producing exceptional genevers since 1975 and currently lists 10 differently flavoured recipes for this traditional Dutch drink. The idea of producing a whisky with peppery, spicy rye as the key ingredient came about in 1997, but owner Fred van Zuidam's enthusiasm for whisky-making needed to match his reputation for precision,

and it was a further decade before the product reached the shelves. The rye whisky, now bottled as a 5-year-old, has been painstakingly well made. The rye is milled using traditional Dutch windmills – in keeping with the distinctly local feel that Zuidam prides itself on. A range of single malt whiskies, distilled using malted barley and bottled under the Millstone label, is also available, matured up to eight years in French and American oak.

TASTING NOTES

Zuidam – 5-year-old Dutch Rye Whisky – 40% abv

Nose Vanilla, pipe tobacco and notes of spicy, peppery rye. Some cinnamon, a little cardamom and clove notes also develop.

Palate A spicy bitter, sweet palate, with notes of dark chocolate, cinnamon, some unripe banana and fragrant vanilla.

Finish Short, with lingering notes of white pepper and clove.

SWEDEN
MACKMYRA

Website **www.mackmyra.se**
Founded **1999**
Location **Valbo, Sweden**

There's something to be said for ideas that begin life when you're out on the piste, which is where the initial embers of the Mackmyra Distillery began to glow as eight friends met at a mountain lodge in 1998 for a skiing holiday. The story goes that each had brought with them a bottle of whisky for the host and that the topic of making whisky had come up – in particular they discussed why no one had ever made a Swedish whisky before, given the climate and abundance of quality water.

After developing over 170 recipes for a malt whisky, the first spirit from the then very much experimental distillery began to flow from the small stills, and by 2002 an integrated distilling operation had begun, with a new full-sized distillery built in the densely wooded area of Valbo about 180km (112 miles) north of Stockholm. Initial bottlings were met with widespread approval from the whisky community and the new Mackmyra Distillery flourished, beginning to focus on the key aspects of what made its whisky different. The use of roasted Swedish oak has added a unique spiciness to the whisky, and the distillery has started to use Swedish peat from Karingmossen, an area near to the

distillery, which is laden with juniper twigs, giving the smoke a distinctly aromatic style.

In 2008 Mackmyra released its long anticipated First Edition, which typifies the developing house style of the distillery and it has already won numerous international awards. Recently, Mackmyra embarked on perhaps its most ambitious plan to date, with building work beginning on the Mackmyra Whisky Village in the nearby forests of Gävle. The new facility will allow Mackmyra almost to quadruple its whisky production.

TASTING NOTES
Mackmyra – The First Edition – 46.1% abv

Nose A spicy, woody note develops first, with freshly cut pine, some vanilla sweetness and a touch of dried apricot and raisins.

Palate A distinctly woody overtone hits first, but no dryness, leading the way for gentle, soft fruit notes (plums and pears), some light floral honey and a hint of clove.

Finish Long and dry, with dried fruits and a touch of citrus.

WALES
PENDERYN DISTILLERY

Website **www.welsh-whisky.co.uk**
Founded **2000**
Location **Brecon Beacons, Wales**

With its Celtic origins, Wales has had an undeniably lengthy association with whisky or *wysgi* as it is written in Welsh, which it is said dates back to the 4th century. The first commercial distillation of a Welsh whisky can be traced back to Pembrokeshire in 1705. This distillery was once owned by the family of one of the founding fathers of American whiskey, Evan Williams, who emigrated from Wales to the USA to become one of the very first distillers in Kentucky.

The area surrounding the Brecon Beacons provides not only an abundant mineral-enriched water source for making whisky, but also a climate similar to that of the Scottish Highlands. Penderyn is the first Welsh distillery for over 100 years and has the honour of being the only current producer of a Welsh malt whisky.

The distillery first produced a whisky in 2004, taking its malty wash from the Brains Brewing Company, based in Cardiff. Penderyn produces roughly one cask of spirit per day, which is an incredibly small amount, considering how popular the whisky has become in the UK. The distillery has also developed a innovative copper pot still created by Dr David Faraday, a direct descendant of the legendary Victorian scientist Sir Michael Faraday. As a result, a high-strength new-make spirit of around 92% can be produced using just one still, as opposed to the traditional two still set-up in Scotland and the triple distillation used in the production of Irish whiskey.

Most Penderyn whisky is matured in ex-Bourbon casks but then transferred for a short time into much larger vessels: Portuguese barriques. These have previously held sweet, fortified Madeira wine, which helps to give the house style of whisky a sweet, fruity characteristic. Other Penderyn releases come in limited editions, including peated versions, which see the whisky finished in casks previously containing peated Scotch whiskies and the more traditional Sherry wood finishes.

TASTING NOTES

Penderyn – Madeira-finished single malt Welsh whisky – 46% abv

Nose Notes of sweet, fruity wine, rich toffee, cinnamon pastry and a touch of leather.

Palate Fresh and zesty but balanced by a lovely oiliness and flavours of dried fruits, creamy fudge, apricots and a hint of oak.

Finish Lengthy, with notes of well-rounded fruit and malt, followed by an oaky dryness.

ABOVE: Checking the casks soon to be filled with the new spirit at Penderyn Distillery, Wales.

OTHERS TO TRY

BLAUE MAUS DISTILLERY

Website www.fleischmann-whisky.de

Founded 1980

Location Eggolsheim, Germany

The Blaue Maus (Blue Mouse) Distillery has been producing whisky since 1983 and built a new distillery in 2012. The first commercial whisky was released in 1996 and there is a 25-year-old among the impressive range of single malts. Well worth seeking out.

Tipple to try Blaue Maus – Single Cask Malt Whisky – 40% abv

THE OWL DISTILLERY

Website www.belgianwhisky.com

Founded 2004

Location Grâce-Hollogne, Belgium

Etienne Bouillon is the owner of the Owl Distillery, which started out as a dream back in 1993. He has drawn on his in-depth knowledge of traditional fermentation techniques, as well as a successful stint spent on Islay, studying distillation under the Bruichladdich Distillery's master craftsman, Jim McEwan.

Tipple to try Belgian Owl – 3-year-old Belgian single malt whisky – 46% abv

SLYRS DISTILLERY

Website www.slyrs.de

Founded 1928

Location Schliersee, Germany

A short distance from the Austrian border, the Slyrs Distillery is also only a stone's throw from the beautiful Schliersee lake, which nestles in the middle of the Bavarian Alps. It is a location extremely important to the distillery's owner,

Florian Stetter, a skilled brewer who clearly understands the importance of combining pure spring water with quality malted barley to make a perfectly balanced whisky. He has been producing whisky since 1999, and one of the most unique aspects to his production process is the drying of the locally grown malted barley, which is partly smoked above fires fuelled by beech wood, imparting a sweet, aromatic flavour to the mash. The range also includes a 12-year-old and a new Sauternes cask finish.

Tipple to try Slyrs – 2007 – 3-year-old Bavarian single malt whisky – 43% abv

WHISKY CASTLE DISTILLERY

Website www.whisky-castle.com

Founded 2002

Location Elfingen, Switzerland

Ruedi Käser is the owner of this promising distillery, north of Zurich. He has been experimenting with different grains and a wide range of different cask types; one notable wood is chestnut, deemed to be outside the Scotch Whisky Association's rules (which specify only oak can be used to mature whisky in Scotland). However, Whisky Castle is not bound by any such rules and Käser has created an appealing range of different flavours, occasionally bottled under the Castle Hill label, which include whiskies from beech-smoked barley, spelt and rye whiskies, Port cask finishes, the intriguingly titled 'Girl's Choice', which is a lighter style whisky, matured in white wine casks, and 'Edition Cheese' (actually named after Kaser whose name translates as 'Cheese'.

Tipple to try Castle Hill Double Wood Swiss Whisky – 43% abv

ASIA

The consumption of whisky across Asia has increased rapidly over the past five years, with China, Taiwan and South Korea all developing a huge thirst for predominantly blended Scotch whiskies, such as Johnnie Walker and Chivas Regal. In addition, many Scotch whisky companies are now producing exclusive limited-edition expressions specifically for sale in Asian markets.

INDIA

With a drinking scene as diverse as its culture, India is unquestionably one of the global hotspots when it comes to whisky. Surprisingly, India currently stands as the largest whisky-drinking nation in the world, but what is actually being enjoyed on a grand scale is a far cry from the whisky we know and love in Europe.

Most Indian whisky is made in a completely different way from the traditional barley-based spirit drunk in the West. Instead of grain, molasses is fermented and distilled, then coloured, to resemble a more traditional whisky. The process has more in common with the production of rum, but brands of molasses whisky such as Bagpiper, 8pm and McDowell's are enormously successful in India, selling millions of cases each year. Under the guidelines set out by the Scotch Whisky Association, it is unlikely that Indian molasses whisky will be available in the UK.

Scottish blended whiskies such as Cutty Sark, Johnnie Walker Black Label and Chivas Regal have gained a foothold in many of India's most exclusive bars, but their popularity is still extremely limited due to the high taxes levied on imported Scotch whisky. However, one Indian company, Amrut, has been distilling a whisky in the more traditional style and its launch kicked off in Scotland in 2004, several years before the brand was released in India.

Long before Amrut began to garner international interest, the Kasauli Distillery (established in the 1820s by Edward Dyer, high in the Himalayas) was producing a single malt whisky using distillation equipment imported from Scotland. Solan No 1 was one of India's most popular whiskies before the advent of the molasses-based whiskies that reign supreme today. Another interesting player is the Sikkim Distillery (founded in 1954 in the foothills of the Himalayas), which has carved out a niche with several of its malt-based whiskies, distilled using spring water from the region. Hot on its heels comes the John Distillery, which in 2012 released its first single cask whisky into the UK.

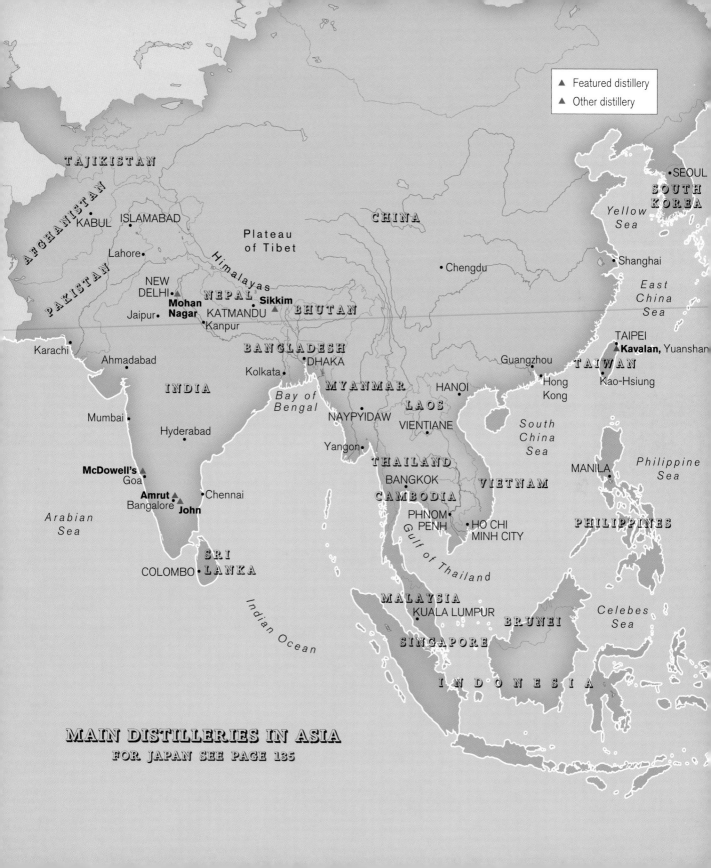

TAJIKISTAN

AFGHANISTAN

KABUL

ISLAMABAD

PAKISTAN

Lahore

Karachi

Mohan
NEW
DELHI
Nagar
Jaipur
KATMANDU
Kanpur

Himalayas

Plateau
of Tibet

NEPAL **Sikkim**

BHUTAN

CHINA

• Chengdu

• Shanghai

SEOUL

SOUTH
KOREA

Yellow
Sea

East
China
Sea

TAIPEI
▲ **Kavalan,** Yuanshan

BANGLADESH
DHAKA

Kolkata

INDIA

Ahmadabad

Mumbai

Hyderabad

Bay of
Bengal

MYANMAR

NAYPYIDAW

Yangon

LAOS

VIENTIANE

Guangzhou

Hong
Kong

TAIWAN

Kao-Hsiung

Philippine
Sea

HANOI

South
China
Sea

McDowell's
Goa

Amrut ▲
Bangalore **John**

Chennai

Arabian
Sea

SRI
LANKA

COLOMBO

Indian Ocean

THAILAND

BANGKOK

CAMBODIA

PHNOM
PENH

Gulf
of Thailand

VIETNAM

HO CHI
MINH CITY

MANILA

PHILIPPINES

MALAYSIA
KUALA LUMPUR

SINGAPORE

BRUNEI

Celebes
Sea

INDONESIA

MAIN DISTILLERIES IN ASIA
FOR JAPAN SEE PAGE 135

▲ Featured distillery
▲ Other distillery

INDIA
AMRUT

Website **www. amrutwhisky.co.uk**
Founded **1948**
Location **Bangalore, India**

The Amrut Distillery was founded in 1948, and since then has produced a variety of spirits, including vodka and rum. In 2001, while studying in the UK, Rick Jagdale, Executive Director of Amrut, decided to test the water with the company's very first single malt, made from home-grown Indian barley. The whisky was deemed a hit, and in 2004 Amrut single malt whisky was launched on the international market. It was to take a further five years before the domestic market woke up to embrace the whisky.

The aging conditions between India and Scotland could not be more different. Amrut matures most of its whisky 915m (3000ft) above sea level in Bangalore. The temperature there in summer reaches 40°C (104°F), with the coolest period averaging around 20°C (68°F), so the amount of alcohol evaporation from the casks is around six to seven times greater than that experienced in Scotland. As a result, it is impractical to age the whisky for any more than six years.

Amrut has released several standard bottlings, including a peated single malt (using Scottish barley) and several cask-strength editions. One of the distillery's most popular releases, Amrut Fusion, has already won a handful of awards internationally for

its innovative recipe, using Indian and a slightly peated Scottish barley.

TASTING NOTES
Amrut Fusion Single Malt Whisky – 50% abv

Nose A big-hitting nose of dark chocolate, wafts of peat and pepper, with some lighter vanilla notes developing as the aromas open up.

Palate An initial oaky dryness leading into malted dark chocolate, a big swathe of peat smoke, some black coffee notes, dried apricots, raisins and cinnamon.

Finish Long-lasting, with the spices, peat smoke and dark chocolate notes coating the mouth, refusing to let go.

TAIWAN
KAVALAN

Website **www. kavalanwhisky.com**
Founded **2005**
Location **Yuanshan, Taiwan**

The popularity of whisky across the whole of the Pacific region has created an exciting arena for domestic distillers. Here you will find a whisky based on the traditional methods developed and refined in Scotland, but one that has been fine-tuned for the demands of a new audience, whose members are more liberal about how they view the spirit and how they drink whisky.

Kavalan Taiwanese whisky, produced by the King Car Group in the town of Yuanshan, is a prime example of how far the image of 'world whisky' has now come.

Far from being a small, experimental 'tip of the hat' in the direction of Scotland, the distillery, built in 2005 and fully opened to the public in December 2008, is one of the largest distilling operations in the world. It produces nearly six million bottles a year, with a capacity for a further three million. The company worked closely with some highly respected names in the world of whisky production in order to understand the complexities of producing a consistently high-quality spirit, including Dr Jim Swan, the man behind the developing success story of Welsh whisky Penderyn. The distillery now receives around one million visitors a year, showing just how much an impact Kavalan has had, not only on the domestic market of whisky-drinkers, but also right across Asia, including China.

As with Indian whisky, the warm, humid conditions that surround the distillery are higher than those in Scotland, so the aging process is significantly escalated. As a result, Kavalan is predominantly bottled as a 3-year-old whisky, using a mixture of first-fill ex-Bourbon, Sherry, wine and Port casks.

A word of warning for the sceptics out there: a recent blind whisky tasting held on Burns Night in Edinburgh for a number of eminent whisky writers and journalists included several highly regarded Scotch whiskies and a sample of Kavalan. Guess which whisky unexpectedly came out on top?

TASTING NOTES
Kavalan Solist – Sherry cask release – 58.7% abv

Nose Aromas of dried fruits steeped in thick, sweet Sherry, woody spices (cinnamon and clove), some lighter citrus notes, a hint of marzipan and some dark chocolate.

Palate Laden with dried fruit flavours, including figs, dates and raisins, with some orange zest and sugared almonds.

Finish Lengthy, with a wonderful array of dried fruit notes and some drying oak notes.

SOUTH AFRICA

Anyone doubtful about the popularity of whisky in South Africa only needs to take a seat at the splendidly appointed Bascule bar in the Cape Grace Hotel in Cape Town to realize that whisky is seriously hot property there. The bar has over 400 different malts and blends from just about every whisky-producing country and its popularity has never been greater in the country.

But what is surprising is the fact that South Africa's domestic whisky production has a legacy dating back a little over a century. The James Sedgwick Distillery, first established in the late 19th century, has in more recent years been revered by numerous whisky writers and journalists for its innovative approach to making great whisky – and given the popularity of the fabulous Cape wines it is surely high time that South African whisky received its share of international attention.

Drayman's Brewery, near Pretoria, became South Africa's second whisky distillery in 2006. The micro-distillery operates an interesting 'solera' system at the aging stage, whereby 18-year-old whisky is married together with whisky as young as 3-year old in larger casks before being transferred to smaller casks.

JAMES SEDGWICK

Website **www.threeshipswhisky.co.za**
Founded **1886**
Location **Wellington, South Africa**

James Sedgwick Distillery was established around 1886 in the foothills of the Bain's Kloof Pass, and since then it has been run by just six managers. In 2011 *Whisky Magazine* acknowledged that it was one of the most innovative whisky operations in the world.

The distillery is named after Captain James Sedgwick, originally of Yorkshire descent and formally of the British East India Company, who settled in the Cape in 1850 and established a prosperous business, dealing in liquor and tobacco. After his death, his sons established the distillery on the banks of the Berg River, as well as providing the local residents with imported whisky from Scotland. Whether or not the local population developed a taste for whisky, the Boer wars later finished off any interest in the spirit.

In 1977 the distillery launched Three Ships, a blend of South African and Scotch whiskies, whose popularity highlighted the possibilities for a successful home-produced whisky, and since that time James Sedgwick hasn't looked back.

Under the stewardship of current manager Andy Watts (who,

coincidentally, hails from the same area of Yorkshire as Sedgwick), the distillery's next pioneering break was the release of Three Ships Bourbon Cask Finish in 2005 (the distillery's first blended whisky, which is made from 100% South African grain, and malt whiskies, to receive additional maturation in ex-Bourbon casks).

The flagship whisky is Three Ships 10-year-old single malt, which has won international awards for its smooth, smoky, yet distinctively unique flavour, something the pioneering Captain would no doubt be delighted to hear about.

TASTING NOTES

Three Ships – Single Malt Whisky –10-year-old – 43% abv

Nose A very alluring, soft and aged peat gently wafts in first, almost reminiscent of a lightly peated Islay malt.

Palate Initially sweet and fragrant, rather like a sweetened Earl Grey tea; creamy cereal, soft red summer fruits and chocolate-covered hazelnuts.

Finish The sweetness lingers and the cereal notes coat the tongue.

AUSTRALIA'S DISTILLERIES

Featured distillery ▲
Other distillery ▲

Arafura Sea

Timor Sea

Cape York

Darwin

Gulf of Carpentaria

Hoochery ▲
Kununurra

Great Barrier Reef

Cairns

Coral Sea

Townsville

Indian Ocean

Broome

NORTHERN TERRITORY

QUEENSLAND

Lake Mackay

Alice Springs

△ Uluru (Ayers Rock)

WESTERN AUSTRALIA

Lake Eyre

Toowoomba• •Brisbane

SOUTH AUSTRALIA

NEW SOUTH WALES

Perth •

•Newcastle

•Sydney

Great Southern ▲ Albany

Great Australian Bight

▲ **Southern Coast**
Adelaide

•CANBERRA

Australian Capital Territory

VICTORIA

Geelong •Melbourne

▲ **Timboon**

▲ **Bakery Hill**

Bass Strait

TASMANIA

HOBART

Inset (Tasmania)

Marrawah •

Hellyers Road
Burnie
•Devonport

Tasman Sea

Launceston

Nant ▲
Bothwell

New Town ▲▲ HOBART
Tasmania ▲▲ **Sullivans Cove**
Lark **Old Hobart**

AUSTRALIA

For a continent perhaps known better for its sporting endeavours, indigenous (and fairly unusual) fauna, several brands of lager and, of course, its wine, it will no doubt come as a surprise that Australia is currently one of the most exciting whisky-producing nations in the world. The growth of micro-distillation, particularly in Tasmania, has given rise to a rich seam of well-crafted whisky. Historically, Tasmania has been the hub of whisky distillation in Australia since 1822, when the first distillery was established on the island, then called Van Diemen's Land. By 1824, 16 distilleries were operating, but their death knell was abruptly sounded a little over a decade later, when distilling was made illegal and a once-thriving distillery scene fell silent. Cue a 150-year wait until a new breed of Tasmanian distiller felt it was high time to fire up the copper stills once again.

BAKERY HILL

Website **www.bakeryhilldistillery.com.au**
Founded **1998**
Location **Boroondara, Victoria**

Bakery Hill is the best-known distillery on the Australian mainland. It is the playground of an impassioned Aussie gent, David Baker, who has been distilling whisky in his small copper still since 2008. The distillery predominantly uses local barley, which is well known for its high quality and excellent alcohol yield, but on occasion peated malt, imported from the UK, has been used to produce a more experimental whisky.

Each batch of whisky is bottled from single casks, rather than blended batches, which gives each of the releases an air of exclusivity – something, which aficionados of the growing Australian whisky scene are relishing. The whisky is predominantly matured in ex-Bourbon casks, but for one of the distillery's top releases, Double Wood, additional French wine casks are used, giving the already light and fruity whisky a more intense spicy, citrussy edge. Recently, the distillery has been expanded and 1000-litre (220-gallon) batches of wash are double distilled in the single Bakery Hill Pot still, which will be operating nearly 24/7 to meet demand for the whisky.

Baker has also been producing a whisky from malted barley smoked with Australian peat, which he describes as being 'intense, without being over the top, with notes of toffee honeycomb, with a suggestion of peat saltiness'. When he's not manning

the stills, Baker has found time to lead whisky enthusiasts through a regularly run intensive seminar about whisky production, including, of course, several expressions of his own brilliant whisky.

The distillery benefits from the temperate climate in Melbourne, the warmer temperatures aiding a faster aging in the oak casks that Baker has been experimenting with, helping to produce a characterful spirit with plenty of bite and spice.

Bakery Hill also uses smaller casks (ranging from 50–100 litres/11–22 gallons) which helps maturation occur faster, thanks to the greater surface to wood contact.

TASTING NOTES

Bakery Hill – Australian Cask Strength Classic Single Malt – 60.5% abv

Nose Initial notes of sourdough mix, malty breakfast cereal and some creamy vanilla notes. Given time, some dark demerara sugar notes develop, along with some lighter orchard fruits.

Palate Powerful, with more malted cereal notes, some sweet marzipan, toasted oats and a few spicy undertones. With water, the sweet notes begin to melt into the mouth, with the release of more aromatic vanilla.

Finish Lively and medium in length, with lingering liquorice notes and a return of the toasted oats.

LARK

Website **www. larkdistillery.com.au**

Founded **1992**

Location **Hobart, Tasmania**

Tasmania has been going through a revival of distilling – helped by the laws concerning building distilleries being relaxed, the current worldwide interest in craft distillation and the huge popularity of Australian whiskies across the UK and Europe, thanks to their continued successes in international spirit competitions. Leading the Tasmanian charge is the Lark Distillery, under the watchful eye of Australian distiller extraordinaire Bill Lark, who is considered to be the father of modern Australian whisky distillation, since building his distillery in 1992. Lark changed the landscape of distilling since the last Tasmanian distillery closed in the 1830s by helping bring major changes to the legislation regarding the minimum size of still needed.

Looking at Tasmania's landscape, it is easy to see why the region is so ideal. Not only is the temperate climate perfect for maturing whisky, it also has a wonderfully clean and abundant water supply, as well as a rich agricultural system producing some world-class barley.

Tasmania also has its own highland peat, which Lark has used to great effect in its flagship bottlings of 5-year-old whisky. This is drawn from separate single casks, maintaining the artisanal nature of the distillery.

Making Lark whisky is not a labour of love reserved for Bill Lark. The distillery has truly become a family affair, with Bill's daughter Kirsty winning a scholarship from the Institute of Brewers and Distillers, making her one of the youngest female distillers in the world.

The distillery offers guided tours where visitors can learn about the history of Tasmanian distilling as well as Lark's production techniques.

TASTING NOTES

**Lark – Tasmanian Single Malt Whisky –
small cask aged –
58% abv**

Nose Overly malty notes initially, with some woody spice, a hint of aromatic and oily peat and some sweet vanillas.

Palate The malty notes continue in the mouth, with some creamy vanilla ice cream, some stewed apple and ripe plum notes and drying oak.

Finish Lengthy spiced notes, with a delicate sweet vanilla emerging at the end.

SULLIVANS COVE

Website www.tasmaniadistillery.com.au
Founded 1994
Location Cambridge, Tasmania

Hot on the heels of Tasmania's first modern distillery, Lark came Sullivans Cove. The distillery was originally located on the banks of the River Derwent in Hobart, Australia's second-oldest city. After nearly a decade of producing whisky there, the distillery moved to the village of Cambridge, where it continues to produce a range of three different single malt whiskies, as well as a gin and vodka.

The output is fairly small compared to many other international craft distilleries, with around 120 casks per year, but for Sullivans Cove, quality is more important than quantity, and the whisky has been picking up international awards since 2005.

The barley used in the distillation process is all grown locally in Tasmania. Like many of the other artisanal distilleries in Tasmania, the different whiskies come in batches from single casks, using a variety of different wood types, including French wine, Port and ex-Bourbon. Finally, each bottle is filled and labelled by hand.

With a mission statement that reads 'Distilled with Conviction' it's no surprise that the hard work of such a small operation

is beginning to pay off and the whisky is now exported to a number of markets.

Recently, Sullivans Cove picked up perhaps the ultimate accolade for a small-time distillery – The World's Best Single Malt at the World Whiskies Awards in 2014 for its French Oak Cask release. The distillery also offers enthusiasts the chance to purchase individual casks of Sullivans Cove whisky in either 2- or 4.5-litre sizes, which is perhaps the ultimate home whisky experience for the self-confessed enthusiast.

TASTING NOTES

Sullivans Cove – Australian Double Cask Single Malt Whisky – 40% abv

Nose Initial wafts of cereal, some malted brown bread and some very light fruit and floral notes, with apricot skins.

Palate Light on the palate with mild citrus notes, some sweet cereal and vanilla.

Finish Short, with lingering malt notes and some sweet fruit.

WHISKY VOCABULARY

ABV Alcohol by volume. This measurement determines the strength of the whisky in the bottle, ranging from 40% to over 60%.

Age By law, Scotch whisky must be matured in wood for a minimum of three years, as must Irish and Canadian whisky, while in the US the minimum legal requirement for bonding is two years. Most reputable single malt whiskies are matured for at least eight years, and if a blended whisky carries an age statement, it must refer to the youngest whisky in the blend.

Alembic A traditional distillation device, comprised of two parts: one to heat and vaporize a liquid and the other to convert the vapour back to a more concentrated liquid form.

Angels' share A distillers' term for maturation losses. In Scotland, some 2% of all maturing whisky evaporates through the porous oak casks each year, but in hotter and more humid climates, for example in India, the losses may be much greater.

Barley The principal raw material used in the whisky-making process in Scotland, Ireland and Japan. *See* also Malting.

Barrel Sometimes used as a generic term for a cask, but in the Scotch whisky industry a barrel is specifically a cask with an approximate capacity of 180 litres (40 gallons).

Blend Many countries produce blended whiskies, using a variety of cereals, some malted and some unmalted. A blended Scotch whisky is one made from a mixture of grain and malt spirit. Theoretically, the higher the malt content, the better the blend, although this is not always the case. Much depends on the quality and age of grain and malt whiskies used.

Blended malt Previously known in Scotland as 'vatted malt', blended malt is a mix of two or more malt whiskies, and contains no grain spirit.

Blended whisky To create consistently good blended whiskies, different casks of whisky from a variety of distilleries are expertly balanced by a master blender to create the perfect recipe.

Bourbon Classic American style of whiskey, which must by law be made from a mash of not less than 51% corn grain. The spirit is matured in new, white oak barrels that have previously been charred or thermally degraded.

Bourbon, small batch Following the success of Scotch single malt whiskies, a number of American distillers have developed the concept of small-batch Bourbons, namely carefully chosen, exclusive bottlings of their finest whiskeys, which generally command premium prices.

Brewing The process that follows malting in the production of malt whisky, and consists of mashing and fermentation, though in Irish distilling circles it is usually taken to mean just mashing, with fermentation being considered a separate, successive operation.

Butt The second-largest size of cask regularly used by the whisky industry for maturation purposes. The butt contains approximately 500 litres (110 gallons), twice the amount of the hogshead.

Campbeltown The smallest of the generally recognized Scotch whisky regions, now boasting just three distilleries. Campbeltown is located on the Kintyre Peninsula in Argyllshire.

Cask A generic term applied to containers of varying capacity in which spirit is stored during maturation.

Cask strength Whisky sold at cask strength has not been diluted to the standard 40% or 43% abv, but is bottled at the strength at which it leaves the cask. This varies depending on the age of the whisky, as older whiskies lose considerable strength during extended maturation.

Chill-filtering The process of refrigerating whisky and finely filtering it to ensure it retains its clarity in the bottle and when water is added by the consumer. Many connoisseurs consider that chill-filtration detracts from the character of the whisky in subtle ways, and a number of bottlers now make a virtue of not chill-filtering their products and will state so on the label.

Classic Malts collection A line-up of six single malts chosen and marketed by United Distillers in 1988 to represent the stylistic diversity of the various single malt whisky-producing regions of Scotland. United Distillers was taken over by Diageo when that company was formed in 1997. The six single malts are Cragganmore, Dalwhinnie, Glenkinchie, Lagavulin, Oban and Talisker.

Clearic New-make spirit, straight from the still. Clear in colour and high in strength, this was a popular drink with distillery workers when the practice of dramming was still extant.

Coffey still Patented in 1830 by former Irish Inspector-General of Excise Aeneas Coffey, this still revolutionized whisky-making. Also known as the column, continuous or patent still, it allowed large quantities of spirit to be distilled much more quickly than in the traditional pot still, paving the way for the development of blended Scotch whisky. Essentially, the stills used in Scottish grain distilleries, in Ireland and in most US distilleries are very similar to Coffey's original, consisting of two tall 'columns', the first being the analyser, which separates the spirit from the wash, while the second, known as the rectifier, concentrates the spirit to a greater degree.

Column still *See* Coffey still

Condenser An important piece of distillery equipment, used to convert the hot spirit vapour back into liquid form, by using cooling water. *See* Shell & Tube and Worm.

Continuous still *See* Coffey still

Corn The cereal at the heart of most North American whiskies, notably Bourbon. 'Corn whiskey' is also a generic term for a rural, unsophisticated form of US whiskey, which has strong associations with 'moonshining' and is considered to improve very little with aging. Once a staple of Scottish grain whisky, corn has now largely been replaced by wheat, as it is considerably less expensive to purchase and gives a higher yield of alcohol.

Cutting During distillation, the stillman, or stillhouse computer programme, 'cuts' from collecting foreshots to the middle cut or heart of the run, before then cutting back to collect feints (see page 206). 'Cut points' are crucial to the character of the spirit produced, and every distillery has its own formula for them, based on alcoholic strength and/or timescale.

Dark grains Cubes or pellets of high-protein animal feed produced by treating pot ale with dried draff. Pot ale evaporates into a dark brown syrup, hence the name.

Deluxe A term usually applied to blended whiskies, and one with no legal definition. Any blended whisky, regardless of quality or age, may be labelled as 'deluxe', although the consumer would expect a reputable deluxe whisky at least to contain a higher proportion of malt to grain and/or embrace older whiskies than a 'standard' blend.

Distillation Distillation follows the process of fermentation in whisky-making, and is characteristic of all spirit production. During distillation the alcohol is separated from the wash by heating it in stills. Alcohol boils at a lower temperature than water and is driven off as vapour, leaving behind the water. It is subsequently condensed back into liquid form.

Draff The spent grist left behind in the mash tun after the mashing process has been completed. Being high in protein it makes excellent cattle food, and is either sold off to farmers in its 'raw' state or converted into dark grains.

Dram A measure of Scotch whisky of unspecified size, although in some Scottish bars a 'dram' is taken to mean a large or double whisky. 'Dramming' in distilleries was the semi-official practice of offering employees amounts of spirit at regular intervals during the working day. The advent of drink-driving laws and health and safety legislation finally ended the custom.

Dunnage Traditional warehousing for whisky maturation, which consists of a stone or brick building, ideally with an ash- and earth-covered floor. Casks are stacked no more than three high on wooden runners. Most experts believe such warehousing creates the optimum maturation conditions for Scotch malt whisky.

Esters Fruity flavours found in new-make spirit, predominantly developed during the fermentation period.

Expression A particular variant of a brand, e.g. Johnnie Walker Blue Label is an expression of Johnnie Walker.

Feints The final flow of distillation, produced after the middle cut has been collected. The feints consist of the heavier compounds and less volatile components of the low wines, such as fusel oil. Although not desirable in large quantities, a small amount of feints contributes to the overall character of the whisky being made.

Fermentation Along with mashing, fermentation is part of the brewing process of whisky production. Yeast is added to the wort in the fermenters or washbacks and the result is wash. This is the first time during whisky-making that alcohol has been produced.

Fillings New-make spirit, once filled into casks.

Finish The practice of 'finishing' whisky is a relatively new phenomenon. Essentially, after a substantial period of maturation in its original cask, the whisky is transferred into a different one, which has previously held another alcoholic drink, for a period of finishing. This provides variations on the distillery's 'house' style. The most common finishes feature various styles of Sherry, but others include rum, Madeira, Burgundy and Port.

Foreshots The initial flow of distillation, produced before the middle cut is collected. It contains an excess of acids, aldehydes and esters, but, like feints, a small quantity of foreshots contributes to the character of the whisky. As with feints, the amount present depends on the distillery's 'cut points'.

Grain In Scotland grain whisky is distilled principally from wheat or corn in continuous stills. Although a number of single and blended grain whiskies are available, nearly all grain whisky distilled is used for blending.

Green malt At the point when germination is halted during malting, the barley is referred to as green malt.

Grist Ground, malted barley ready for mashing.

Heart of the run *See* Middle cut.

Highball or hi-ball Whisky and soda, as popularized in Japan.

Highland One of the principal regions of Scotch malt whisky production, the Highland area lies north of a theoretical line that runs between Greenock on the Firth of Clyde in the west and Dundee in the east. Although geographically part of the Highland region, Speyside is usually considered to merit its own classification.

Hogshead Often colloquially referred to as a 'hoggie', the hogshead is a common size of whisky cask, having an approximate capacity of 250 litres (55 gallons).

Irish By law, Irish whiskey (as it is customarily spelled) has to be distilled and matured in Ireland for a minimum of three years. Although Irish pot still whiskeys (usually using malted barley and unmalted cereal) are still made, most of today's available Irish whiskeys are blends of pot still whiskey and continuous still grain whiskeys.

Islay An Inner Hebridean island off the west coast of Scotland famed for its distinctive malt whiskies. Islay currently has eight working distilleries, and at their most extreme, Islay malts are characterized by brine, peat and iodine notes. In recent years Islays have developed a cult following among malt whisky-drinkers.

Kiln During malting the green malt is dried in a kiln in order to prevent germination proceeding too far and using up the starch essential for the production of alcohol. During kilning, peat smoke may be introduced to flavour the malt, though the principal fuel used in the kiln is coke.

Lowland One of the principal whisky-producing regions of Scotland, the Lowland area has suffered from many distillery closures over the years, and now just five Lowland distilleries are in operation. Stylistically, Lowlands are light-bodied, gentle whiskies, ideal as aperitifs.

Low wines In the pot-still whisky-making process, low wines are the product of the first distillation in the wash still. They are impure and weak, and a second distillation in the spirit or low wines still is subsequently necessary.

Lyne arm or pipe also known as a lye arm or lye pipe, this is the pipe connecting the head of the still to the condenser or worm. The angle of the lyne arm has a significant effect on the style of spirit produced. *See* also Reflux.

Maize Dried corn, often used in the production of grain whisky and especially in the Bourbon industry as part of the trio of grains contained in a mash bill.

Make The product of a distillery: whisky. *See* also New make.

Malt Barley or other grain is prepared for whisky-making by steeping, germinating and kiln-drying. The purpose of malting is to break down the cell walls of the cereal in order to release the starch and begin the process of converting that into sugars, which will subsequently produce alcohol.

Marriage The practice of vatting whisky before bottling in order to achieve a greater degree of harmony. A selection of casks of single malt may be married before bottling, and many blenders marry their blends in a similar fashion.

Mash Malt mixed with hot water to form wort. Mashing follows malting and precedes fermentation in the whisky-making process, and the mash of grist and hot water is mixed in a large, circular vessel known as a mash tun. Mashing extracts soluble sugars from the malted grain.

Mash bill The recipe used to distil Bourbon whiskey, usually comprising 51% corn maize, rye and malted barley. Other grains are also used, including wheat.

Maturation The practice of storing whisky in casks in order to achieve a more mellow and well-rounded spirit. Many countries specify a legal minimum maturation period. During maturation the porous casks allow the whisky to interact with the external atmosphere, and the spirit takes colour and flavour from the wood. At the same time, some of the higher alcohols are transformed into esters and other compounds with attractive aroma profiles.

Micro-distillery A small artisanal distillery, with a still capacity of around 1800 litres (400 gallons) or less. The movement of micro- or craft distilleries has become very popular worldwide.

Middle cut The most pure and desirable spirit collected during distillation. Also known as the heart of the run. *See* Cutting.

Mizunara A strain of oak (*Quercus mongolica*), which is used by Japanese whisky-makers, that gives a distinct cedary quality to the maturing whisky.

Mizuwari A popular way to drink blended whisky in Japan, using quality ice and very pure mineral water.

Moonshine A term used in the USA to denote illicitly distilled whiskey, often harsh and new. It was originally distilled during the hours of darkness using the light of the moon in order to minimize the chances of detection.

Neat Unmixed or undiluted. *See* also Straight.

New make Freshly distilled whisky. *See* Fillings.

Nose The aroma or bouquet of a whisky. Along with colour, body, palate and finish, the 'nose' is used to quantify and describe a whisky. Most whisky professionals, particularly blenders, use their noses as the principal means of analysing whiskies.

Pagoda The distinctive style of roof found on distillery malting kilns in Scotland and sometimes in other countries, e.g. Japan.

Patent still *See* Coffey still.

Peat Peat has an important influence on whisky character when it is used to flavour malt in the kiln, but much of the process water used in Scottish distilleries flows over peat, and this also plays a minor part in influencing the finished product.

Piece The term applied to a quantity of germinating barley while it is on the malting floor.

Pipe A type of cask sometimes used in whisky maturation that formerly contained Port.

Poitin Irish term for illegally distilled spirit; it is often anglicized to poteen.

Pot ale The high-protein waste liquid left in the low wines still after the first distillation has taken place.

Pot still A copper distillation vessel. The size and shape of pot stills varies from distillery to distillery, and pot still variables play an important part in determining the character of spirit produced.

Proof Measurement of the strength of spirits, expressed in degrees, calculated using a hydrometer. Although still employed in the USA, the proof system has now been superseded in Europe and the rest of the world by a measurement of alcohol strength as a percentage of alcohol by volume.

Reflux During distillation some of the heavier flavours with comparatively high boiling points condense from vapour back into liquid form before leaving the still and are redistilled. This is known as reflux, and the greater the degree of reflux, the lighter and 'cleaner' the spirit produced. Short, squat stills produce little reflux, compared with tall, slender stills. The angle at which the lyne arm is attached also affects the levels of reflux.

Run The flow of spirit from a still during a specific period of distillation.

Rye Grain used for whiskey-making, most notably in the USA, where rye whiskey was once more popular than Bourbon. Now something of a niche product, rye is making a stealthy comeback among US connoisseurs.

Scotch Whisky distilled and matured in Scotland, but usually with the colloquial implication of blended whisky.

Scotch Whisky Association (SWA) The SWA is a trade association set up in 1942 to represent the interests of Scotch whisky around the world, helping to protect and preserve its provenance. www.scotch-whisky.org.uk

Shell & tube A modern method of condensing spirit vapour, which comprises a number of smaller pipes housed in an outer 'shell'. The pipes (or tubes the spirit vapour travels along) are cooled by a continuous flow of cold water, passing through an inlet and outlet in the shell.

Shiel A wooden shovel used for turning barley during malting in traditional floor maltings.

Silent Just as a closed theatre is said to be 'dark', so a closed, though potentially productive, distillery is described as 'silent'.

Single A single malt whisky is the product of one distillery, not vatted or blended with any others.

Single cask Most bottles of single malt will contain spirit from between 100 and 150 casks, vatted to give consistency, but a single cask bottling comes from one individual cask. It is frequently sold at cask strength and is prized for its individuality.

Speyside The geographically defined region of northeast Scotland that is home to approximately half of all Scottish malt whisky distilleries.

Spirit Until it has been matured for three years in its country of origin, Scotch and Irish whisk(e)y officially known as spirit. It is produced in a spirit still, monitored and separated in a spirit safe and collected in a spirit receiver.

Spirit safe A secure, brass and glass box within which cutting takes place, without the stillman being able to have direct physical contact with the spirit. The spirit safe was invented by Septimus Fox during the early 1820s, and its use became compulsory in 1823.

Steep The vessel in which barley is soaked or steeped during malting.

Still Whether a pot or continuous still, operation is on the principal that alcohol boils at a lower temperature than water and is driven off as vapour, leaving behind the water. It is subsequently condensed back into liquid.

Straight Unmixed or undiluted. *See* also Neat.

Switcher A mechanism consisting of rotating arms which is fitted to a washback to reduce excessive frothing during fermentation.

Tennessee Tennessee whiskey is made in the eponymous US state and is characterized by charcoal filtration, called the Lincoln County Process that is intended to produce a purer, smoother whiskey.

Top dressing A blending term used to denote high-quality malts that are known to marry well and are used to give a blended whisky a veneer of depth and character.

Triple distillation The practice of distilling whisky three times rather than the usual two in order to achieve a light, pure style of spirit. Triple distillation is a traditional characteristic of Irish whiskey, and also of Scottish Lowland whisky-making.

Tun A large vessel in which mashing takes place, usually known as a mash tun. However, in a distillery the 'tun room' is home to the washbacks.

Vatting The process of mixing or blending components in a vat. For Scotch whisky, vatting was formerly most often applied to 'vatted malts': more than one malt vatted together before bottling. The term has now been dropped by the Scotch Whisky Association and most distillers in favour of the expression 'blended malt', which is thought to be less confusing for consumers.

Wash The liquid at the end of the fermentation process, ready for distillation.

Washback or fermenter The vessel in which fermentation takes place, traditionally constructed of wood, but now often made of stainless steel, which is easier to keep clean.

Water One of the key components of whisky-production. Water is necessary for steeping during the malting process, for mashing and for cooling the vapour from the stills back into liquid form. As a source of reliable, pure water is crucial to distilling, most distillery sites have been chosen with this in mind.

Wood Generic term for casks used in the whisky industry.

Worm A long, coiled copper tube attached to the lyne arm of the pot still, and fitted into a large wooden vat filled with cold water, known as a worm tub. Before the introduction of 'shell and tube' condensers, the worm tub was the only means of condensing alcohol vapour back into liquid form. A number of distilleries continue to use worm tubs, as experts insist that the character of whisky made using a worm tub differs significantly from that cooled in a modern condenser.

Wort Essentially unfermented beer, wort is produced in the mash tun. *See* mash.

WHISKY BARS

Detailed below are whisky bars, throughout the world, that have been carefully selected by *Whisky Magazine*. Telephone numbers are listed only when there is no website.

AUSTRALIA
Eau de Vie Darlinghurst, NSW
www.eaudevie.com.au
Shady Pines Saloon Darlinghurst, NSW
www.shadypinessaloon.com
Tokonoma Shochu Bar & Lounge
Surry Hills, NSW *www.toko.com.au*

BELGIUM
The Bull
Roeselare *www.thebull.be*

CANADA
The Feathers, Toronto *www.thefeatherspub.ca*
Highlander Pub, Ottawa
www.thehighlanderpub.com
The Lunar Rogue Pub, Fredericton
www.lunarrogue.com
Via Allegro, Toronto
www.viaallegroristorante.com

CHINA
Bar Constellation, Shanghai
Tel: +86 21 5404 0970

CYPRUS
Babylon Bar & Restaurant, Lefkosia
Tel: +357 665 757

ENGLAND
Albannach, Trafalgar Square, London
www.albannach.co.uk
Boisdale, Belgravia and Bishopsgate, London
www.boisdale.co.uk

Britons Protection, Manchester
www.britonsprotection.co.uk
Lanesborough Hotel, Hyde Park Corner,
London *www.lanesborough.com*
Moti Mahal, Covent Garden, London
www.motimahal-uk.com
Salt Whisky Bar and Dining Room, Marble
Arch, London *www.saltbar.com*
The Fisherman's Retreat, Bury, Lancashire
www.fishermansretreat.com

FINLAND
St Michael Irish Pub, Oulu *www.stmichael.fi*

FRANCE
Aspen Café, Samoens, Haute-Savoie
www.aspencafe.fr
Wallace Bar, Lyons Tel: +33 4 7200 2391

GREECE
Cosmos, Athens Tel: +30 10 672 9150

HUNGARY
The Caledonia, Budapest *www.caledonia.hu*

INDIA
360°, The Oberoi, New Delhi
www.oberoihotels.com
Aer, Four Seasons, Mumbai
www.thefourseasons.com/mumbai
The Bar, Grand Hyatt, Mumbai
www.mumbai.grand.hyatt.com
Blue Bar, Taj Palace Hotel, New Delhi
www.tajhotels.com

Bombay High, Mumbai Tel: +91 22 2830 3030
Chipstead, Taj Coromandel, Chennai
www.tajhotels.com
Dome, Intercontinental, Mumbai
www.intercontinental.com
Harbour Bar, The Taj Mahal Palace Tower,
Mumbai *www.tajhotels.com*
ITC Hotel Maurya, Diplomatic Enclave, New
Delhi *www.itchotels.in*
ITC Hotel The Windsor, Bangalore
www.itchotels.in
Library Bar, The Leela Palace, Bangalore
www.theleela.com
Nero, Hotel Le Meridien, New Delhi
www.standwoodhotels.com/lemeridien
Pan Asian, Sheraton New Delhi Hotel, New
Delhi
www.itchotels.in
Polo Lounge, Hyatt Regency, New Delhi
www.delhi.regency.hyatt.com
Reflections Bar, J W Marriott, Mumbai
www.marriott.co.uk/JW-Marriott
Wink, Taj President Hotel, Mumbai
www.tajhotels.com

REPUBLIC OF IRELAND
Jasmine Bar, Brooks Hotel, Dublin
www.slh.com
L. Mulligan Grocer, Dublin
www.lmulligangrocer.com
The Palace Bar, Dublin *www.thepalacebar.
com*
The Shelbourne, Dublin *www.marriott.com*

ITALY
Sbrizzai Alessandro, Trieste
Tel: +39 40 771 834

JAPAN
Bar Talisker, Chuo-ku, Tokyo
Tel: +81 3 3571 1753
Campbelltoun Loch, Chiyoda-ku, Tokyo
Tel: +81 3 3501 5305
Cask, Minato-ku, Tokyo *www.cask.jp*
Park Hotel Tokyo, Minato-ku, Tokyo
www.parkhoteltokyo.com
Star Bar, Chuo-ku, Tokyo *www.starbar.jp*
The Mash Tun, Shinagawa Ku, Tokyo
www.themashtun.com

LITHUANIA
Bar W, Kaunas, Lithuania *www.viskiobaras.lt*

NORWAY
Grand Terminus Whisky Bar, Hordaland
www.grandterminus.no

SCOTLAND
The Anderson, Fortrose
www.theanderson.co.uk
Bon Accord, Glasgow
www.bonaccordweb.co.uk
The Bow Bar, Edinburgh Tel: +44 131 226 7667
The Canny Man's, Edinburgh
Tel: +44 131 447 1484
Cuillin Hills Hotel, Portree, Isle of Skye
www.cuillinhills-hotel-skye.co.uk
Drumchork Lodge Hotel, Aultbea, Wester
Ross
Tel: +44 1445 731 242
Duffies Bar, The Lochside Hotel, Bowmore, Isle
of Islay *www.lochsidehotel.co.uk*
Fiddler's, Drumnadrochit, Inverness-shire
www.fiddledrum.co.uk
Gleneagles Hotel, Auchterarder, Perth and
Kinross *www.gleneagles.com*

The Grill, Aberdeen
www.thegrillaberdeen.co.uk
Highlander Inn, Craigellachie, Speyside,
Banffshire *www.whiskyinn.com*
Òran Mór, Glasgow *www.oran-mor.co.uk*
Seaview Hotel, John o' Groats, Caithness
www.seaviewjohnogroats.co.uk
Torridon Country House Hotel, Torridon,
Achnasheen, Wester Ross
www.thetorridon.com
A Wee Drop, Creag Mhor Lodge, Ballachulish,
Invernesshire
www.creagmhorlodge.com
Whiski Bar and Restaurant, Edinburgh
www.whiskibar.co.uk

SOUTH AFRICA
Bascule Whisky & Wine Bar, Cape Grace
Hotel, Cape Town *www.capegrace.com*
Wild about Whisky, Dallskroom
www.wildaboutwhisky.co.za

SOUTH KOREA
Off, Seoul Tel: +82 2 516 6201

SPAIN
Scanlan's Tavern, Bizcaya
www.scanlanstavern.blogspot.com

SWITZERLAND
Hotel Waldhaus am See, St Moritz
www.waldhaus-am-see.ch

TAIWAN
Whisky Gallery, Scotch Malt Whisky Society,
Taipei City *www.smws.com.tw*

USA
The Bar at Blu, Louisville, Kentucky
www.blugrille.com
Baxter Station, Louisville, Kentucky
www.baxterstation.com
Bourbon's Bistro, Louisville, Kentucky
www.Bourbonsbistro.com
Brandy Library, New York
www.brandylibrary.com
Char No. 4, New York *www.charno4.com*
DBA, New York *www.drinkgoodstuff.com*
Death & Company, New York
www.deathandcompany.com
Delilah's, Chicago, Illinois
www.delilahschicago.com
Desha's, Lexington, Kentucky
www.deshas.com
Dram, New York *www.drambar.com*
Dundee Dell, Omaha, Nebraska
www.dundeedell.com
Jockey Silks Bourbon Bar, Louisville,
Kentucky *www.galthouse.com*
The Last Hurrah, Boston, Massachusetts
www.omnihotels.com
Maker's Lounge, Louisville, Kentucky
www.makerslounge.com
Old Talbott Tavern, Bardstown, Kentucky
www.talbotts.com
Proof on Main, Louisville, Kentucky
www.proofonmain.com
Seelbach Hilton, Louisville, Kentucky
www.seelbachhilton.com
Twisted Spoke, Chicago, Illinois
www.twistedspoke.com
Z's, Louisville, Kentucky
www.zoysterbar.com

SPECIALIST RETAILERS

AUSTRALIA
www.oakbarrel.com.au

EUROPE
Celtic Whiskey Shop, Ireland
www.celticwhiskeyshop.com
James Fox, Ireland www.jamesfox.ie
La Maison du Whisky, France www.whisky.fr
Mara Malt Rarities, Germany
www.maltwhisky-mara.de
Van Wees Whisky World, Holland
www.whiskyworld.nl
Whisky Paradise, Italy
www.whiskyparadise.com
Whiskyhuis, Belgium www.whiskyhuis.be
Whisky Shop Tara, Germany
www.whiskyversand.de
The Whisky Store, Germany www.whisky.de

JAPAN
www.shinanoya.co.jp

SOUTH AFRICA
www.whiskyshop.co.za

UK
Arkwright's www.whiskyandwines.com
Berry Bros & Rudd www.bbr.com
Cadenhead's www.wmcadenhead.com
Gordon & MacPhail
www.gordonandmacphail.com
Robert Graham www.whisky-cigars.co.uk
Loch Fyne Whiskies www.lfw.co.uk
Master of Malt www.masterofmalt.com
Milroy's of Soho www.milroys.co.uk
Royal Mile Whiskies
www.royalmilewhiskies.com
Soho Whisky.com www.sohowhisky.com
Duncan Taylor Scotch Whisky
www.duncantaylor.com
The Wee Dram www.weedram.co.uk
The Whisky Exchange
www.thewhiskyexchange.com
The Whisky Shop www.whiskyshop.com

USA
Astor Wines & Spirits www.astorwines.com
Binny's Beverage Depot www.binnys.com
Federal Wine & Spirits www.federalwine.com
Park Avenue Liquor Shop
www.parkaveliquor.com
Twin Liquors www.twinliquors.com

WHISKY SOURCES

WHISKY WEBSITES

Caskstrength
www.caskstrength.blogspot.co.uk
Neil's very own blog, co-written with fellow whisky writer Joel Harrison.

Dr Whisky *www.drwhisky.blogspot.co.uk*
The Doctor (Sam Simmons) is here with your daily prescription of irreverent reviews and whisky news. A dram a day keeps the doctor at play!

Edinburgh Whisky Blog
www.edinburghwhiskyblog.com
A smartly written blog, with a youthful outlook on whisky.

Miss Whisky Woman *www.misswhisky.com*
An up-to-date and well-written blog from enthusiast, Alwynne Gwilt.

Nonjatta *www.nonjatta.com*
Japan-based whisky expert Stefan Van Eycken has assembled the best online resource on Japanese whisky. Highly recommended.

Spirit of India *http://amrut-spiritofindia.net*
The first blog site dedicated to Amrut Indian single malt.

Whisky Advocate Blog
www.whiskyadvocateblog.com
One of the premier US sites, written by John Hansell with contributions from a number of well-known international whisky writers.

Whisky Boys *www.whiskyboys.com*
The home of Jim and daughter Nicola. A no-nonsense approach to appreciating whisky and hosting successful tastings.

Whisky for Everyone
www.whiskyforeveryone.com
A very useful online site, demystifying the jargon which surrounds whisky.

Whisky Fun *www.whiskyfun.com*
Top online resource for reviews of rare bottlings and new releases, written by witty Frenchmen, Serge Valentin.

Whisky Intelligence
www.whiskyintelligence.com
Probably the most up-to-date online resource for new releases and press information.

Whisky Israel *www.whiskyisrael.co.il*
Spirited musings on whiskies from around the globe from founder Gal Granov.

Whisky Magazine *www.whiskymag.com*
The website of *Whisky Magazine* which has useful links to other sites.

Whisky-Pages *www.whisky-pages.com*
Gavin's informative online site.

Whisky Wire *www.thewhiskywire.com*
Written by whisky enthusiast Steve Rush, Whisky Wire hosts numerous Twitter whisky tastings and interviews with industry insiders.

MAGAZINES

Unfiltered *www.smws.com*
The official magazine of the Scotch Malt Whisky Society. Well worth a look.

Whiskeria *www.whiskyshop.com*
A regular and very informative magazine, available through the The Whisky Shop, a chain of independent whisky retailers.

Whisky Advocate *www.maltadvocate.com*
Arguably America's leading whisky publication, now more than 20 years old. Well written.

Whisky Magazine *www.whiskymag.com*
Now published in six languages and distributed around the globe, *Whisky Magazine* covers all the hot issues.

CLUBS & SOCIETIES

Connosr *www.connosr.com*

An online community of international whisky fans, sharing tasting advice hints and tips and the best place to buy whiskies via their 'Whisky Marketplace'.

Malt Maniacs *www.maltmaniacs.net*

Self-confessed whisky anoraks! Read their musings here.

Scotch Malt Whisky Society *www.smws.com*

In our opinion, one of the best and most open-minded whisky members clubs, with outlets all over the world focusing on the individual flavours of whisky, not brand names.

Whisky Squad *www.whiskysquad.com*

Run from a small London pub, the Whisky Squad organize tastings on all kinds of whisky, with a good dose of humour thrown in for good measure.

FESTIVALS & EVENTS

Most things taste better in the open air and whisky is no exception. The following whisky festivals are the best gatherings around the globe for like-minded imbibers.

Feis Ile, Islay Festival of Whisky and Music
www.theislayfestival.co.uk

A truly magical week of distillery open days, traditional music and local cuisine from the island of Islay, one of the world's greatest whisky-producing regions.

Maltstock *www.maltstock.com*

A three-day event held at a woodland retreat in Nijmegen in the Netherlands, Maltstock is a great opportunity to meet members of other international whisky clubs, attend master classes from whisky writers and distillers, and try some of the rarest whiskies on the planet. Don't forget to bring a bottle, too...

Kentucky Bourbon Festival
www.kyBourbonfestival.com

With the Bourbon Trail attracting thousands of visitors a year, the Kentucky Bourbon Festival in mid-September is one of the area's major highlights, with a mixture of music, entertainment, barbecues and great whiskey.

Spirit of Speyside Festival
www.spiritofspeyside.com

A virtual distillery crawl across Speyside's many legendary names, interspersed with music and other cultural events.

Sydney Whisky Fair, Australia
www.sydneywhiskyfair.com.au

The country's premier whisky fair, celebrating both international and domestic whiskies.

Uisge, Finland

Finland's first dedicated whisky event, run in Helsinki by members of the Finnish Whisky Society. No website because of Finland's alcohol restrictions.

Universal Whisky Experience
www.universalwhiskyexperience.com

Las Vegas' own take on the more luxury end of whisky, with master classes from well-known distillery ambassadors and equally rare, expensive bottlings.

Victoria Whisky Festival, Canada
www.victoriawhiskyfestival.com

Tastings and masterclasses at this lively festival on Vancouver Island.

Viking Line Whisky Festival
www.vikingline.se

A whisky festival – but on a Scandinavian ferry. Lots of fun, assuming you've got sea legs!

Whiskyfest
www.maltadvocate.com/whiskyfest

Run in New York, Chicago and San Francisco, Whiskyfest was set up by *Whisky Advocate* magazine and covers a range of whiskies from around the world.

The Whisky Festival, Germany

www.festival.whiskyfair.com

One of the ultimate whisky events for the enthusiast. There are some seriously rare whiskies on offer.

Whisky Live www.whiskylive.com

Now operating in over 17 countries, including Russia, Taiwan, China and South Africa, Whisky Live has truly opened up the modern-day whisky event to a global audience.

The Whisky Lounge

www.thewhiskylounge.com

Eddie Ludlow and his wife have bought a laid-back atmosphere to the whisky-tasting experience with the Whisky Lounge concept, appearing at cities all over the UK.

Whisky Luxe

www.whiskylive.com/whisky-luxe

The Indian version of Whisky Live deserves a mention on its own, with a focus on the more luxurious, high end of the market, with some very rare bottlings on offer.

BOOKS

101 Whiskies to Try Before You Die, by Ian Buxton

Alt Distilleries, by Darek Bell

An A–Z of Whisky, by Gavin D Smith

Drinking Japan, by Chris Bunting

Malt Whisky Yearbook, edited by Ingvar Ronde

The Whisky Bible, by Jim Murray

The Whisky Distilleries of the United Kingdom, by Alfred Barnard

World Whisky Atlas, by Dave Broom

INDEX

Italic page numbers refer to
  maps
Bold page numbers refer to
  main entries

Aberfeldy 77, 84
Aberlour 61, *86*, 93
Abhainn Dearg *112*, 119
abv (alcohol by volume) 25, 27,
  29, 31, 40, 49, 50, 53, 55, 204
  and food combinations 58
  and maturation 38
additives 48
Adnams 25, *180*, **184**
  Copper House North Cove
    Creek Aged Vodka 184
age 7, 53, 204
  and character 40
  and quality 17, 40–1, 69
  statement of 40, 41
Ailsa Bay *94*, 98
air quality 39
Akuto, Ichiro 140
Alberta Distillers *172*
alcohol
  by volume *see* abv
  early distillation of 12
  fermentation process
    23–4
alembic stills 12, 204
Allason, Rob 6
Allied Distillers Ltd 101
Allied Domecq 116, 158
Allt a Bhainne *86*
Alltech *149*
American whiskey
  distilleries 148–71
  legal definition 19
  production process 30–1
  quality of 150
  types of 30
  with/in food 62
  see also Bourbon; corn
    whiskey; Kentucky;
    rye whiskey; Tennessee
    whiskey; United States
Amrut 194, *195*, **196**
  Cask Strength Indian 62
  Fusion 62, 196
  Peated 59
  Indian Single Malt 52
Anchor Distilling *162*
'Angels' Share' 38, 204

Angostura *163*
  bitters 57
Annandale *94*
appearance 48
Ardbeg 59, 60, 68, *100*, **101**
  Uigeadail 62
Ardmore 77
Ardnamurchan 77
Armstrong, Raymond 96
aroma 33, 42–4
  memories of 450
  and tasting 48–50
Arran 61, *112*, **113**
  Machrie Moor 113
artisanal whisky 125, 203
Asia
  distilleries 194–7
  map 195
  see also Japan
Auchentoshan 60, *94*, **95**
  Three Wood 65
Auchroisk *86*
auction houses 66, 67, 69, 70
Aultmore *86*
Australia
  bars 211
  distilleries 200–3
  map 200
Austria 182
authenticity 72–3

Bagpiper 194
Baker, David 201
Bakery Hill *200*, **201**
Balblair 77
Balcones *163*, **164**
  Baby Blue 164
  Brimstone 164
  Rumble 164
Ballantine's 121
Ballast Point *162*
Ballindalloch *86*
Balmenach *86*
Balvenie, The 23, 68, *86*, 93
  Double Wood 61, 65
  Signature 93
Banff 67
barley 13, 174, 204
  malted 22–3, 23, 26, 28, 150,
    158, 175, 186, 207
  new varieties 45
  types of 22–3, 39
Barrel House *149*

barrels 204
  kits 165, 203
bars *see* pubs and bars
Beam family 151, 155, 157
Beam Inc 123, 129, 158
Belgian Owl 41
Belgium 193, 211
Bell, Darek 166
Bell's Original 121
Belmont Farms *163*
Ben Nevis 77
Ben Wyvis 109
BenRiach *86*, 93
  Curiositas 93
Benrinnes 61, *86*
Benromach *86*, 93
  Traditional 93
Berry Bros & Rudd 122
Bertrand, The *180*
Biltmore Hotel (New York) 56
bitters 57
Black Bottle 122
Black Velvet *172*, 179
Bladnoch *94*, **96**
Blair Atholl 77
Blaue Maus Distillery *180*, 193
blended grain Scotch whisky,
  legal definition 18
blended malt 204
blended malt Scotch whisky
  consistency of manufacture
    45
  legal definition 18
'Blended Malt Whisky' 52, 125
blended Scotch whisky, legal
  definition 18
blends 204
  aged 9
  art of 120, 124
  best-selling 121–3
  history of 13
  home blending kits 124
  Japanese 136–7
  legal definitions 18
  modern flavour-based
    approach 125
  quality of 7, 17, 120, 124
  sales of 120, 121
  Scotch 120–5
blue corn 164
Boehm, Jacob 157
boil ball stills 25, 144
Bonham's 66, 67, 70

books on whisky 217
bootleg operations 151
bottles
  condition of 68
  design 70, 71, 92
Bouillon, Etienne 193
Bourbon casks 35, 37, 38, 58
Bourbon whiskey 6, 52, 53, 148,
  150, 204
  casks 35, 37, 38, 58
  distilleries 152–3, 155, 157–
    61, 170, 171
  legal definition 19
  production process 30–1
  and Prohibition 151
  small-batch and limited
    edition 9, 157, 204
  with/in food 62
Bowmore 68, *100*, **102**
  Darkest 60
  Mutter 67
Box *180*
Braeval *86*
Braunstein *180*
Brazil 16
brewing 204
Bronfman, Samuel 176
Broom, David 45
Brora 67
Bruichladdich 25, 59, 60, 62, 66,
  100, **103**
  'The Laddie' 103
Buffalo Trace 53, *149*, **152**
Bulleit Bourbon 71
Bunnahabhain *100*, 107
Bunting, Chris 147
Burn Stewart Distillers 118, 122
Burns' Night 63, 197
Burns, Robert 13, 63
Bushmills *127*, **128**
  Original 128
butt casks 35, 204
buttery, smooth and sweet
  flavours 43
    food combinations 61
buying whisky 51–3

Cadenheads (Edinburgh) 51
Campari company 90
Campbell, Daniel 102
Campbeltown 204
  distilleries 108–11
  map 108

Canada
  bars 211
  distilleries 175–9
  legal definitions 19
  map 172–3
Canadian Mist *173*
Caol Ila 52, 59, 60, *100*, 107
Caperdonich 67
Capone, Al 151, 178
caramel colouring 48, 120
Cardhu *86*, **87**
cartons, condition of 68
Cashel (Ireland) 12
cask strength 205
casks 204
  barrels 204
  buy your own 165, 203
  chestnut 193
  first-fill 37
  and flavour 41
  and food combinations 58
  Japanese 134, 136, 137, 142
  manufacture of 36
  and maturation process 37–8
  oak 27, 31, 35–6, 134, 136, 165
  pipe 208
  single 53, 209
  Spanish sherry 35, 36
Ceimici Teoranta distillery 129
Celts 12
Charbay *162*
Charles Mackinlay & Co Ltd 115
cherry flavour 16
Chichibu *135*, **140**
  Ichiro's Malt 140
chill filtration 48, 205
China 9, 16, 194, 197, 211
  ancient distillation techniques 12
Chivas Brothers 15, 113, 116, 122
Chivas Regal 122
Christie's 66, 67, 70
cigars, and whisky 64–5
Classic Bourbon Mint Julep 56
Classic Malts collection 205
Clear Creek *162*
clearic 25, 205
cloudiness 48
clubs and societies, whisky 215
Clynelish 61, 62, *77*
cocktails 8, 56, 57, 138–9
coffee, Irish 133

Coffey stills 18, 130, 137, 138, 144, 174, 205
cola, mixing with 55
collecting whisky 66–71
  and counterfeiting 73
colour
  and aroma and flavour 42, 48
  and maturation 38
colourants 48
column stills *see* Coffey stills
Compass Box 62, 125
  Asyla 125
  Flaming Heart 125
  Orangerie 125
  Peat Monster 125
  Spice Tree 52, 62, 125
computers 20, 45
condensers 205
Constellation Brands Inc 179
continuous stills *see* Coffey stills
Cooley 18, *127*, **129**
  Connemara 129
coopering 34, 35, 36
the copper 24–5
Copper Fox *163*, **165**
Cork Distilleries Company 131
corn 13, 148, 167, 174, 175, 205
corn whiskey 170, 174
  legal definition 19
  production process 30–1
Cornish whiskey 185
Corsair *163*, **166**
cost *see* prices
Cotswolds *180*
counterfeit whisky 72–3
County Antrim (Ireland) 13
Cowan, Jessie 'Rita' 145
craft distilleries 148, 150, 174
Cragganmore *86*, 93
Craig, Rev Elijah 13, 155
Craigellachie *86*, 109
Crow, James 161
Cumming, John and Elizabeth 87
Currie, Harold 113
cutting 205
Cutty Sark 60, 122
Cyprus 211
Czech Republic 183

Daftmill *94*, 98
Dailuaine *86*
Dalmore, The 36, 68, *77*, **78**
  Cigar Malt Reserve 64, 65
  Kidermorie 67

Oculus 67
  Trinitas 78
Dalwhinnie 61, *77*, **79**
dark grains 205
Deanston 77
Death's Door *163*
deluxe 205
Des Menhirs *180*
Destilerias y Crianzas Del Whisky *180*
Dewar's 15, 68, 84
  White Label 122
Diageo plc 20, 45, 82, 87, 97, 104, 105, 117, 120, 121, 123, 128, 154, 176, 179
Dickel, George A 154
Dingle *127*
distillation 206
  American whiskey 31
  ancient practice of 12
  development of 13
  grain whisky 29
  modern methods 24–5
  single malt 27
  triple 18, 25, 95, 209
  two-stage 25, 27
distilleries
  Asia 194–7
  Australia 200–3
  boom and bust of 15
  Canada 172–9
  consistent manufacture 45
  craft 148, 150
  Europe 180–93
  first division 68
  global explosion of 75
  innovation 9
  investment in 16
  Ireland 127–33
  Japan 140–7
  Kentucky and Tennessee 148–61
  lost 66–7
  micro 200, 208
  modern 20–5
  other United States 162–71
  Scotland 76–119
  South Africa 198–9
draff 206
drams 47, 54, 55, 63, 69, 73, 206
Drayman's Brewery 198, *198*
Dry Fly *162*
Dufftown 62, *86*
Duncan Taylor, Glencraig 52
dunnage 206
Dyer, Edward 194

E150 48
East London Liquor Company *181*
Echlinville *127*
Eden Mill *94*
Edgefield *162*
Edinburgh 97
Edradour 20, *77*, 84
  Caledonia 84
Edrington Group 122
Egyptians 12
Eigashima *135*, **141**
  Akashi 141
Ellensburg *162*
Emperador 123
England
  bars 211
  distilleries 184–6
enjoyment of whisky 47
environment, and character of whisky 39
Erenzo, Ralph 170
esters 206
Eunson, Magnus 114
Europe
  distilleries in 180–93
  map 180–1
evaporation 38, 40, 68, 70, 196
Excise Act (1823) 91
expression 206

Famous Grouse 53, 122
Far East, *see also* China; Japan; South Korea; Taiwan
Faraday, Dr David 191
fault-finding 68
feints 206
fermentation 23–4, 206
  American whiskey 30–1
  grain whisky 28
  single malt 27
fermenters 23
festivals and events 216–17
Fettercairn *77*
fillings 206
Finger Lakes *163*
finish 49, 50, 206
Finland 187, 211
Fitt, David 186
flavour 33, 42–4
  and age 40–1
  and casks 37, 38
  map 44
  tasting 50
floral flavours *see* fresh, floral and fruity aromas and

flavours
food
  whisky with Japanese 138
  whisky with 58–63
foreshots 206
Fortune Brands Inc 158
Forty Creek *173*, **175**
Four Roses *149*, **153**
  Single Barrel Bourbon 62
France 188, 211
fresh, floral and fruity aromas
  and flavours 43
    food combinations 60
fruity flavours *see* fresh,
  floral and fruity aromas and
  flavours
Fuji-Gotemba *135*

gentlemen's clubs 64
'Geographical Indication' status
  73
Georg T. Stagg 53, 152
George Dickel 31, *149*, **154**
Germany 193
germination 23
Gibson's Seagram *173*
  Finest 179
Gillies, Maeve 71
Gimli *173*, **176**
  Crown Royal 176
ginger ale, mixing with 55
Glann Ar Mor *180*, **188**
Glaser, John 125
Glasgow 95
Glasgow Distillery Company *94*
glassware 52, 54–5
  warming 7
Glenallachie *86*
Glenburgie *86*
Glencadam *77*
Glencairn glasses 54
GlenDronach 36, *77*
Glendullan *86*
Glen Elgin *86*
Glenfarclas 21, 36, 61, 65, *86*,
  88
  Family Casks range 88
Glenfiddich 15, 37, 61, 65, 68,
  76, *86*, **89**
    64-year old 67
    Janet Sheed Roberts Reserve
      67
    vintage reserve 89
Glen Garioch *77*
Glenglassaugh *77*
Glengoyne 65, *77*, **80**, 85

Glen Grant 20, *86*, **90**
Glengyle *108*, **109**
  Kilkerran Work in Progress
    109
Glenkinchie 25, 60, *94*, **97**
Glenlivet 15, *86*, **91**
  Nadurra 61
Glenlossie *86*
Glenmorangie 25, 68, *77*, **81**,
  101
  Original 60
Glen Moray *86*, 93
Glenora *173*, **177**
  Glen Breton 177
Glen Ord 77
Glenrothes 65, *86*
Glen Scotia *108*, 109, **110**
Glen Spey *86*
Glentauchers *86*
Glenturret *77*, 84
Gordon & MacPhail 67
Graber, Jess 169
Graham brothers 122
grain 22–3, 170, 174, 206
  malted 21, 22–3, 23
grain whisky
  and blending 121
  production process 28–9
  single Irish 133
Grant, George 21
Grant, Major James 90
Grant, John and James 90
Grant family 88, 89
Grant's Family Reserve 122–3
Great Lakes *163*
Great Southern *200*
Greece 211
  ancient 12
green malt 28, 45, 206
Green Mountain *163*
Green Spot 131, 133
green tea, mixing with 9, 56,
  138
Greenore 133
grist 23, 26, 206
Guillon *180*

haggis 63
Haider, Johann 182
Haig 68
Hakushu 59, 61, 62, *135*, **142**
Hall, John 175
Hammerschmiede *181*
Hanyu 66, *135*, **140**
headspace 70
heart of the run 208

Heaven Hill *149*, **155**
  Bernheim Original Straight
    Wheat Whiskey 155
  Elijah Craig 155
  Evan Williams Vintage
    Single Barrel Bourbon
    52, 155
  Pikesville Rye 155, 171
  Rittenhouse Rye 53, 155
Hebrides 13, 119
Hellyers Road *200*
hi-tech equipment 20
Hicks & Healey *180*, **185**
highballs 138–9, 142, 206
Highland Park 23, 52, 53, 61, 65,
  68, *112*, **114**
  bottle design 71
Highlands 207
  distilleries 25, 77–85
  map 77
High West *162*
Highwood *172*
Hiram Walker 116, 158, *173*,
  174, **178**
  Canadian Club 178
history of whisky 12–16
hogshead casks 35, 207
Holinshed, Raphael 12
honey infusion 16, 164
Hoochery *200*
hot toddies 138
Hungary 211
Hunter, Ian 106
Hven *180*

Ian Macleod Distillers Ltd 80
ice, in whisky 55, 56, 138, 139
Immature Spirit Act (1915) 40
Inchgower *86*
India
  bars 211–12
  distilleries 194–6
  Indian whisky 17, 52
  Indian whisky with/in food
    59, 60, 62
  map 195
  production process 194
  whisky-drinking in 194
ingredients 6, 18, 21–2
inhalation 49
Inver House Distillers Ltd 83
investing in whisky 16, 66–71
Ireland
  bars 212
  distilleries 127–33
  map 127

and origin of whiskey 12,
  13, 17
Irish coffee 133
Irish Distillers 131, 132
Irish Mist Liqueur Company
  Ltd 132
Irish whiskey 8, 52, 126–33, 207
  with food 60
  legal definition 18
  pot still 9, 18, 25, 57, 131
  sales of 126
Isaiah Morgan *163*
Islands
  distilleries 112–19
  map 112
Islay 39, 52, 207
  distilleries 100–7
  map 100
Isle of Arran Distillers Ltd 113
Italy 212

J&B Rare 123
Jack Daniel's 31, *149*, **156**
Jagdale, Rick 196
James Sedgwick 198, *198*, **199**
  Three Ships 62, 199
Jameson 14, 126, 131
  Original 131
Japan
  bars 212
  blends 136–7
  character of whisky 136
  development of whisky 136
  distilleries 140–7
  history of whisky 15, 16
  map 135
  whisky 6, 17, 22, 52, 57,
    134–47
  whisky with food 59, 60, 62
Jim Beam *149*, **157**
  Baker's 157
  Basil Hayden's 157
  Booker's 157
  Knob Creek 157
John *195*
John Jameson & Son 131
John Power & Son 131
Johnnie Walker 15, 16, 76, 87,
  123
  Gold Label 61
Jones, Paul Jr 153
Jura *112*, **115**
Justerini & Brooks 123

Karuizawa 66, **143**
  Asama 147

Kasauli 194
Käser, Ruedi 193
Kavalan *195*, **197**
    Classic 41
    Solist 57, 62, 197
Kentucky 8, 13, 19, 38
    distilleries 148–50, 152–3,
        155, 157–61, 171
    map 148–9
Kentucky Bourbon Trail 150
Kilbeggan *127*, **130**
    Distillery Reserve 130
Kilchoman 23, *100*, **104**
    Machir Bay 41
kilns 26, 45, 207
King Car Group 197
Kininvie *86*
Kingsbarns *94*
Kittling Ridge Winery &
    Distillery *173*, 175
Knob Creek, Kentucky Straight
    Bourbon 171
Knockando *86*
Knockdhu *77*

labels
    age statement 40, 41
    condition of 68
Lagavulin 59, 60, *100*, **105**
Lakes *180*
Lalique 67, 92
lantern stills 25
Laphroaig 15, 53, 59, *100*,
    106
Lark *200*, **202**
Lark, Bill 202
Lark, Kirsty 202
laser technology 72
laws 13, 40, 72–3, 91, 125, 204
Lee, Brian 170
legal definitions 18–19
'legs' 48, 49
Leibovitz, Annie 92
lemonade, mixing with 55
Lewis, Isle of 119
Lincoln Country Process 19, 31,
    154, 156
Linkwood *86*
Lithuania 212
Littlemill 95
Loch Lomond Distillers *77*, 109
Lochside 67
Locke family 130
London Distillery Company,
    The *181*
Longmorn *86*

low wines 207
Lowlands 207
    distilleries 25, 94–9
    map 94
lyne arm or pipe 207
Macallan, The 36, 68, 70, *86*, **92**
    60-year old 67
    Cire Perdue 66, 67
    Fine Oak 61
    Vintage 67
MacCallum, Duncan 110
McCormick *163*
Macdonald & Muir Ltd 81
McDowell's 194, *195*
Macduff *77*
McEwan, Jim 103, 193
Machlachlans 95
Mackmyra *180*, **190**
    First Edition 190
McMenamins *162*
Macsween, Jo 63
McTear's 66, 67, 69, 70
magazines on whisky 215
maize 28, 158, 207
Makalanga, Biawa 90
make 207
Maker's Mark 62, *149*, **158**
Malcolm, Dennis 20
malting 207
    and character 39
    single malt 26
    variables in 45
malting floors 21, 23
maltose 23
Manhattan 56, 57
Mannochmore *86*
marketing 45
marriage 207
Mars Shinshu *135*
mash bill 150, 207
mash tun 23, 26, 209
mashing 23, 207
    American whiskey 30
    and character 39
    grain whisky 28
    single malt 26
Master of Malt 124
maturation 9, 37–8, 207–8
    American whiskey 31
    Asia 196, 197
    Canadian whisky 174
    casks 35–6
    and character 37, 38, 41
    chip and barrel 165
    evaporation during 38, 40
    grain whisky 29

secondary 125
single malt 27
medicinal properties 13
micro distilleries 200, 208
middle cut 208
Midleton *127*, **131**, 133
    Very Rare 52
milling
    American whiskey 30
    and character 39
    grain whisky 28
    single malt 26
Miltonduff *86*
miniatures 51
Mint Julep 56
Mitchell, William 109
mixers 7, 17, 55–6
Miyagikyo 60, *135*, **144**
Mizunara 136, 142, 208
Mizuwari 138, 142, 208
Mohan Nagar *195*
molasses whisky 194
Moloney, Michael 132
monasteries 12
Monkey Shoulder 23
moonshine 19, 208
Moors 12
Morrison Bowmore Distillers
    Ltd 95, 102
Mortlach *86*
Mount Vernon *163*
Mull, Isle of 118
myths 17, 49

name, origin of 13
Nant *200*
Nashoba *163*
National Prohibition
    Enforcement Act (Volstead
    Act) (1919) 151
neat 17, 208
Nelstrop family 186
Netherlands 189
New Holland *162*
new make 25, 27, 31, 35, 208
New Zealand 8
Nichols, Austin 160
Nikka 136, 146
    All Malt 61, 137
    'Black' Pure Malt Whisky
        147
    Coffey Grain 147
    From The Barrel 138
    Taketsura 147
Noe, Fred 157
Northern Ireland 128

Norway 212
nose 42, 48–9, 208
Number One Drinks Co
    143

oak, for casks 35, 136, 142
oats 170
Oban 53, 61, *77*, **82**
Old Buck *181*
Old Bushmills 13, 128
Old Fashioned 56, 57
Old Hobart *200*
Old Midleton 131
Old Potrero Hotalings Single
    Malt 53
Old Pulteney 65, *77*, **83**
old whiskies 40
olfactory gland 49, 50
onion stills 25
orange flavour 125
Orkney isles 39, 71, 114, 116
Owl Distillery 193
oxidization 69, 70
Owl *180*
Oyuwari 138

Paddy and Power's 131
pagodas 208
palate 49
Pappy 53
patent stills *see* Coffey stills
Paterson, Richard 64–5, 120
peat 22, 26, 39, 202, 208
peaty aromas and flavours
    see smoky and peaty aromas
    and flavours
Pemberton *172*
Penderyn 25, *180*, **191**
    Madeira finished single
        malt 191
    Sherry Cask Welsh whisky
        62
    Single Malt 52
Penobscot Bay *163*
Pepper, Oscar 161
Pernod Ricard 91, 120, 121, 128,
    131, 178, 179
piece 208
Piedmont *163*
pipe casks 208
Pleasanton, General 19
poitin/poteen 208
Port Ellen 15, 67, 107
pot ale 208
pot stills 12, 18, 20, 208
    combination 169

copper 25, 161, 167, 177,
    184, 191
  design and types of 25
  different shaped 136
  single 18, 131, 133
Pradlo *180*, **183**
  Hammerhead 183
prices
  at auctions 67
  and counterfeiting problem
    73
  and quality 17
Prichard's *163*
production methods 9
  American whisky 30–1
  consistency 45
  grain whisky 28–9
  modern 20–5
  single malt 26–7
Prohibition 15, 16, 148, 151, 154,
    156, 160, 170, 174, 178
proof 208
Proximo Spirits Co 169
pubs and bars
  Japanese 138–9
  whisky bars 211–13
  whisky menus 52–3
Pulteney, Sir William 83
Pyysing, Anssi 187

Raman signature 72
Rankin 92
rare whiskies 53, 66–7, 160
Redbreast 57, 60, 131, 133
reflux 208
region, grouping bottles by
  51, 53
Rémy Cointreau 103
retailers, specialist 214
Reynier, Mark 103
rice 170
rich and spicy aromas and
    flavours 43
  food combinations 61
Ridley, Neil 6, 8
Ripy brothers 160
Rogue *162*
Rosebank 15, 67, 68, 95, 97, 98
Roseisle 16, 20, 24, *86*
Rosenstiel, Lewis 179
Roughstock Montana *162*, **167**
Royal Brackla *77*
Royal Lochnagar *77*, 82
run 209
Rupf, Jorg 168
Russell, Jimmy 160

Russia 16
Rutledge, Jim 153
rye 13, 150, 174, 175, 184, 209
rye whiskey 53
  distilleries 150, 152, 153,
    155, 166, 167, 170, 171,
    174, 179, 182, 189
  legal definition 19
  production process 30–1

St Andrews University 72
St George (US) *162*, **168**
  Breaking & Entering 168
St George's (England) *180*, **186**
  Chapter 6 186
St James *162*
St Magdalene 67, 95
sales, global 16, 75
Samuels family 158
Sazerac Rye American whiskey
  53, 62, 152
Scapa *112*, **116**
Schenley Industries 154
Schultz, Bryan and Kari 167
scientific analysis 45, 72
Scotch whisky 6, 8, 209
  blending 120–5
  casks 35–6
  counterfeiting 72–3
  distilleries 76–119
  first division 68
  single malt production 26–7
  with/in food 60–3
Scotch Whisky Association 40,
  72, 125, 177, 193, 194, 209
  Legal Affairs Department
    (LAD) 72
Scotch Whisky Auctions 70
Scotch Whisky Experience
  (Edinburgh) 7
Scotland
  barley 22–3
  bars 212–13
  Campbeltown 108–11
  distilleries 76–119
  Highlands 13, 77–85
  history of whisky-making
    13–15
  Islands 112–19
  Islay 100–7
  legally defined categories 18
  Lowlands 25, 94–9
  not all the best whisky made
    in 17
  Speyside 86–93
  water quality 22

whisky exports 6, 9
  whisky synonymous with 6
Seagram 176
  VO 179
Sedgwick, Captain James 199
serving whisky 54–7
Shapira brothers 155
shell and tube condensing 24,
  209
Shelter Point *172*
Sheridan, Jim 133
sherry casks 35, 36, 37, 38, 58
shiel 209
shops, whisky 51, 214
Sikkim 194, *195*
silent distilleries 209
single grain, legal definition 18
single malts 6, 209
  age of 40–1
  availability of 9
  blended 125
  counterfeiting 73
  legal definition 18
  limited editions 45
  older bottlings of 'standard'
    68
  production method 26–7
Singleton 62
sipping 50
Skye, Isle of 39, 117
Slyrs Distillery *180*, 193
smell *see* aroma
Smith Bowman *163*
Smith, Gavin D 6, 9
Smith, George 91
Smith, John Gordon 91
smoky and peaty aromas and
    flavours 39, 43
  food combinations 59, 60
smooth and sweet flavours *see*
    buttery, smooth and sweet
    flavours
sniffing 49
snifters 54–5
soda water, mixing with 55,
  138, 139
Soho Whisky Club 64
Solan No. 1 194
Solas *163*
Sonic 142
Sotheby's 66, 67
South Africa
  bars 213
  distilleries 198–9
  grain whisky 6, 62
  map 198

South Korea 194, 213
Southern Coast *200*
Spain 213
spelt 170
Speyburn *86*
Speyside 209
  distilleries 86–93
  Malt Whisky Trail 87, 88
  map 86
Speyside (distillery) *86*
spirit 209
spirit safe 29, 209
Springbank 52, 68, 69, *108*, **111**
  1938 67
  Hazelburn 111, 145
  Longrow 111
  Vintage 61
Stauning *180*
steep 23, 26, 30, 209
stills 12, 209
  destruction of illegal 19
  see also alembic stills; boil
    ball stills; Coffey stills;
    column stills; lantern
    stills; onion stills; pot stills
Stillwater *162*
Still Waters *173*
Stitzel-Weller 158, 159
storing whisky 69–70
straight 209
Stranahan, George 169
Stranahan's Colorado *162*, **169**
  Snowflake 169
Strathearn *77*
Strathisla 60, *86*
Strathmill *86*
Sullivans Cove *200*, **203**
  American Oak Bourbon
    Cask Matured 203
  Australian Double Cask
    Whisky 203
Suntory 136
  Kakubin 137
  see also Hakushu; Yamazaki
Swan, Dr Jim 197
Sweden 6, 190
swirling whisky 7, 48
switcher mechanism 23, 209
Switzerland 193, 213

Taiwan
  bars 213
  distilleries 194, 197
  whisky 8, 16, 57, 62
Taketsura, Masataka 134, 144,
  145, 146

Talisker 15, 59, 60, 63, 65, *112*, **117**
Tamdhu *86*
Tamnavulin *86*
Tasmania 200, 202–3
Tasmania (distillery) *200*
tasting 48–50, 125
   blind 197
   link with smell 48–50
   notes 50
   steps 50
   whisky menu 52–3
Tate, Chip 164
taxation 13
Tayburn, Mark 119
Taylor, Duncan 52
Taylor, E.H. Jr 152
Teacher's 68
   Highland Cream 69, 123
Teaninich *77*
Teeling *127*
Teeling, John 129, 130
Teerenpeli *181*, **187**
Tekel *181*
temperature
   and character 39
   of warehouses 39
Templeton Rye *163*
   Small Batch Rye Whiskey 171
Tennents 95
Tennessee whiskey 148–50, 209
   distilleries 148–9, 154, 156
   legal definition 19
   map 148–9
   maturation 38
   production process 30–1
terroir 39
Thomas H. Handy rye whiskey
   53, 152
Timboon *200*

Tirril *180*
Tobermory *112*, **118**
Tomatin *77*
Tomintoul *86*
Tom Moore *149*
tonic water, mixing with 55,
   139
top dressing 209
Torii, Shinjiro 22, 145
Tormore, The *86*
Triple Eight *163*
Tullamore Dew *127*, **132**
tulip-shaped glasses 54
Tullibardine *77*
tumblers 54
tuns 23, 26, 209
Tuthilltown *163*, **170**
   Hudson Baby Bourbon 170

uisge beathe 12, 13
United Distillers 96, 105
United States 148–71
   bars 213
   distilleries 164–71
   history of whiskey-making
     in 13, 15, 16
   Kentucky and Tennessee
     148–61
   legal definitions 19
   maps 148–9, 162–3
   other distilleries 162–71
   see also American whiskey;
     Bourbon; Kentucky;
     Tennessee whiskey

Valleyfield *173*
Van Eycken, Stefan 147
Van Winkle *149*, **159**
Van Winkle, Julian 'Pappy'

158, 159
vatted malt 125, 204
vatting 71, 210
vermouth 57
Victoria Spirits *172*
viscosity 48

Waldviertler Roggenhof *180*,
   182
Walker, Hiram 178
warehouse, and flavour 39
Warenghem *180*
wash 24, 25, 27, 29, 31, 210
washbacks 23, 27, 210
Wasmund, Rick 165
water 210
   quality of 22, 39, 148
   types of 39
   with whisky 7, 50, 55, 138
Watson, Albert 92
Watts, Andy 199
websites 214–15
   Canadian distilleries 179
   collecting and investing 70
   Japanese whisky 147
Welsh whisky 13, 52, 62, 191
West Virginia Distilling *163*
   wheat 150, 155, 158, 159, 167,
   174, 184
Wheatley, Harlen 152
Whisky Castle Distillery *180*,
   193
   Castle Hill 193
Whisky Highland 70
Whisky Magazine 67, 70, 215
whisky menus
   jargon 53
   understanding 52
Whisky Sour 56, 57

White Horse 68
Whyte & Mackay 103, 115, 123
   Special 123
Wild Turkey *149*, **160**
William Grant & Sons Ltd 89,
   98, 132, 170, 179
William Larue Weller 53
Williams, Daniel Edmond 132
Williams, Evan 13, 52, 191
Wills, Anthony 104
wine, terroir 39
Wiser's Deluxe 179
Wolfburn *77*
women, as whisky-drinkers
   9, 17
wood *see* casks
Woodford Reserve 61, *149*, **161**
Woodstone Creek *163*
World Whisky Awards 137,
   144, 203
worldwide interest in whisky
   6, 9
worm 25, 210
wort 23, 26, 206, 207, 210
Wright, Hedley 109, 111

Yamazaki 22, 52, 53, 57, 60, 62,
   135, **145**
   Hibiki blends 137, 145
   White Label 136
yeast 21, 23–4
Yellowstone *162*
Yoichi 60, *135*, **146**
young people, as whisky-
   drinkers 9, 16, 138
young whiskies 41

Zuidam, Fred van 189
Zuidam Distillery *180*, **189**

Authors' acknowledgments

The authors would like to thank the following people for their help in writing this book: Rob Allanson, Eugene Bacot, Derek Bell, Dave Broom, Chris Bunting, Bert Cason, Ryan Chetiyawardana, Jason Craig, Georgie Crawford, Susie Davidson, Ben Ellefsen, Ralph Erenzo, Tim Forbes, Rosemary Gallagher, John Glaser, George Grant, Ken Grier, Daryl Haldane, Emily Harris, Joel Harrison, Wendy Harries Jones, Mickey Heads, Andy Hogan, Mika Jansson, Brian Kinsman, Alice Lascelles, Jim Long, Dr Bill Lumsden, Neil MacDonald, Ian Macmillan, Chris Maybin, Joe McGirr, Frank McHardy, Marcin Miller, Dr Nick Morgan, Hans Offringa, Bill Owens, Richard Paterson, Carrie & Lois Ridley, Pat Roberts, David Robertson, Ingvar Ronde, Darren Rook, Colin Ross, The Scotch Malt Whisky Society, Darrell Sheehan, Sukhinder Singh, The Soho Whisky Club, Cat Spencer, Jeremy Stephens, David Stewart, Richmond Towers, Chip Tate, Jackie Thompson, Gerry Tosh, *Whisky Advocate*, *Whisky Magazine*, Alan Winchester.

Picture Acknowledgments

Alamy 7, 16 (above)

Corbis 2–3, 10, 16 (below), 19, 21, 22, 23 (above), 24, 26, 32, 37, 38 (right), 42, 43 (all), 46, 56, 57, 59, 74, 126, 134, 137, 151, 174

Diageo/David Broom 44

www.flickr.com © DuncanR 100, © Inverness Whisky Festival 6, © Jody T. Photography 39, © The Macallan Single Malt 66, © Donald Ogg 51, © David Roberts 108, © Mark Sawinski 38 (left)

Fresh Food Images front cover

Getty Images 35, 69, 138 (both)

Paragraph Publishing 1, 23, 85, 192, 210

Ridley, Neil 8, 139

Science and Society Picture Library 13, 14

Scottish Viewpoint back cover, 17, 20, 25, 34, 36, 48, 49, 50, 63, 76, 98, 99 (both), 107

Smith, Gavin D 9

The Soho Whisky Club 64

Whisky Magazine Bar listings 213–219

Whyte & Mackay 120

The publishers would like to thank the following for supplying images. Abhainn Dearg, Compass Box, Corsair Distillery, Hicks and Healey Distillery, Master of Malt, Quercus Communications, Royal Mile Whiskies, St George Spirits, Stock Spirits Group, Touch PR, Waldviertler Roggenhof, The Whisky Exchange, Whyte & Mackay.

Maps and illustrations Barking Dog Art
Bottle and glasses photography David Forcina

This edition published in the United Kingdom in 2015 by
Pavilion
1 Gower Street
London WC1E 6HD

Copyright © Pavilion Books Company Limited 2013, 2015
Text copyright © Neil Ridley and Gavin D Smith 2013, 2015

All rights reserved. No part of this book may be reproduced or utilized in any form by any means electronic or mechanical, including photocopying, recording or by an information storage and retrieval system, without the prior written permission of the publisher.

ISBN 978 1 862059658

A CIP catalogue for this book is available from the British Library

10 9 8 7 6 5 4 3

Commissioning editor Fiona Holman
Produced by Posthouse Publishing
www.posthousepublishing.com

Colour reproduction by Rival Colour Ltd, UK
Printed by TIMES OFFSET (M) SDN BHD, Malaysia

This book can be ordered direct from the publisher at
www.pavilionbooks.com